The Prussian Spirit
1914–1940

THE PRUSSIAN SPIRIT

A Survey of German Literature and Politics
1914–1940

by
S. D. STIRK
M.A. (Oxon.), Dr. phil. (Breslau)

KENNIKAT PRESS/Port Washington, N.Y.

THE PRUSSIAN SPIRIT

First published 1941
Reissued 1969 by Kennikat Press

Library of Congress Catalog Card No: 68-8245
SBN 8046-0447-9
Manufactured in the United States of America

Preface

One of the best ways of answering the familiar questions:
'What are we fighting for?' and 'What are our war aims?' is to
answer the less frequent question: 'What are we fighting
against?'

This book is an inquiry into the psychology of the German
people, their habits of mind, the subject-matter of their thoughts
and feelings, their spiritual background and tradition, as re-
flected and expressed in recent German literature. It approaches
the difficult and complex problem of present-day Germany from
the standpoint of Prussia and the Prussian spirit; and its main
thesis is that Hitlerism is fundamentally a continuation of Prussianism. Without the 'Prussianization' of Germany, a process
which became definite and decisive in 1871 and was much
accelerated by the Great War, there would be no National
Socialism; without Frederick the Great, Bismarck, Moltke, Hindenburg, and the other great Prussians there would be no Hitler.
At the same time it must be stressed that Hitlerism is for the
most part Prussianism of the very worst kind, so much so that it
may even be regarded as a perversion of Prussianism.

Many books have been written about Hitler and National
Socialism. Here is an attempt to go behind Hitler, and to get at
the German people, or at any rate at a very characteristic type
and a large and dominating section of the German people,
namely, the Prussians; and it attempts to explain why the Prussians accepted so blithely and so tragically such an unworthy
leader, and why most of them have continued to accept him for

7

so long. The reader will soon perceive that the word Prussian is not used here in any strict geographical or racial sense, and is not applied exclusively to the inhabitants of the former kingdom of Prussia. The Prussian spirit is active all over Germany; and although the Prussian type is most in evidence among the land-owners east of the Elbe, the state officials centred on Berlin, and the staffs of the Prussian universities, it is to be found among all classes and conditions of Germans, and includes many workers and peasants and small shopkeepers. It will also be noted that Prussianism is not treated as something fixed and given, and that there is no attempt to define it in an abstract and formal way, but rather to describe and illustrate it by an abundance of examples. Finally, it may as well be stated at the outset that all sweeping indictments and condemnations of the Prussians are avoided, and that their good and enduring qualities are appraised.

Most of the recent books about Germany concentrate on the years *after* 1932, which makes Hitler and National Socialism appear far more novel and unique and terrifying than they really are, and gives a wrong perspective. One of the chief aims of the present survey is, therefore, to fill in the gap between 1919 and 1933 by the analysis of certain books which were read by many Germans, particularly by young Germans, during these years, but which for the most part never became known in England and America. These books serve to show how in spite of the apparent successes and superficial stability of the Weimar Republic the Prussian spirit continued to be active, and how the Prussianism of this tragic interlude prepared the way for and finally secured the triumph of Hitler. Some of the books dealt with are of great value and perhaps even essential for the under-standing of Germany's political and spiritual development be-tween the two great wars; others have been chosen not so much for their outstanding importance or intrinsic literary merits, but because they are so representative of the Prussian or the Nazi spirit.

This book maintains that the Prussian approach to the prob-lem of Germany is valuable and illuminating; but it does not pretend to give a complete picture of the last twenty-five years either in literature or in politics. Moreover, it is primarily concerned with ideas, and with the broad battles of spiritual and intellectual forces, rather than with single events, and their place in any systematic and chronological pattern. To quote the words placed by Thomas Mann at the head of his essay on 'Friedrich und die Grosse Koalition' (1914), it is 'A sketch written for the day and the hour' ['Ein Abriss für den Tag und die Stunde']. It is intended as a 'war-book', and as such it should be judged.

S. D. STIRK, M.A. (Oxon.), Dr. phil. (Breslau)

May 1941

Contents

CONTENTS

Introductory

Chapter I

Introductory

---

1. English Opinion on Prussia, 1914–18 and 1939–40

If there was one thing of which English people from 1914 to 1918 were convinced, it was that the fight was against Prussia and Prussianism. Brief consideration of some of the 'war-books' of the first Great War will suffice to bring this conviction to mind.

Shortly after war broke out in August 1914 a book appeared entitled *Britain's Case against Germany (An examination of the historical background of the German action in 1914)*, by Ramsay Muir, who was at that time Professor of History at the University of Manchester. In the preface he declared that the great issue for which England was fighting was no new thing, and had not emerged suddenly out of diplomatic difficulties in the Balkans. 'It is the result of a poison which has been working in the European system for more than two centuries, and the chief source of the poison is Prussia.' In Chapter 4 he discussed in detail 'How Prussia rules Germany', and came to the conclusion that in spite of its superficially democratic form (including the Reichstag), the German Empire set up by Bismarck was fundamentally a monarchist and a militarist state, a reproduction on an enlarged and modernized scale of the older Prussia. 'The German Empire is now permeated by the Prussian spirit.'

An even more detailed and striking indictment of Prussia was contained in W. H. Dawson's book *What is Wrong with Germany?* which also appeared early in the war. More than any other Englishman before 1914, W. H. Dawson had tried to interpret Germany to England, and the preface revealed his great sadness

INTRODUCTORY

at having to write such a book. The following passages are typical of his views on Prussia. 'After 1870–71 a new and virile influence entered into German national life, or rather an old influence began to assert itself under new and more favourable conditions. This was the influence of the Prussian spirit, which in its various manifestations has more than anything else transformed the Germany of the past and given to it a new, though not higher culture. This spirit has ever been a hard and immalleable element in the life of Germany; it is still the knot in the oak, the nodule in the softer clay.' 'It is essentially the Prussian spirit which has made Germany to so large a degree unsympathetic to the modern world.' 'Inspired and led by Prussia, Germany has staked its whole existence, its present and its future, on military power.' 'No-one in Germany doubts that the Prussian spirit has greatly helped to bring Germany to its present position of pre-eminence both as a political and an economic power, but indebtedness for past services does not make that spirit any more acceptable to the South Germans.'

This idea of the 'Two Germanys', a Prussian and a non-Prussian, appeared in varying form in nearly all these war-books. In one of the essays in the symposium *War and Democracy* (1915), by Seton-Watson, J. Dover Wilson, Alfred Zimmern, and Arthur Greenwood, Zimmern described first of all what he called 'the real Germany, the Germany of the south and west. This Germany, the Germany of the Rhine country, Frankfurt, Heidelberg, Cologne, Nürnberg, is the Germany which so many Englishmen know and admire.' He then turned to a consideration of 'the second and more powerful of the two Germanys, namely, Prussia'. And in a tone of regret he declared that in order to understand Prussia and the Prussian spirit we must plunge ourselves into an atmosphere wholly different from that of the Germany which he had just described. He spoke of the origins of Prussia in the activities of the Teutonic Knights: 'Here we see the strange, stern, medieval, crusading atmosphere which lies behind the unpleasant combination of soldiers and religion, of culture and violence, of "Germanization" and devastation. . . . The Prussian outlook is entirely foreign to Western habits of mind.' Zimmern, like many of his contemporaries, was apparently filled with the hope—if not with the conviction—that the

16

process and verdict of German history could and would be reversed, and that somehow or other non-Prussian Germany would subordinate and triumph over Prussia. In this respect it is interesting to compare the more pessimistic, but certainly more realistic, views expressed by Edmond Holmes in his book *The Nemesis of Docility* (1916), in which he declared it was inevitable that the Prussian, not the Weimar, type should dominate Germany. 'For military absolutism could give to Germany what the princely patronage of culture could not give—the political unity and the material strength which would enable her to hold her own against the possibly hostile nations that surrounded her. It is idle to speculate on what might have happened if Germany had allowed herself to be Weimarized instead of Prussianized. In point of fact she has been Prussianized.' In a later passage Edmond Holmes wrote: 'If I have devoted a seemingly disproportionate amount of space to Prussia, my reason for doing so is that Prussia can no longer be distinguished from Germany, which is now either incorporated in Prussia or in course of being Prussianized. The influence of Prussia has grown steadily since 1870, and is now all-powerful. And the ascendancy of Prussia in Germany means that the German character is gradually acquiring the characteristic Prussian features of militarism, officialism, coercive discipline, and mechanical obedience. Slow, patient, resolute, painstaking, methodical, materialistic, unimaginative, the Prussian is making himself master of the soul as well as the outward life of the German people; and the Prussian is at heart a drill-sergeant—and a serf.'

Now one would have thought that the leaders of public opinion at the outset of the second Great War, and above all those responsible for our propaganda at home and abroad, would have made a special study of the war-books of 1914–18, and would have been only too eager to correlate and identify Prussianism with Hitlerism. But apart from a few isolated attempts, this did not happen: which is surely one reason why our propaganda in the early stages of the war lacked direction, consistency, and drive.

Mr. Eden was one of the first and one of the few statesmen to point out the close similarity and affinity between Prussianism and Hitlerism. In a speech on the 2nd December 1939 he declared: 'But let us not delude ourselves. It is Britain's power, influence, and authority that Germany is out to break. Germany made the war of 1914 in order to impose her military supremacy over Europe. She has made this war for precisely the same purpose. Hitler is not so unique as all that. He is merely the latest expression of the Prussian spirit of military domination. The fact that he is not a Prussian makes him rather worse. His purpose is the same as that of Bismarck and Kaiser Wilhelm—to rule Europe.'

One had the impression that this was a new idea to many people; that it stirred up old memories and gave them a cue they had been waiting for. Mr. Eden's speech was of course reported in the press, and commented on in leading articles. But the interest went further than that; at any rate for a brief period. The specialists and feature writers took up the idea. Two examples may be given. On the 12th December 1939, that is to say a few days after the speech, the *Daily Telegraph and Morning Post* published a long middle-page article by J. B. Firth, with the main headline: 'Hitler's Rule is in the Tradition of Prussian Tyranny', and as a second headline: 'And the German People have Assented and Applauded'. In the course of the article Firth quoted with effect the well-known simile from Lord Rosebery's essay on 'Frederick the Great': 'Prussia has ever since (i.e. ever since the time of Frederick the Great) been like a pike in a pond, armed with sharp teeth and endless voracity, poised for a dart when the proper prey shall appear.' The conclusion of the article reads: 'Let us not be deluded! (cf. Mr. Eden's speech?) The pike is in the pond and the pond will need a thorough netting before it is safe for decent fish.'

Two days later (14th December 1939) G. Ward Price wrote one of his articles for the *Daily Mail* with the title: 'It's So if Goebbels Says So'. Ward Price asserted: 'If Britons accustomed to travel on the Continent were asked in which country they felt most at home, the commonest answer would be—Germany.' He then proceeded to ask: 'How is it that the German, often so likeable as an individual, behaves so detestably in the mass?' And his answer ran: 'I think one must distinguish between the Prussians and the rest. This is no longer a geographical difference. Germany has been so thoroughly Prussianized, especially under the Nazi régime, that the Prussian character appears everywhere. People in every part of the country with inborn tendencies to brutality, arrogance, and tyranny are encouraged in the development of these instincts by the Nazi Party. Alongside this species, and much outnumbering it, is the pleasanter German type with docility as its predominant characteristic.'

Another statesman who pointed out the connexion between Prussianism and Hitlerism was Sir Nevile Henderson. In his *Failure of a Mission*, which appeared in April 1940, he wrote: 'It is no coincidence that in the last war it was the Prussians rather than the Germans whom we regarded as our real enemies. Though few of the actual leaders of the National Socialist Party are Prussians by origin, it is the Prussian ideology, and particularly their methods, which are no less dominant to-day in Germany than they were in 1914 or in 1870.'

But for a really comprehensive and thoroughgoing condemnation of Hitlerism as a continuation of Prussianism, one must turn to the collection of essays by G. K. Chesterton, published posthumously in February 1940 under the title: *The End of the Armistice*. In the 'Compiler's Note' F. G. Sheed explained that when going through a mass of Chesterton's essays, he came to realize that as far back as the middle twenties and continuously up to his death in 1936 Chesterton's mind had been dominated by the storm of war which was to break in September 1939. 'These essays represent Chesterton's analysis of the whole problem of Germany in Europe. They were written at various dates, not in any particular order nor as chapters of a future book. Yet they form a unity because of the unity of Chesterton's own mind.' Chesterton had formed a certain theory of Germany, which Mr. Sheed summarizes as follows: 'There is a reality called Europe, which makes sense when you see it as Christendom. To this reality Germany belongs, and Prussia does not belong. The problem for Europe is the healing of Germany by the exorcizing of Prussianism, a force which by its very nature is an abiding trouble to Germany and so to the world. Prussia must be restrained. And to be restrained it must be understood. If we misconceive its nature, we shall repeat the mistake of Versailles—we shall build our dams in the wrong places.'

INTRODUCTORY

The title given by Mr. Sheed to this collection was taken from the introductory essay on 'Arms and the Armistice'. 'The first fact to be noted about the Armistice', wrote Chesterton in most typical vein, 'is the rather remarkable fact of the name itself. For, you will notice, it has never at any time been called The Peace. The world, weary of war as it has hardly ever been weary in all the ages, yet has an instinct guiding even its language, and it has never dared finally to announce Peace with Prussia. And if anybody thinks that the world was very wrong to feel like this, or that I am wrong to put it into plain words, let him look at Prussia to-day and see.'

Again and again Chesterton made clear that all his sympathies were with Catholic Austria. Prussia, he declared, was simply a revolt against Germany; it always was, and still is, the enemy of Germany. In an article on Dollfuss, the Austrian Chancellor who was murdered by the Nazis on the 25th July 1934, he wrote: 'The one really big and bad blunder in the Versailles settlement was that we did not punish Prussianism in Prussia; we only punished it in Austria. We ought to have weakened Prussia and if anything strengthened Austria. We did in fact weaken Austria and relatively strengthen Prussia. And at this moment every man in his five senses is wishing we had done the opposite.'

Chesterton was quick to realize the significance of the meeting of the Reichstag in the Garrison Church at Potsdam on the 21st March 1933; and early in April he wrote an article with the heading 'The Return of Prussianism—Hitler's Repudiation of German War-Guilt over the Tomb of Frederick the Great', in which he pointed out that humour could hardly be Hitler's strong point, and in any case 'some of us are but little reassured by a man abjuring piracy over the bones of Captain Kidd or perjury upon the holy relics of Titus Oates'. In a later article on National Socialism he declared: 'Prussia begins to reappear, which means that War begins to reappear. Prussia means Prussianism now exactly as it did in 1914; it always did, it always does, and (short of a spiritual conversion) it always will. Prussia is a patch of eighteenth-century heathenry and heresy, which never did believe, nor (to do it justice) generally pretended to believe, in any sort of international ideal or common code of

20

Christendom. From the first command of Hohenzollern to the last appeal of Hitler, it is the most simple, one-sided, savage tribal patriotism, and nothing else.'

It can hardly be said that Chesterton's book received the attention it deserved, just as his repeated warnings of the revival of the very worst kind of Prussianism—warnings expressed in the essays and articles when they appeared singly—had gone almost unheeded. In their astonishment and excitement at the new and nasty phenomenon of Hitler, people tended to overlook Germany's Prussian past; or in other words they forgot to inquire into Hitler's political pedigree, and into the family tree of National Socialism. Throughout 1940 mention of 'Prussianism' appeared sporadically and spasmodically in the news; and a spate of such phrases as 'Prussian tyranny', 'Prussian militarism', 'the Prussian jackboot' occurred from time to time in speeches, leading articles, and 'letters to the editor'. But there was no widespread, firm, and consistent realization that Hitlerism—no matter what else it might be—was Prussianism 'writ large'.

2. 'Refugees from Nazi Oppression' Disagree

A few days before the publication of Chesterton's essays a book appeared entitled *Exit Prussia, a Plan for Europe*, by a distinguished 'refugee from Nazi oppression', Edgar Stern-Rubarth. From a brief biographical note one learnt that he was born at Frankfurt-am-Main, had been editor-in-chief and managing director of the Wolff news agency, and was the creator of the *Diplomatisch-Politische Korrespondenz*, the daily bulletin of the German Foreign Office. Dismissed when Hitler came to power, he came to England in 1935. The dust-cover of the book showed two hands tearing Prussia out of the map of Europe. The theory of the 'Two Germanys', so familiar in the first Great War, and half-heartedly revived in the early days of the second, was here given in an extreme form and carried to its most logical and most drastic conclusion.

With rather astonishing *naïveté* Stern-Rubarth explained: 'All my life I had known that something was wrong. I did not know what it was and neither did many of my contemporaries who felt as I did. It was not until I went into exile and so became able to view my native land from a distance that it dawned upon me. It dawned slowly.' As if Prussianism had never been attacked and denounced before! It is clear that Stern-Rubarth is very proud of his connexions with Frankfurt, and he relates many of the old jokes against Prussia current in that city, for example: When an old gentleman of Frankfurt was asked where the boundaries of the city ended, he replied: 'Just dip your finger in the River Main, and smell at it. Where it begins to stink, it is Prussian!' Stern-Rubarth's West-German origin and his hatred of Prussia make him idealize non-Prussian Germany and the Middle Ages. 'If Germany as a whole, and especially since the creation of the Prusso-German Empire in 1871, seems different from the Germany of the Middle Ages and the earlier years of modern times, it is because she has been pervaded by the Prussian spirit, dominated by Prussian officials, Prussian law, and the Prussian concept of aggressive nationalism.' Chapter 2 is entitled 'Hitler, the Arch-Prussian'. 'It was the Prussian soul upon which Hitler played, although his first success was won in anti-Prussian Bavaria. It was to the music of Old Prussian military marches and army songs that the Brownshirt recruits displayed their mass adherence, and it was upon a phraseology full of Prussian concepts of service, sacrifice, efficiency, and racial superiority that they were fed.'

His conclusion was that if one could only eliminate Prussia from Germany and wipe out Prussian domination of Germany, then Europe and the world would be well on the way to peace. In other words, Stern-Rubarth talked about the 'de-Prussianization' of Germany, just as other people might talk about the decarbonization of a car. He admitted that it might be a hard task to overcome the concepts that decades of specific Prussian teaching all over Germany, and years of a ruthless Nazi propaganda outdoing even those teachings, had hammered into the brains of the German masses. But he had no doubt that the scales would finally fall from the eyes of the 'real' Germans, who would come to realize that they had been the victims as well as the tools of Prussian megalomania, and that their most recent rulers were the last and most ruthless representatives of the Prussian spirit.

With Stern-Rubarth's proposals for the creation of a 'Western

Slav Federation' which would include Prussia, a resurrected
Poland, and a newly formed Czechoslovakia, and with his further plans for a well-balanced Europe, in which international,
social, and economic justice shall prevail, it is not our business
to deal. Suffice it to say that the whole book is dominated by a
naïve and bland optimism, and by a most ostrich-like refusal to
face facts, which are astonishing in a man of such distinction and
experience.

By an interesting coincidence almost identical views and suggestions about Prussia were expressed at almost the same time—
yet quite independently—by an even more distinguished German *émigré*, Emil Ludwig. This writer, whose real name is Emil
Ludwig Cohn, is best known to English readers for his uncon-
ventional and thought-provoking biographies of Kaiser Wilhelm
II, Napoleon, and President Roosevelt. He left Germany several
years before Hitler came to power, and settled in Switzerland,
where he became naturalized in 1932. Needless to say his person
and his works were always anathema to the Nazis, who, when
they did not ignore him altogether, furiously attacked him. On
the 10th February 1940 the first part of a long article by Ludwig, entitled 'Krieg gegen Preussen' ['War against Prussia'] appeared in *Das Neue Tage-Buch*, a violently anti-Hitler weekly,
published in Paris and Amsterdam.[1] The continuation and conclusion of the article appeared in the next number (17th February). Ludwig began by pointing out that for more than a hundred years the world has puzzled over the 'Two Germanys'
existing alongside each other, the one constantly attracting
foreigners, and the other repelling them. How is it possible, the
foreigner asks himself, that in the land of Goethe, Kant, and
Beethoven barbarism again and again raises its head? The answer,
so Ludwig declared, was much simpler than such foreigners
believed, and might be summed up in the following way: Every-

[1] *Das Tage-Buch* was a well-known and influential left-wing periodical,
founded in 1922 by an able German journalist Leopold Schwarzschild, who
was its editor till 1933. When Hitler came to power he left Germany, and
founded *Das Neue Tage-Buch*. After the defeat and occupation of Holland and
France the periodical unhappily ceased to appear, and it was assumed for a
time that Schwarzschild had fallen into the hands of the Germans when they
occupied Paris. It later became known, however, that he had escaped and
was in the United States.

thing which ennobles the German name in the world comes from non-Prussians, but the threat, the danger, the brutality, comes exclusively from Prussia. The obvious thing to do is, therefore, to separate the bad from the good, and to isolate Prussia. In this sense the present war ought to be described as a war against Prussia, and not as a war against Hitler. A Germany without Hitler does not offer any guarantee of peace; for Hitler is a man who can be replaced at any moment by another man like him. But Prussia is a disease which one can and ought to put into quarantine!

Non-Prussian in Ludwig's opinion are not only Austria, Bavaria, Suabia, Baden, but also Saxony, the Saar, and the Rhineland. Of the seventy millions of Germans (counting the Austrians), only thirty-two millions live to-day in Prussia, and further, the territory of Prussia is less than half of Germany. So that on the analogy of the constitution of the United States Prussia ought to have 50 per cent of the power. In reality it has 100 per cent.

Ludwig declares: Anybody who has studied the Prussian spirit will attribute entirely and absolutely to Prussia the responsibility for what Germany has become during the last eighty years. Prussia has never given up anything, but has always taken. For hundreds of years the rulers of Prussia have pursued a policy opposed to the best interests of Germany as a whole. The Hohenzollerns were continuously envious of the Habsburgs, and their primary aim was always to increase their own territory and power. Then follow examples of the anti-German policy of the Great Elector, Frederick William I, and Frederick the Great, similar to those which we shall quote from other sources in later chapters, after which Ludwig gives a devastating account of the internal development of Prussia, stressing above all the privileged position of the Junkers, and how they have always terrorized and exploited the peasants. Service in the army, the whip, fear, discipline, obedience: all these things led to the creation of a type which was absolutely 'un-German' ['undeutsch']. By intermarriage with the inhabitants of the territory east of the Elbe, Prussia became 'half-Slav'. With Bismarck and the foundation of the Empire, Prussia and the Prussian Junkers gained the upper hand in Germany.

INTRODUCTORY

Emil Ludwig continues: 'All the Germans of first rank in the world of the mind and the spirit come from South Germany or at any rate from non-Prussian Germany; not a single one comes from Prussia.' Prussia has not produced a single great musician. In literature the only two great Prussian names are Herder and Kleist. Herder, according to Ludwig, hated the Prussians, and about Kleist he discreetly says nothing, but passes on to Kant. He admits that Kant is usually claimed as a Prussian philosopher, but maintains with heat that Kant is not really a Prussian, for his mother came from Nürnberg, and his paternal ancestors from Scotland!

Eventually Ludwig reaches the present day, and Hitler. He repeats his earlier assertion that Hitler's downfall would by no means result in a new Germany. Millions of Germans have voted for Hitler of their own free will. The root of the matter is that Hitler is an absolutely Prussian phenomenon. Everything he accepts and everything he rejects, his methods, and his ideals are 'Old Prussian' ['altpreussisch'], and things are only made worse by the fact that he is a convert to Prussianism. Everything Hitler says, and above all the way he says it, is typically Prussian, and for that reason he is nowhere so completely understood as in Prussia. What the world is at present fighting against is not a single adventurer, but the symbolical leader of millions of Germans, who if they had not found Hitler would have chosen another leader of the same sort.

Finally, Ludwig makes proposals very similar to those of Stern-Rubarth: the separation of Germans into north and south, into Prussians and non-Prussians. Some of the names he suggests for the 'real' and purified Germany are rather amusing: Südreich, Ostreich, Donaureich (Danubian Empire!), Alpenreich (Empire of the Alps!). Like Stern-Rubarth he admits that there are certain difficulties in the way of such a division, but he simply pooh-poohs them, and refuses to see that they are insuperable. 'Prussianism', he quite rightly points out, 'is not the territory of a state, the extent and population of which may be ascertained from statistics. Prussia is an attitude of the mind and spirit, more sharply outlined than that of Germans as a whole.' But in spite of all this, he refuses to admit the impracticability of his plans. In future Prussia could only be tolerated on the map of Europe as a state of second rank. Prussia must be isolated and made smaller, say about the size and importance of Rumania. Deprived of its leadership of all the German tribes, it would cease to be a danger to Europe. The world would finally receive German 'gifts and values' without Prussian 'threats'.

The next number of *Das Neue Tage-Buch* (24th February) brought an article in defence of Prussia by Joachim Haniel, who declared that Ludwig's theory of Prussian responsibility for German backslidings was far too simple a solution to such a huge and complicated problem. Haniel concentrated on Ludwig's assertion that Prussians have contributed little or nothing to German 'culture', and tried rather unconvincingly to prove that this was wrong by giving a long list of 'great Prussians'. Towards the end, however, he put forward the interesting and at first sight rather surprising theory that the evil in Germany was really due to 'Pan-Germanism and the psychology of world-domination' ['Alldeutschtum und die Weltbeherrschungs-Psychologie']; mental diseases which were not produced originally by Prussia and which were not specially at home in Prussia. The truth is, so Haniel declared, that the founders, the early fathers, the chief preachers of Pan-Germanism, were all of them non-Prussians: Ernst Moritz Arndt, Fichte, Hegel, and so on. One must also remember that Hitler, Göring, Hess, Frick, and the other leaders of the 'gangster's racket' now prevailing in Germany are not Prussians, that the Nazi movement became really strong in Bavaria, and that even before 1914 the centres of Pan-Germanism were Mainz, Leipzig, and München. Haniel went even further, and defended the view that Prussia did not 'Prussianize' Germany, but that Germany 'Teutonized' Prussia! The bacillus of Pan-Germanism and world-hegemony was only carried into Prussia after the breakdown of 1806, after which Prussia was reorganized by non-Prussian Pan-Germans. Prussia only gradually came to be penetrated and dominated by these ideas and throughout the nineteenth century many of the Prussian Junkers and officials opposed them bitterly. It is true that to-day Prussia is infected through and through by this ideology, but it did not originate in Prussia, nor has Prussia at any time fallen a victim to it to a greater extent than any other part of Germany.

This article not surprisingly called forth a very sarcastic (and at times personal and rude) reply from Ludwig in the next number, and a week later (9th March) the cudgels were taken up by Hugo Bieber, well known in the Weimar Republic as a writer and publicist. Bieber wrote: 'I wish to express my agreement with Haniel's views. The German spirit of to-day is not a Prussian product.' Prussia came into existence at the earliest in the seventeenth century, and the Hohenzollerns were not important before 1415. Nevertheless, historians have testified to the existence of all the characteristic features of the Pan-Germans, yes, and of the Nazis too, centuries before this. What Cæsar and Tacitus said about the Germans might be applied almost equally well to-day! Bieber also quoted more obscure authorities like the Roman writer Apollinarius Sidonius (fifth century) and the Slav chronicler Kosmos of Prague (eleventh century) to prove his case. He then described how the romantic and imperialist and essentially non-Prussian spirit infected Prussia in the nineteenth century, and how Prussia was 'Teutonized'. To-day Prussia and Germany had become such a unity ['ein Amalgam'] that it was impossible any longer to make a distinction. But it was only fair to Prussia to point out that originally the dangerous and evil part of this amalgamation was Germany, and not Prussia.

It is clear, therefore, that even the German *émigrés* and refugees from Nazi oppression disagree on the thorny question of Prussia, and this fact alone goes a long way towards justifying an inquiry into the nature and influence of the Prussian spirit from 1914 to 1940. Even more important is the fact that all these writers, who by their origins, upbringing, and tragic experiences are well qualified to judge, regard the Prussian spirit as a fundamental aspect and in many ways the crux of the problem of modern Germany.

3. A Note on Prussian History with special reference to the Question of Slav Blood, and the Teutonic Knights

This is not the place to give a survey or summary, however brief, of Prussian history up to 1914. So many good books are available on Prussian history and individual great Prussians that it is unnecessary to try to compete with them here. But the two general points mentioned in the heading above are of such importance and crop up so often nowadays that I propose to deal with them briefly before starting on the main field of my inquiry.

The Question of Slav Blood

One of the most striking innovations in the last few decades—in thought and scholarship as well as in practical politics—has been the ever-increasing influence and application of theories about race. In the English war-books of 1914–18 little or nothing was said about race, except that contemporary Germans were associated with the Huns, and this was of course a general rather than a strictly racial term of abuse. But it has now become quite the fashion to assume that the Prussians are racially distinct from the Germans and that they are really Slavs, or at least a strange and unhappy mixture of German and Slav blood, with the Slav blood predominating. This is simply the old theory of the 'Two Germanys' in a more up-to-date and fashionable form, that is to say, with a racial bias. Incidentally such a theory is not at all polite to the Slav races in general, including our allies the Poles, the Czechs, and the Russians; but that is another matter.

One would have expected a man like Stern-Rubarth, whose brilliant career in Germany was cut short at any rate partly because of his Jewish blood, to be extremely careful about questions of race. However, such was not the case. He wrote in Chapter 3 of *Exit Prussia*: 'The racial nonsense of Hitlerism is of course universally exploded, but the word "race" still has its uses; in the scientific sense of an ethnic unit with characteristics of its own as regards habits, folk-lore, outlook on life, organization, nutrition, etc. In these and many other respects the Prussians are a race distinct from the Germans: they are a trans-Elbian, Slavonic, at best Slav-German mongrel tribe.' Later he asserts: 'We must admit that the physical characteristics of the Slav race are visible all over Prussia so far as it was made a unit by Frederick the Great: the same prominent cheek-bones and often slanting eyes prevail, which in the Russian betray the old Asiatic influence.' Does he mean that the Prussians are Mongols as well as Slavs? Or perhaps Red Indians? A final 'gem': we are solemnly informed that Bismarck and Hindenburg are Slavonic types!

Sir Nevile Henderson gave expression to similar ideas at the beginning of his *Failure of a Mission*, when describing his trip on a German liner from Buenos Aires, on his way to Berlin to take up his appointment as ambassador. 'I had several talks with the Captain, and on one occasion, pointing to his own high cheek-bones, he drew my attention to the considerable admixture of Slav blood in many of the Germans, particularly of the Prussians.' It was no doubt this 'revelation' which made Sir Nevile write a few lines lower down: 'In what proportion militant Prussianism is due to its Slavonic blood mixture is an open question.' (In which case the Poles and the Russians ought to be even more 'militant'?) He continues: 'But the fact remains that the Prussians, of whom even Goethe spoke as barbarians (Why 'even' Goethe, and where did he speak of them like this?) are a distinctive European type, which imposed itself and its characteristics upon the rest of Germany (in which case the idea of the 'Two Germanys' is no longer valid?) and from the point of view of the Western world, has prostituted, or is prostituting, the great qualities of order and efficiency, probity and kindliness of the purer German of the north-west, west, and south Germany, with whom an Englishman on his travels abroad finds himself in such natural sympathy.' But surely the qualities of 'order and efficiency' have always been recognized as essentially and typically Prussian? And are there no Prussians capable of 'probity and kindliness'? Did an Englishman on his travels abroad never find himself in natural sympathy with a Prussian? And why should the German of north-west, west, and south Germany be 'purer'?

Now as far as one can see the great majority of German writers on this question of Slav blood and similar questions are always most eager to stress the 'colonizing activities' of Germans in the Middle Ages, and later the efforts of the Great Elector, Frederick William I, and Frederick the Great to attract settlers. Thus they describe the land east of the Elbe as 'colonized land' ['Kolonialland']. At the same time it is maintained with vigour and often with heat that the whole area was originally German, in spite of the inconvenient Slav inhabitants whom the German 'colonists' discovered on arrival. And at this stage in the argument the writers rush back to the 'migration of the peoples' ['Völkerwanderung'] of the fourth and fifth centuries A.D., and going back further still they ransack the museums and ancient burial grounds and encampments for broken pottery and ornaments and weapons, in an endeavour to prove that the Germans, or at all events Germanic peoples, were there first. Probably they were; but this does not alter the fact that after they had left various Slav peoples took their place and lived there for centuries until the tide of migration turned. Nor does proof that wide areas were inhabited by Germanic tribes two thousand years ago justify the German claim to dominate the areas to-day. It is true, therefore, that many of the arguments used by German writers on these questions are specious, but on the other hand there can be no doubt about the German 'urge to the east' ['Drang nach dem Osten'], and the steady flow of Germans eastwards from the time of Charlemagne to that of Frederick the Great. Obviously many of the German settlers and their descendants intermarried with the Slav peoples they subjected and partly ousted, but they still remained Germans, above all in such matters as language and culture. And there is accordingly not the slightest reason for lumping together the inhabitants of Brandenburg, East Prussia, and Silesia, and calling them Slavs. There is this further point, namely, that the 'Prussen', the heathen tribe which caused the German colonists in the Middle Ages more trouble than any other, and whose powers of endurance and sturdy opposition are shown in the significant fact that they gave their name first to the territory, then to the state, and finally to the type and the spirit, were racially quite distinct from their Slav neighbours. They were of the same blood as the Letts, the Lithuanians, the Estonians, and the Finns, and belonged to the same group of Baltic peoples; in other words they were not Germanic, but they were also not Slav.

The Teutonic Knights

In the entire colonizing activities of Germans in the Middle Ages, and more particularly in the fight against the Prussen, pride of place must be given to the Order of Teutonic Knights. It would be an interesting and worth-while study to trace how the Teutonic Knights have conquered the modern German consciousness and modern German literature, particularly during the last few decades. We shall frequently come across them in the course of our inquiry. In 1191 German merchants from Bremen and Lübeck who were taking part in the Third Crusade started a hospital at Acre by making tents out of the sails of their ships. They later founded the 'Deutsches Haus' at Acre, and called themselves 'Brothers of the German House' ['die Brüder vom Deutschen Hause'], and it was out of this brotherhood that in 1198 the Order of Teutonic Knights [der Deutsche Ritterorden] arose. The members accepted the customary vows of poverty, chastity, and obedience, and set themselves two main tasks: to care for the sick and fight against the heathen, always in the service of the Virgin Mary. Both the Emperor and the Pope showed them favour; they were granted a special coat of arms—a black cross on a white shield; and they took to wearing white cloaks with a black cross on the left shoulder. In 1226 a Polish duke, Conrad of Masovia, invited the Order to help him in his desperate struggle with the Prussen. The call was answered, and in the spring of 1231 the army of the Order crossed the Vistula. Their path during the next few decades is best shown by the fortified centres which they in turn founded, and which later developed into some of the chief towns of East Prussia: 1231 Thorn, 1233 Marienwerder, 1237 Elbing, 1254 Königsberg (so named in honour of Ottokar, the Czech King of Bohemia, who helped in the 'crusade' against the Prussen), 1270 Marienburg. By about 1280 the Prussen and the other heathen tribes had been completely subjugated, and the Teutonic Knights could then turn their attention to more peaceful pursuits, such as the preaching of Christianity, the cultivation of the soil, and the development of trade. In 1309 Marienburg became the residence of the High Master [Hochmeister] and the headquarters of the Order; and the wonderful castle was built, undoubtedly one of the finest buildings of the Middle Ages.[1]

[1] It is a sad thought that the Marienburg should now be one of the chief temples and training headquarters of the Hitler Youth. But this is yet another example of the way in which the Nazis have seized on and exploited

In 1410 Poles, Lithuanians, Russians, and Tartars overcame the Order in the first battle of Tannenberg. By the Peace of Thorn in 1466 the Order was assured possession of East Prussia, but only as a fief of the Polish King. In 1511 Albrecht, Markgrave of Brandenburg, was elected High Master, and in 1525, acting partly on the advice of Luther, he secularized the Order, and became the first Duke of Prussia. In 1660, by the Treaty of Oliva, the Great Elector succeeded in throwing off Polish suzerainty. In 1701 Frederick, Elector of Brandenburg, took the title of King of Prussia.

'The heroic work of the Order of Teutonic Knights was the foundation-stone of the Prussian State and the corner-stone of the German Empire.' This sentence from a recent Nazi history-book for schools represents the accepted and fashionable view among patriotic Germans to-day; and this idealization of the Teutonic Knights has become an indispensable element of the Prussian myth, and a characteristic manifestation of the Prussian spirit. It is further part of a general tendency to put less stress on Brandenburg and far greater stress on Prussia—or what is now usually called 'East' Prussia—in the combination 'Brandenburg-Prussia', whose rise we have briefly indicated in the preceding paragraph. In his historical survey of Germany on the basis of the various 'districts' and 'tribes' (*Das stammhafte Gefüge des deutschen Volkes*, first published in 1934) Josef Nadler, Professor of German Literature at the University of Vienna, asks the rhetorical question: 'What would have become of Brandenburg without Prussia?' And his answer is that it would probably have developed on the same lines as most of the other German principalities, a prey to particularism, provincialism, and political sloth. But the acquisition of the large and difficult and unexploited territories at some considerable distance to the east

everything that is sacred and symbolical and politically vital in the Prussian past.

The Nazis were no doubt thinking (in a romantic and rather confused way) of the Order of the Teutonic Knights and similar medieval orders when they built the three *Ordensburgen* or 'Castles of the (Knightly) Order' (Crössinsee in Pomerania, Vogelsang in the Rhineland, and Sonthofen in Bavaria). These *Ordensburgen* are the new political universities, at which carefully selected specimens of Nazi youth are given a final training to fit them to become the leaders of the Party, the administration, and the state.

PART I

Weimar and Potsdam, 1919–1933

Weimar and Potsdam, 1919–1933

It is said that a Cambridge History don arranged to spend in Germany a sabbatical period of six months, from October 1932 to March 1933, with the avowed and laudable object of studying the 'Weimar Constitution'. But alas, his studies were roughly interrupted by the advent of Hitler to power, which at once reduced the Weimar Constitution to shreds, and he returned with his mission unfulfilled, and was compelled to cancel the course of lectures on the 'Weimar Constitution' which he had announced for Trinity Term 1933. This was very sad, but in a way typical of English public opinion after the first Great War. Once the War had been won, the Versailles Treaty signed, and the League of Nations set up, most English people settled down, and tried to make their lives as much pre-1914 as possible. They fell into a complacent attitude of 'as-it-was-in-the-beginning-is-now-and-ever-shall-be', refusing stubbornly to see that Europe, and indeed the world was in a chaotic state, that tremendous changes—political, social, economic, cultural, and religious—were taking place, that 'things were in the saddle and riding mankind'. From this dream-like state they were rudely awakened by the vulgar shouts and wild gesticulations of a nasty little German called Adolf Hitler, who simply would not 'live and let live'.

Like the Cambridge don, most English people never expected, up to 1933, any great and sudden changes in Germany. Those Germans, nice people some of them, seemed to be quite satisfied with their Weimar Republic; of course, there were occasional

37

rumours of a monarchist movement, and the Reds also seemed to be gaining ground; but Stresemann (pity he died so soon; a sound fellow!) had done a good piece of work; Germany had entered the League of Nations, and had signed the Locarno Pact. It is of course easy, as always, to be wise after the event, but there were signs and portents enough between 1919 and 1933 that the Weimar Republic was faced with a powerful and ever-increasing opposition, and that it was simply an interlude on which the curtain would soon go down, and that the Germans, or at any rate, the Prussians, would revert to type.

Admittedly it had seemed in the first few months of the Weimar Republic as if Prussia's day was done and her glory departed: the spirit of Weimar had triumphed (Heaven be praised!) over the spirit of Potsdam, and Goethe over Frederick the Great. Prussia had few friends in the National Assembly which deliberately and significantly enough met at Weimar in the spring of 1919 to draw up the new constitution. Hugo Preuss, who was chiefly responsible for the drafting of the constitution, declared at a meeting of the drafting committee: 'The relationship of Prussia to Germany can only be either that Germany stands under Prussian hegemony, or that Prussia is absorbed into Germany. If there is anything in politics which amounts to a mathematical certainty it is this.'

A member of the (Catholic) Centre Party put forward in this committee a plan for the setting up of a separate and independent Rhineland-Westphalian, or West-German, republic, and many South Germans also favoured proposals to divide up Prussia. But too many political cooks spoil the broth, and the opponents of Prussia were too numerous and too disunited to agree. So that all they did was to include an article in the constitution (Article 18) which provided for a re-distribution of the territories of the various states within the Reich at some future date. The belling of the Prussian cat was, of course, again and again postponed. And the result was an awkward dualism between the government of the Reich and the government of Prussia. Compared with the other states Prussia was far too large and powerful: but theoretically she had forfeited the position of leadership of the Reich which Bismarck had secured for her. The seat of both governments was Berlin, and there was frequent overlapping and friction. One of Hitler's first acts on coming to power was to abolish the separate government of Prussia and to place Prussia under the central government of the Reich. This was done by a law published on the 6th February 1933, that is to say, within a week of Hitler's appointment as Chancellor. From the 20th July 1933 Prussia was governed by a 'Commissioner' ['Reichskommissar'], who was none other than Hitler's chief henchman, Göring. On the 7th April 1934 a great step was taken in the unification and Nazification of the Reich by the appointment of 'Reich Governors' ['Statthalter'] to the various states, rather on the medieval model whereby a strong Emperor sent his representatives to hold sway over subjected territories. It is significant that Prussia was not given a 'Statthalter', and that Hitler reserved the rights and duties of Statthalter in Prussia for himself. Thus the governments of the Reich and of Prussia were once again united, and even more closely than in the empire of Bismarck. This all serves to show the great importance which Hitler and the Nazis attached to Prussia. They realized that once they had secured control of Prussia they were sure of controlling the whole Reich.

Far more important, however, than the failure of the opponents of Prussia to destroy her in a physical and territorial sense was their failure to suppress the Prussian spirit and to blot out the Prussian tradition. But here in all fairness it must be pointed out that most of them did not try to do this; or at any rate, they soon gave up trying. Perhaps they realized instinctively, and as Germans they were better fitted than anybody else to judge, that it was then (and probably always will be) impossible to replace the spirit of Potsdam by the spirit of Weimar. Perhaps they noticed the Prussian stirrings in their own hearts and minds: 'Scratch a German, and you will find a Prussian', no matter how non-Prussian and anti-Prussian he may seem! And no doubt many of them felt at bottom that Germany needed the spirit of Potsdam if she were to rise again, and recover anything like the political and economic power she had enjoyed just previous to 1914. Even the most ardent devotee of Weimar, of 'noble simplicity and serene greatness' ['edle Einfalt und stille Grösse'], must find it hard at times to resist the temptation of Prussian 'Machtpolitik', Prussian uniforms, and Prussian marches, above all if they are accompanied by the convenient if specious excuse of spreading German 'Kultur' and 'Zucht' (discipline) among benighted neighbours.

It is also worth while stressing that the times were far less favourable to the idealistic and other-worldly spirit of Weimar than to the more commonplace, realistic, and grasping spirit of Potsdam. The friars in the Middle Ages acted on the theory that if one is to improve the condition of a man's soul, one must also look to his body: if the body politic is ravaged by hunger (the blockade), amputation (the Versailles Treaty), poverty (the inflation years, 1921-3), and similar ills, then it is perhaps unreasonable to expect a healthy and normal development of the political soul. Quite soon after the November revolution, therefore, the tendency set in towards compromise with the Prussian spirit. Early in 1919 the Social Democrats found it necessary to co-operate with the Army: in an effort to restore order and to keep down their most serious rivals, the Communists. The new government could not continue to exist without some kind of military force at its disposal, and in desperation President Ebert permitted the establishment of a 'Freikorps' out of officers and men of the old Imperial army. On the 6th January 1919 the first squads of volunteers marched into the suburbs of Berlin. From that time on, the Weimar Republic was an uneasy partnership which was bound to lead to disaster. In 1925 Hindenburg, the representative of the army and the old order, was elected President. Frederick the Great was allowed to continue as a great national hero. The Prussians, the die-hard Conservatives, the Catholics, the Communists, and, indeed, men and women of every conceivable group and outlook, were given freedom to organize themselves and join in the political game. German party politics degenerated into haggling and wire-pulling behind the scenes; and it is therefore not to be wondered at if the coalition governments which resulted, and which rapidly succeeded each other, were often characterized by weakness and indecision. If the Weimar Republic had preserved something of the repressive nature of its Prussian and Imperial predecessor, and if only it had anticipated a tithe of the wonderfully efficient repressive methods of its Nazi (and in many ways Prussian) successor, it would no doubt have found more favour with the

German people, and would not have come to such a sudden and tragic end.

It would certainly have found more favour with the Prussians, and all Germans with Prussian leanings. For the fact that the Weimar Republic was so democratic and liberal and cosmopolitan simply had the effect of making them more Prussian than ever before, and, in many cases, far more Prussian than they would normally have become. The opponents of Prussia were ready and often eager to compromise: the opponents of the Weimar Republic were steadfastly determined to overthrow it.

On this question of compromise between the spirit of Potsdam and the spirit of Weimar, we may quote one of the profoundest and most clear-sighted thinkers of our time, the Italian philosopher Benedetto Croce (*History of Europe in the Nineteenth Century*): 'In vain and only by way of rhetorical vagueness did some speak emotionally of the idyllic marriage or the friendly disagreement between the "two souls" of the empire, that of Prussia and that of Germany, that of Potsdam and that of Weimar, whereas in fact only one soul was supreme, that of Prussia and Potsdam.' It is clear from the context that Croce is referring to the empire of Bismarck; but his verdict applies with even greater force to the Weimar Republic and the Third Reich. It is like trying to mix oil and water: Prussia, like the oil, will always in the end come out on top.

In the chapters which follow the spirit of Potsdam is represented by Moeller van den Bruck, Oswald Spengler, Wilhelm Stapel, Walter Flex, Ernst Jünger, by panegyrists of Frederick the Great, and finally by Hitler and Rosenberg; and the spirit of Weimar by Fritz von Unruh, Carl Zuckmayer (*The Captain of Köpenick*), and Werner Hegemann (*Anti-Frederick*). It is at once clear, therefore, that a selection has been made of outstanding personalities and works, and that it is a somewhat arbitrary selection with a heavy bias towards Prussia. Admittedly this does not give anything like a complete or accurate picture of German literature from 1919 to 1933; but such is not our aim. Our aim is to draw attention to certain factors and features in the Weimar period which have hitherto been sadly neglected.

Chapter I

Moeller van den Bruck on 'The Prussian Style' and 'The Third Empire'

Moeller van den Bruck was born in Solingen in 1876. His father was an architect, but in choosing this profession he had rather departed from the family tradition. Most of Moeller's ancestors on his father's side were Protestant pastors or Prussian officers, and Moeller himself was destined at first to become an officer. It was in honour of his mother that he called himself in his first publications Moeller-Bruck, later Moeller van den Bruck; she came from the Rhineland, and is said to have had Spanish as well as Dutch blood in her veins. Moeller went to school at Düsseldorf, but he was unhappy and unsuccessful there, and did not stay long enough to take the usual leaving examination. In the spring of 1896 he went to Leipzig, where he attended a few lectures at the University, but was not enrolled as a student. In the meantime his parents had died, and had left him a considerable sum of money; so in August 1896 he went to Berlin, married, and began to write. His chief interests at the outset of his career as a writer were art and literature, and for a time he contributed articles to Maximilian Harden's well-known periodical *Die Zukunft*. With the help of his wife he also tried his hand at translating French writers like Maupassant. He soon had a large circle of friends and acquaintances, including such men as Richard Dehmel, Arno Holz, Rudolf Steiner. But the longer he stayed in Berlin, the more isolated and restless he felt. The 'Rheinländer' in him protested against Prussia and Prussianism; and he found himself becoming more and more

42

opposed to the Prussian state and Prussian society. He finally decided to go to France, although this meant giving up not only his country, but also his wife and his son. His first great work, *Die moderne Literatur*, a volume of over eight hundred pages, the importance of which literary historians would seem not yet to have realized, appeared in 1902, and in the autumn of that year he left Germany. He is said to have thought seriously of going to America, but Paris held him for several years, and after Paris he spent some time in Italy. It was in Paris that he wrote the greater part of *Die Deutschen*, his second great work, the eight volumes of which appeared at intervals from 1904 to 1910. Here too he translated into German, with the help of his second wife and her sister, practically the whole of Dostoevski, whom he may be said to have discovered for Germany. Moeller planned a third great work, a kind of cultural history of the nations, which was to bear the title *Die Werte der Völker*; but only the first volume was finished—*Die italienische Schönheit*, which appeared in 1913. By this time Moeller was back in Berlin, and apparently quite happy there. It was as if he had been fated to leave Prussia and Germany for a long period in order to find his real German self and the burning patriotism that henceforth dominated him. He who had once fled from Berlin became an enthusiastic admirer of Prussia and one of her most loyal and devoted supporters. He began to write his book *Der preussische Stil*, in which he idealized and glorified Prussia as no-one before him. When war came in August 1914 he joined the army, and fought in the wearisome campaigns in the east. Later he was employed in the foreign propaganda branch of the Army High Command in Berlin, a post for which his years abroad and his literary abilities made him very suitable. The manuscript of *Der preussische Stil* was finished in 1915, and the book appeared in 1916.

Moeller steeled himself to regard Germany's defeat in November 1918 with unwavering optimism and a grim refusal to despair. In a letter (dated the 20th January 1919) to his friend Hans Grimm, with whom he had worked in the propaganda office in Berlin and who was later to write the most famous novel on life in the German colonies: *Volk ohne Raum* ['The Nation without Living Space'] (1926), he speaks of the confidence in the future which he has observed everywhere in Germany, but particularly among young Germans, in spite of the war and the revolution. Moeller already believed, or made himself believe, that the lost war would turn out in the long run to Germany's advantage.

Early in 1919 he published an essay called 'Das Recht der jungen Völker' ['The Rights of the Young Peoples']; it had the approval of the German Foreign Office, and was addressed to President Wilson. Moeller here took up and developed ideas he had outlined as early as 1906 in that section of his work *Die Deutschen* which bore the title 'Die Zeitgenossen' ['Contemporaries']. He divided the peoples and nations into young and old, into those which are still active and creative, and those which are only capable of enjoying the fruits of past labours. Among the young nations he included the Bulgars, the Finns, the Japanese, the Prussians. Most of the other nations were old; the Romance nations like France and Italy were definitely so; and England he regarded as a degenerate Germanic nation, a nation of shopkeepers, not of heroes. He stressed the contrast between the victorious nations, with their declining populations, and the defeated states, which were sadly over-populated. The old, victorious nations kept to the ideas of 1789; the new nations lived and acted according to new ideas. Moeller confidently expected from Germany a complete reorientation and renewal of political ideas, and the creation of a new political world in which Prussia was to shine forth as the great model for all the young peoples. 'The time will come once again in which all peoples that are young, and everybody who feels young, will recognize in Prussian history the most beautiful, the noblest, the most manly political history of all the European peoples.' In passing, we may note that this idea of the 'rights' of the young, virile, and over-populated nations quickly became a mainstay and an ever-recurring feature of German, Italian, and Japanese propaganda; and it is interesting, therefore, to discover its Prussian creator and its Prussian origins. The more one thinks about it the more one realizes that it is essentially a Prussian idea, and altogether in line with Prussia's historical development and with the Prussian spirit and tradition.

In March 1919 Moeller helped to found the 'Juni-Klub', and took a leading part in its activities. This club was chiefly made

44

up of nationalist and right-wing intellectuals, who decided on their name after the signing of the Treaty of Versailles on the 28th June 1919. They had their own periodical, *Das Wissen, eine Wochenschrift für politische Erziehung* ['Knowledge, a Weekly Periodical for Political Education'], and Hans Grimm and Paul Ernst were among the contributors. It strongly opposed Versailles, Weimar, Marxism, Democracy, and was for a time one of the best-known organs of the nationalist opposition. There is indubitable evidence to show that in 1921 Adolf Hitler found in this circle a friendly and sympathetic welcome. It was here that he met Moeller for the first time, and he is said to have been greatly impressed. That Hitler and the National Socialists owe much of their political Weltanschauung to Moeller will become increasingly clear as this inquiry proceeds.

We must now pass on to an examination and analysis of Moeller's greatest work, *Der preussische Stil*. Perhaps one notices first of all the photograph on the dust-cover: the head of Frederick the Great from the well-known equestrian statue by Rauch which stands on the Unter den Linden near the university and the State Library, in Berlin. The binding is in black and white, the Prussian colours. After looking at the title-page, we turn to the dedication, which runs 'Dedicated to the Prussian officer Lieutenant-Colonel Rudolf Moeller, my dear uncle and true friend, as a confession of faith in Hegel and Clausewitz.' It would be difficult to find anything more Prussian than that! On the next page stands the motto of the book—the words are Moeller's own: 'Prussia is the greatest act of colonization undertaken by Germans, just as Germany will be the greatest political act of the Prussians.'[1] In this somewhat cryptic statement, of which the English translation is inadequate to express the full meaning, we have in a nutshell a typical Prussian conception of Prussian and German history. The preface is by Hans Schwarz, the special guardian of the memory and heritage of Moeller van den Bruck, above all in his capacity as Director of the 'Moeller-van-den-Bruck-Archiv' in the Dorotheenstrasse, Berlin. (His play, *Prinz von Preussen*, will be discussed in Chapter XII.) Schwarz writes in the enthusiastic style of the disciple and

[1] 'Preussen ist die grösste kolonisatorische Tat des Deutschtums, wie Deutschland die grösste politische Tat des Preussentums sein wird.'

devotee, and only two points need detain us. The first is his account of the decisive experience ['das grundlegende Erlebnis'] which led Moeller to write the book. He had just finished his *Italienische Schönheit*, when one day he found himself standing in front of the Hauptwache [Guard-House], Unter den Linden, one of the best-known creations of the architect Schinkel. (Many English visitors to Berlin will remember it, because after the war of 1914-18 it was turned into the chief national memorial to the German dead.) Suddenly he realized that this building represented a style of architecture, an artistic form, a spirit, a Weltanschauung, and a way of life just as independent and self-sufficient as the classicism of Italy and the ancient world. Here was a real style in its own right, a 'Prussian style', which it was no longer feasible to explain simply by relating it to similar structures of the Italian or French Renaissance. This style could only be explained by reference to Prussian and German history. Prussia, he suddenly realized, meant the beginning of a new period in European history, and the Prussian style was really the last great style to develop in Europe. The second point worthy of note in the preface appears in the concluding paragraph. Schwarz quotes the opening words of the book: 'Prussia is without a myth' ['Preussen ist ohne Mythos'], and declares that by writing this book Moeller provided Prussia with a 'myth', and thus disproved his own introductory statement.

The first chapter of the book bears the title 'Genesis', and is of special interest and importance for the general ideas it contains. Moeller declared the spirit of Germany as a whole to be essentially 'romantic', and that the Prussian spirit was a necessary counterbalance and antidote. The chief task facing Germans was to organize their tremendous creative powers, which had so often been extravagantly wasted on side-issues and unworthy ends; and to discipline their longings and dreams by the application of Prussian principles of political power, unity, and reality. Germany needed Prussia, in order to overcome its dangerous romanticism. Only in this way could Germany become really 'lebensfähig'—capable of successful existence. Moeller then surveyed the past, and gave in broad outline an essentially Prussian interpretation of German history. Towards the end of the Middle Ages the Germans ceased to be the first nation of the earth, and this because of political weakness. They became a people of mercenary soldiers, mystics, scholars, craftsmen. A spirit of unreality prevailed. In the north, however, a search for a new reality began, and was carried on with ever-increasing vigour by the Teutonic Knights, the Hansa merchants, the Junkers beyond the Elbe, and the Hohenzollern rulers. Here were Germans who had no time for romantic ideas about Rome, Palermo, Jerusalem, but concentrated on the hard realities of life in the north-German plains. The achievements of these men could be summed up in the word Prussia, and it was through Prussia that Germany ceased to be a nation of troubadours and wanderers and became a nation of pioneers and settlers eager for land and for permanent homes. The sweeping and downright romantic nature of such statements does not need any special emphasis, and significantly enough it was with more than an ordinary measure of German romanticism that Moeller enthused about the Teutonic Knights. These noble fellows in their white cloaks with the big black cross were already 'Prussians before the Prussians': in their vows of poverty, chastity, and obedience, their disciplined lives and minds, their subordination of self to the common cause, they represented the real beginnings of 'Preussentum'. Nor could Moeller refrain from pointing out the 'special aesthetic significance' of the Prussian colours of black and white; he describes them as 'these serious nordic colours, which are really not colours at all', and which represent a typically Prussian renunciation of gaiety.

The next two chapters describe how the Germans pushed across the Elbe and reached the Baltic, how knights and priests conquered the Mark Brandenburg, and were followed by settlers —Saxons, Franks, Frisians, Flemings. The Slav tribes which they encountered were overcome and absorbed, for example, the Wends, whose descendants are still to be found in the Spreewald, the district of woods and waterways to the south-west of Berlin. In all this Moeller was at great pains to stress the German elements in this long process of colonization, and the German character of the communities evolved. He declared that the starting-point of Prussia was German, and that Prussianism could never have come from the Slavs. It arose as 'a special form, a special consciousness' ['eine Sonderbildung, ein Sonderbewusstsein'] of German character and life; and separation from the rest of Germany was necessary in order to allow this development to take place. Later the Prussian stream was again to flow into the main German stream, and to determine its course and volume.

The fourth chapter is chiefly concerned with the Great Elector. 'He inaugurated Prussian politics' ['Er leitete die preussische Politik ein'], but although he had many Prussian characteristics he was still German rather than Prussian. It was above all in his internal policy—in which he was far more successful then in his external policy—that he was already Prussian. One of his first acts was to make the army dependent directly upon himself, by requiring that the soldiers should swear obedience to him, and not as hitherto to their respective commanders. Moeller also describes how he introduced administrative and financial reforms, built canals, invited Dutch and Swiss settlers. In spite of all this Moeller concludes that the age was too 'baroque' to be Prussian.

Here we come upon one of those words, borrowed originally from architecture and the history of art, which in the last few decades have been bandied about in Germany and charged with an indeterminate cultural and spiritual meaning. Expressed in the simplest possible terms baroque is that kind of architecture which developed in the late sixteenth, the seventeenth, and eighteenth centuries, chiefly under the influence of the Counter-Reformation, as a reaction to the harmony in rest, the severe simplicity of the Renaissance style. Baroque architecture aimed at strength in movement; straight lines were replaced by innumerable curves and volutes; simplicity was sacrificed to ornamentation, often of a heavy, florid, and pompous kind. Now it is just these latter defects which Moeller had in mind when he described the age of the Great Elector as too baroque to be Prussian. He uses 'baroque', therefore, pre-eminently as a term of abuse. The same applies to 'rococo', which developed out of, or rather alongside, baroque, and is not so much a style of architecture as a method of ornamenting interiors by the use of mirrors and gilding and gay colours, and by the application of conventional decorative motifs such as shells. Obviously such a style is little in keeping with the Prussian spirit: it lacks simplicity,

48

severity, monumentality. Yet Moeller was bound to admit the presence of a great deal of baroque and rococo in Prussia, and it is interesting and not a little amusing to see how he disposed of it. Thus he declared: 'In Prussia the baroque was simpler, the rococo nobler.' Schlüter (1664–1714), the great architect and sculptor who built the Armoury [Zeughaus] on the Unter den Linden and whose equestrian statue of the Great Elector on the Castle Bridge, Berlin, is one of the finest creations of its kind, was undoubtedly baroque. But in Chapter 5, which is entitled 'Schlüter', Moeller describes him as a 'Roman in Germany', and discovers that certain 'Roman' elements in his baroque were closely related to the 'Prussian' style which was soon to develop.

In the next chapter the questions of architecture and style with which Moeller had to deal were obviously of a more congenial nature and fitted in better with his general theories. The chapter is entitled 'Zopf' and is chiefly concerned with Frederick William I. 'Zopf' means 'plait', and is difficult to translate architecturally. But it is easy to realize what kind of architecture is meant, for just as the short and tight plaits into which Frederick William I compelled his soldiers to do their hair was in striking contrast to the flowing locks worn by the 'laughing cavaliers' of those days, so the buildings put up by Frederick William I were very different from baroque and rococo. It is as if we were to take the word 'Roundhead' and apply it to architecture. The plain, simple, and sober 'Zopf' style developed in other parts of Europe also, as a reaction to baroque and rococo; but Moeller proudly pointed out that it first made its appearance in the Prussia of Frederick William I, and that whereas in France 'Zopf' followed rococo, in Prussia it preceded.

Moeller described Frederick William I as 'der Soldatenkönig, der Beamtenkönig' ['the Soldier-King, the King who is also a State Official']—both of which titles were of course not new; but he added—'der Nur-Preusse, der Ur-Preusse', which may be translated (inadequately) as 'the only genuine Prussian, the original Prussian type'. Frederick William I was the creator of 'Prussianism', which now supplied Germany with the backbone it had hitherto always lacked; hard and straight as a ramrod, this backbone was thrust by Frederick William I into the German body politic. A highly imaginative and striking metaphor! His vain and extravagant father Frederick I had won the important title of King of Prussia; Frederick William lived up to this title, and made it a powerful reality. He was the first really Prussian figure, and united for the first time all the great Prussian qualities. Moeller hastened to add that this was not so much because of his well-known eccentricities and whims; for example, his preference for pork and pickled cabbage, or the giant soldiers he collected from all over Europe and treated like playthings, or the hours he spent in the evenings smoking a long pipe and drinking beer out of an earthenware mug ['Tabakskollegium']. Prussian was first and foremost the way in which he continuously disciplined and conquered himself, the way in which he moulded his own character and compelled himself to be strenuous and ascetic. He set up duty as the first commandment in Prussia, against which there was no appeal. He stabilized the royal power and the authority of the state—to use his own phrase—'like a rock of bronze'. Provincial particularism was destroyed, the semi-feudal landowners, and all the other 'estates' were subordinated. He declared: 'The nobility must in future recognize only God and the King of Prussia!' He gave the parole 'Mit Gott und dem König!': service to God and service, to the king. The army was reorganized and enlarged. The old uniform known as the 'Schwedentracht', which went back to the armies of Gustavus Adolphus and the Thirty Years War, disappeared. The blue and yellow flowing cloak, the buff coat, the turned-up and wide-brimmed hat, the top-boots, were replaced by the simple dark-blue uniform, tightly buttoned, with no lapels and fringes, the close-fitting cap and leggings. Frederick William himself almost always wore uniform, and the 'King's coat' was given a meaning which it had never had before. Finally, Moeller stresses Frederick William's piety, quoting such statements as 'I have always striven to make myself better and to lead a godly life'. He had a high conception of his duties as a ruler; he was always at work and went on regular journeys of inspection—because he felt himself responsible to God. It was in keeping with his character, therefore, that the numerous buildings he caused to be erected—churches, barracks, schools, orphanages—should all be simple, sober, practical, but at the same time solid and dignified: in a word 'Zopf'. He had no use for 'romantic nonsense'; he was more concerned with form and line than with superfluous ornament; and he had a love for everything tall and aspiring, as revealed, for example, in the Garrison Church in Potsdam. Moeller cannot praise this church too highly; he regards it as Frederick William's greatest and most characteristic architectural achievement. But here in his enthusiasm he goes off the rails, for he declares: 'And when from its lofty spire "Üb' immer Treu' und Redlichkeit" sounded, his pious yet happy heart was no doubt deeply moved,' etc., etc. This is a reference to the well-known chimes which play the tune of the song:

> *Üb' immer Treu' und Redlichkeit*
> *Bis an dein kühles Grab,*
> *Und weiche keinen Finger breit*
> *Von Gottes Wegen ab!*[1]

Unfortunately, Hölty did not write his poem 'Der alte Landmann an seinen Sohn' ['The Old Peasant to His Son']—of which we have just quoted the first verse—till 1775, and these chimes were not installed in the Garrison Church till 1797.

The next chapter—'Potsdam'—is the longest of the book, and consists largely of a panegyric of Frederick the Great. 'Potsdam is Frederick the Great. The soul of this town is the soul of Frederick the Great.' Frederick the Great inherited Potsdam from his father, but it was he who really created Potsdam: here as in other spheres he completed the good work his father had begun. Moeller had to admit the presence of a great deal of rococo in the Potsdam of Frederick the Great, and this obviously troubled him. But he discovered that the rococo of Frederick the Great was not a French rococo, but somehow a German, a Prussian rococo, with classical elements: more in keeping with the spirit of the great king. Finally, he tried to show that Frederick the Great developed away from—or outgrew—the rococo of

[1] 'Always practise faithfulness and uprightness Until you come to your cool grave, And do not depart a finger's breadth From the paths of God!' The first few notes of the chimes—corresponding to the first line of the song— are used by the Deutschlandsender as its interval signal. 'Always practise faithfulness and uprightness' is surely a singularly inappropriate motto for the chief Nazi wireless station!

his early days, of Rheinsberg, the castle where he spent a few idyllic years before his accession to the throne. It is here above all that Moeller's account becomes conventional: everything leads up to and centres round 'Old Fritz'. He describes lovingly how Frederick returned from his wars quiet, meditative, introspective, his character fashioned and tempered by years of self-discipline, self-sacrifice, devotion to duty. In order to become an instrument for the greatness of Prussia, he had been obliged to renounce many pleasures which had delighted his youth. From sensual things he turned to spiritual things, and became the philosopher of Sanssouci. (We shall see later that this idea of Frederick the Great as a 'victim' or 'sacrifice ('Opfer') is a frequent and popular feature of the legend which has grown up round his name.) It is clear, Moeller argues, that Frederick the Great could no longer be satisfied by flimsy rococo. Besides, the new political situation demanded its rejection. Prussia was now clearly separated from Habsburg, and the North Germans were looking more and more to Prussia. Prussia had definitely established itself as the new political and national entity in Germany, and as a new political and ethical principle. Rococo was no longer suitable for this new Prussia! The climax of this huge piece of special pleading is that Frederick the Great turned more and more to ancient styles and models, and above all to Sparta. Here we may conveniently leave him, but we must hold on for a time to this wondrous idea of Prussia and Sparta.[1]

In his book on Stefan George (1930) Friedrich Wolters began the section on 'The Ancient World and Christianity' with the words: 'It is an eternal and inexplicable dowry of the German people that whenever it awakes it remembers the Greeks.' To this one might add that if Prussians experience an 'awakening', they always remember Sparta! As far back as 1756 Ludwig Gleim wrote in his poem 'On the Opening of the Campaign', one of his 'War Songs of a Prussian Grenadier': 'Let Berlin be Sparta!' ['Berlin sei Sparta!']. So that Moeller was not pro-

[1] Since the appearance of Miss Butler's provocative book on *The Tyranny of Greece over Germany* (1935) English readers can readily inform themselves about the pronounced desire on the part of many Germans from about 1760 to associate themselves with ancient Greece and Rome. But Miss Butler was concerned with literature, art, culture, religion and not with politics, so that here is an important side of the 'Tyranny' with which she does not deal.

claiming a new idea when he solemnly declared that Frederick the Great turned to Sparta. What was new was the application of the idea to architecture, in the attempts to prove the existence of a 'Prussian style'. We have already seen that Moeller damned baroque and rococo with faint praise—to the greater glory of 'Zopf'. The next step in his argument was to maintain that from 'Zopf' it is possible to go direct to the ancient world, without troubling about the Italian and the French Renaissance, and that starting from 'Zopf', architects like Langhans (1733–1808) and Schinkel (1781–1841) created a Prussian style which was not 'classical' in the sense that it copied buildings of the ancient world, but 'classical' in that it represented a new 'Classicism' and because its inherent qualities of greatness were similar and by no means inferior to the classical styles of ancient Greece and Rome. Moeller declared that Langhans, the architect of the Brandenburger Tor, transformed into reality the prophetic command which Gleim put into the mouth of his Prussian grenadier: 'Let Berlin be Sparta!' It was for Schinkel, however, that Moeller reserved his highest terms of praise. In the Guard-House, which he described as the most 'classical' building in Berlin, and in which 'the severity of a Doric surface is united with the delicacy of Attic decoration', Schinkel found his own style, which he then applied in masterly fashion to the much greater tasks with which he was entrusted, for example, the Kaiser Friedrich Museum and the Schauspielhaus. In this way the architectural greatness of the Prussian capital took its rise. 'The ancient world was transformed into a Prussian myth.'[1]

Chapter 13 is called 'Deutschland', and deals with the foundation of the German Empire through the agency of Prussia in 1871. We have seen already that the commonly accepted view

[1] It is interesting to surmise how much Hitler owes to the inspiration of Moeller in his grandiose plans for public buildings, but only an authority on architecture or the history of art could deal with this adequately. It is clear, however, that in their striving for simplicity, austerity, straight and aspiring lines, and above all for 'monumentality' (Chapter X of Moeller's book is entitled 'Monumentalität'), Hitler and the Nazi architects conform in high degree to the 'Prussian style' as discovered and described by Moeller, and that in giving vent to his 'grand passion' Hitler is carrying on the tradition of Frederick William I and Frederick the Great, namely, that the head of the state should himself build, patronize builders, and direct and control their activities.

is that Germany was unhappily 'Prussianized' after 1871; but Moeller puts forward with great eloquence the opposite theory, namely, that Prussia was unhappily 'Teutonized'. Prussia, he says, wanted to be more than Prussia. In this desire lay its own destiny and the destiny of Germany as a whole: Prussia had to be, in order that the new Germany could come into being. But this desire was also Prussia's doom, because in assuming the leadership of a united Germany it lost its soul, its spiritual form, its style. The Prussian destiny and the German destiny could not be fulfilled without sacrifice—the sacrifice of Prussia. In the years after the foundation of the Empire, German 'Romanticism' spread to Prussia and destroyed Prussian character. The stoic Prussian State could not sustain the romantic pomp and circumstance of the new German Empire without degeneration. Moeller puts forward as chief proof of this theory the way in which Berlin was architecturally and aesthetically spoilt. Many fine old buildings, even some by great architects like Schlüter and Schinkel, were pulled down or altered; the new buildings which now came to be erected in great numbers were usually in extremely bad taste. There was little or no 'town-planning'. So that within a few decades, Berlin, which Moeller asserted had once been the most ascetic, the most manly, and one of the most dignified of German towns, became one of the ugliest towns in existence. To many English readers this theory that Prussia suffered great loss and harm at the hands of the rest of Germany may come as something new and as something of a shock. But it will not surprise anyone who is familiar with the struggle for German unity in the nineteenth century. For it is certainly true that there were many Prussians, particularly among the landowning aristocracy and among the conservatives generally, who opposed the achievement of German unity under Prussian leadership, because they were afraid that Prussia would be contaminated and would lose her identity in the process, and some of them persisted in these views even after 1871 and indeed right up to the present day.

The last chapter, 'The Prussian Destiny', was added to the new edition which appeared soon after the Great War: conclusive proof of Moeller's unshakable belief in Prussia, even in her darkest hour. He declared that it was impossible to think of

MOELLER VAN DEN BRUCK

Germany without Prussia and Prussianism. There were certain specifically Prussian values and virtues, such as seriousness, will-power, readiness for sacrifice, which were indestructible and which for a long time had been entering more and more into the lives of the other German 'tribes'. The Great War hastened this unifying process, and made Germans recognize that they were all somehow or other Prussians. The outcome of the war, Moeller declared, had taken the sting and the meaning out of the hitherto widespread and firmly rooted opposition to Prussia. We come finally to the long peroration with the words 'There must be a Prussia', repeated defiantly and almost hysterically, as a kind of refrain. 'Germany cannot do without Prussia and Prussianism!' 'Prussianism represents the political will of the German people. The strength of Prussianism has always been and still is the strength to bring together and to unite. Germany depends on the outcome of the struggle for unity. All Germans who to-day struggle for unity are Prussians.'

Moeller began with art and literature; he ended with politics. Early in 1923 he published *Das dritte Reich* [The Third Empire], the book which up to 1933 probably played a greater part in German party politics than any other, not excluding Hitler's *Mein Kampf*.[1] It was in this book that the idea of the Third Empire was conceived, and expressed in such a form that it appealed to millions of Germans. The Nazis took over the idea from Moeller and exploited it in so far as it suited their ends. In typical fashion they never admitted where they got it from or recognized their obligation, partly no doubt because they were jealous of Moeller's influence, and not a little afraid of the rivalry of the 'Prussians' and 'revolutionary Conservatives' for whom Moeller stood. Another reason was that it was impossible to harness him in the service of their race theories, as the following quotation from *Der preussische Stil* clearly shows: 'For in the

[1] A condensed English translation was published by Allen and Unwin in 1934 under the title *Germany's Third Empire*. Here, as in the other cases when I have dealt with books of which an English translation is available, I have preferred to work at the German original, and the translation of passages quoted is my own. But many English readers will be glad to know that these translations exist: Jünger's *Wäldchen 125* (see p. 91 note), Zuckmayer's *Hauptmann von Köpenick* (see p. 98 note), Hegemann's *Fridericus* (see p. 126), Hindenburg's *Aus meinem Leben* (see p. 148 note), Spengler's *Jahre der Entscheidung* (see p. 190 note), and Niemöller's sermons (see p. 204 note).

last resort it is not the race, nor the mixture of races, nor the racial composition which is the decisive factor for a Volk, but the entirety of its culture, to which every racial group contributes.' When the Nazis came to power they soon began to accuse Moeller of being 'reactionary'. So that gradually the book which up to 1933 had been displayed in bookshops even more than *Mein Kampf*, disappeared from view and sank into comparative oblivion.

In the letter, dated December 1922, in which Moeller dedicates *Das dritte Reich* to Heinrich von Gleichen, one of his friends and associates in the 'Juni-Klub', he reminds him how immediately after the War they began their work, convinced that all the misery in Germany's political life was caused primarily by the party struggle. 'And when in June 1919, on the day after Versailles, we gave our work a definite political character (i.e. by founding the 'June-Club') we came across Germans everywhere who said they did not belong to any party. This book contains a criticism of parties, it appeals to Germans of all parties. We substitute for the party system the idea of the Third Empire, a fine old German idea which goes back to the Middle Ages, and is associated with the expectation of the empire of a thousand years. The Second Empire has broken down. Are we at the beginning of a new period in German history in which the German people will fulfil its destiny in the world? At present we see the triumph of all the peoples of the world over Germany, at home the setting up of a parliamentary system on the western model and domination by the parties.... We shall certainly rise again. ... We told each other in June 1919 that the war has been a war to educate us ['unser Erziehungskrieg']. Was it really so? We hope so.'

The first chapter is chiefly concerned with the November Revolution. We realize, said Moeller, that the Revolution cannot be undone, but we intend to win it ['Wir wollen die Revolution gewinnen!']—we intend to make it serve *our* ends, to us it is a means of winning over the German people to *our* political views. Germany lost the war, not because her fighting strength was inferior, but because she lacked the 'political sense' of the English and the French. 'But we are younger than both these nations.... Our national and political development is not complete.' The German people had been so far non-political, which was the reason why they were so easily tricked at the end of the war. They believed that if they stopped fighting all the other nations would stop fighting as well. They were betrayed by demagogues.

The next chapter consists chiefly of an attack on Marx and 'Marxism'. As a Jew, Marx was an alien in Europe, but yet he had the insolence to interfere in the affairs of European nations! Marxism is condemned as materialism, as emanating from a materialist philosophy and a materialist conception of history. The democratic international Socialism of Marx must be opposed at every turn, and in its place a German and 'national' Socialism must be developed, based on authoritarian and corporative conceptions of the state and industry. Real Socialism depends on co-operation from above and from below; it is not simply a question of the socialization of the undertakings themselves, but it demands a mutual interdependence between management and workers, an adjustment of the claims of all, and an equitable share in the returns.

The third chapter bears as its motto the words 'Liberalism is the Death of Nations' ['Am Liberalismus gehen die Völker zu Grunde']. The effect of Liberalism is to disintegrate; it is a moral disease which ruins the political character of a nation. German youth realized that it had been betrayed in the name of Liberalism: instead of Wilson's Fourteen Points, Germany was given the 440 Articles of the Versailles Treaty. It therefore turned away from Liberalism with contempt and disgust, realizing that Liberalism was contrary to its nature, and regarding all Liberals as enemies. When denouncing Liberalism, Moeller also denounced Freemasonry—as anonymous, international, Jewish. England too came in here for a fair measure of abuse. The English have always talked about freedom, but they have always acted for their own freedom and against the freedom of everybody else! This is not hypocrisy, although it appears to be so; it is simply the peculiar English way of thinking, their astonishing *naïveté*!

In the chapter on 'Democracy' Moeller declared that the Reichstag had always been despised by the people in Germany. With rising scorn he asked: 'What is this Liberal chameleon—

Democracy? Who is this Moloch, who devours masses and classes and estates and all human differences?' And then come surprising statements such as: 'The Germans were originally a democratic people—in the time of the early Teutonic tribes!' Or that Prussia was much more democratic than its reputation would suggest, because the king and the nobility had as their motto: Ich dien!

The next chapter is directed against Communism, and then follow two chapters chiefly devoted to making Moeller's own standpoint clear, namely, that of the 'revolutionary Conservative'. He was at great pains to deny that 'Conservative' is the same as 'reactionary', and he defined the conservative aims as national security, maintenance of the family, the state, and the monarchy, and a recognition of the necessity of 'estates' and corporate bodies. The German masses must be won over for the aims of the state. They must be educated politically. It must be made clear to them that an over-populated country like Germany can only be saved by a purposeful foreign policy.

The final section, entitled 'The Third Empire', was a plea for unity, for the settlement of differences. Moeller confidently asserted that the war had greatly intensified the feeling that all Germans belong together. Since the breakdown of the Second Empire, the antagonism between Prussia and the rest of Germany had disappeared behind the consciousness of a community of the German 'Volk', and the time was now ripe for the setting up of the Third Empire. All Germans had become in some way or other 'Grossdeutsche', i.e. they were in favour of a Great Germany, in spite of frontiers and custom duties and other barriers. 'As a result of the war we lost in territory, but as Germans we moved closer to each other!'

It will have been noticed that in the foregoing analysis of *Das dritte Reich* Prussia and Prussianism were hardly ever mentioned; but there can be no doubt that they were continuously in Moeller's mind when he was writing his final work. And unless one is familiar with *Der preussische Stil* it is impossible to understand *Das dritte Reich* and to see it in its proper perspective.

Moeller quickly wore himself out in the political struggle. He became ill with some mysterious nervous disease, and in 1925, when it became clear that there was no hope of recovery, he committed suicide. Or to use the 'heroic' circumlocution favoured by patriotic and nationally minded Germans for such cases: 'He died a Germanic death' ['Er starb einen germanischen Tod']. It would be more accurate to say that Moeller van den Bruck died the unhappy death of a disappointed Prussian; like Heinrich von Kleist and so many other apostles of Prussianism. But his name will long be remembered as one of the chief creators of the Prussian myth, and as the publicist who did so much to prepare the way for Adolf Hitler.

Chapter II

Oswald Spengler on Prussian Socialism

Oswald Spengler (1880–1936) went to the famous school founded by August Hermann Francke in Halle, and later studied science and mathematics at the universities of München, Berlin, and Halle. After teaching for a few years in a school at Hamburg, he settled down in München and devoted himself to his studies and to writing. His chief work, *Der Untergang des Abendlandes* (vol. i, 1918; vol. ii, 1922) created a great stir, far beyond the limits of Germany. It has been so much discussed and is so well known in England that only the briefest reminder of its contents is needed here. Spengler interpreted the history of the world as a succession of 'cultures', each of which passes through various stages of growth. European culture has now passed into the final stage! The work was above all a refutation of the idea of progress, and the climax of that wave of 'Kulturpessimismus' which dominated Europe after the Great War. Much less known to English readers is Spengler's *Preussentum und Sozialismus* (1920); yet it is a book which throws much light on Germany's political development since the Great War, and had a much greater effect on German youth than *The Decline of the West*. The latter was too huge in scope, and too negative in outlook; whereas *Preussentum und Sozialismus* was concentrated and defiantly positive, often to the point of 'tub-thumping'.

The book was written at the end of 1919, and it is clear from the introduction that Spengler, like Moeller van den Bruck, refused to accept Germany's defeat and the November Revolution, and that from the very first he opposed the Treaty of Ver-

OSWALD SPENGLER ON PRUSSIAN SOCIALISM

sailles and the Weimar Republic. He roundly declared that the
Versailles terms meant a continuation of the War; and that Germany must prepare herself for her part in the struggle. He described the Revolution as the most senseless act in German history. It was not an uprising of the people; it was an affair of
party politics, carried out by demagogues. Weimar was an
attempt to introduce democracy and the parliamentary system
into Germany. 'In the heart of the German people Weimar
stands condemned. They don't even laugh. The new constitution has met with absolute indifference. It is certain that this
hypocritical performance will come to a sad end.' Spengler
went on to compare the Weimar revolution with the English and
the French revolutions of 1688 and 1789. They were all three
concerned with the question of power: Is the will of the individual to be subject to the will of the community, or vice versa?
The English 'instinct' decided that power belongs to the individual, that there must be freedom of competition between
individuals; the triumph of the strong, Liberalism, inequality,
no state. If everybody fights for himself, then in the long run all
will benefit. The French 'instinct' decided that power belongs
to nobody; they rejected subordination of any kind, and therefore there was in France no order, no state, nothing at all. The
German 'instinct', or to be more exact the Prussian 'instinct',
so Spengler declared, asserts that power belongs to the whole
community: the community is sovereign, the individual serves
the community. The king is only the first servant of the state.
(This quotation from Frederick the Great was of course inevitable here!) Everybody has his place: some command and some
obey. This, we are suddenly told, is authoritarian Socialism, in
its nature anti-liberal and anti-democratic, and it has existed in
Germany (or rather Prussia) since the eighteenth century!

We have seen that Moeller van den Bruck was violently
opposed to Marx, and to the Socialism associated with his
name; and that he preached the revival and development of
German and Prussian Socialism to take its place. This was the
main theme of Spengler's book, worked out with much greater
force and detail. In his introduction Spengler declared that
German Socialism is older, stronger, and deeper than that of
Marx. 'Only German Socialism is *real* Socialism! Real Socialism

61

lies in the German blood, and blood alone decides the future. We Germans are Socialists and other people cannot be Socialists! The Old Prussian spirit and Socialism, although to-day they seem to be opposed to each other, are really one and the same thing.'

The World War, fought in the evening of Western culture (such phrases remind the reader constantly that Spengler also wrote *The Decline of the West*), was in the last resort the great conflict between the two Germanic ideas: England versus the Prussian State. It was the Prussian State against which the English army was really fighting: that German masterpiece, which other nations cannot understand or imitate, and which therefore other nations hate. And England won because she was aided, and Germany was betrayed, by 'the England within' ['das innere England']. At first sight this seems like nonsensical drivel, but there can be no doubt that Spengler believed it, and that many 'Prussians'—and Nazis—were only too ready to agree with him. For such people England had always been the villain in the piece; England stood in Germany's path; English ideas and customs undermined German strength at home. Spengler identified 'the England within' with 'Michel', a well-known figure in German caricatures, symbolizing such things as narrow-minded provincialism, bourgeois honesty and simplicity, an ostrich-like refusal to face facts. Criticism at the wrong time, the longing for a quiet life at the wrong time, the striving after ideals when rapid action is required, constant grumbling: all this, said Spengler, is the result of English influence on German character.

This discussion is continued in Chapter 3, which bears the title 'Engländer und Preussen'. Here Spengler gave his definition of 'Prussianism'. He began by saying that he did not want to be misunderstood: although the name pointed to one special part of Germany, 'Prussianism' was by no means limited to that area, nor was it a question of birth; there was of course a Prussian 'race', but not all those born on Prussian territory belonged to it. By no means every Englishman by birth was an 'Englishman' in the sense of race, and not every Prussian was a 'Prussian' in this sense. 'Prussians' were to be found in all parts of Germany. Since Rossbach and Leuthen innumerable Germans had possessed deep down in their souls a piece of 'Prussianism'!

Even in the Germany of 1919 there was much that was Prussian: a sense of reality, *esprit de corps*, discipline, energy: indeed all those qualities which 'Michel' did not possess. Once again poor Michel was reviled. He was unpolitical, unpractical, lost in dreams; he had no sense of race, he adorned himself with English rags and ideas; he practised a trivial cosmopolitanism, enthused over friendship among nations and humanitarian aims; he showed a sleepy inclination towards English Liberalism with its hostility to the state, preferred 'Kleinstaaterei' (i.e. a Germany divided into small states), and delighted in petty religious quarrels.

A suitable sub-title for Spengler's book would be 'The Myth of the Vikings'. He argued that the colonization of the Slav territories across the Elbe was carried out by Germans of all tribes, but chiefly by the Saxons, and that therefore the nucleus of the Prussians was very closely related to that of the English. Those same Saxons, who in loosely organized groups of Vikings, often under Norman and Danish names, subjected the Celtic Britons, also conquered the German East! But, we now learn, the spirit of the Vikings and that of the Teutonic Knights was fundamentally different, and each of them gave rise to an ethical code quite opposed to the other. On the one hand freedom of the individual; on the other a community which stood above the individual. To-day they are called 'Individualism' and 'Socialism'! Each of these words signifies virtues of a high order. Self-reliance, self-determination, resolution, initiative on the one hand; fidelity, discipline, denial of self, self-discipline on the other. To be free—and to serve. To serve—that is the old Prussian style. 'Not I', but 'We'; a feeling of community into which one is entirely absorbed. The individual did not matter: he had to sacrifice himself to the whole. Not each for himself, but all for all, with that 'inner freedom' in the sense of the 'libertas oboedientiae', the freedom of service. Such were the characteristics of the Prussian army, the Prussian Civil Service, and the Prussian workers. They were the virtues of the Teutonic Knights! Whereas English people were nothing but Vikings! One is reminded of John Buchan's novel *The Path of the King*, which is based on the idea that no man knows his ancestry, and that kingly blood may be dormant for centuries until the appointed time. The story

63

begins with a Viking's son lost in a raid, and ends with Abraham Lincoln. But what for John Buchan was the excuse for a good yarn had here become a serious political idea, a means of explaining and increasing hatred between two nations.

Such was the origin, according to Spengler, of the English and Prussian types, in the moulding of which geography played an important part. It was the difference, Spengler declared, between a people living on an island, and a people guarding a 'Mark',[1] with no natural frontiers, and exposed on all sides to attack. In England the island took the place of the state; a land without a state was only possible under such conditions. Instead of the state, there was the free and private individual, opposed to the state, and demanding the ruthless struggle for existence, because only in this struggle could he bring his best instincts, his old Viking instincts, into play. Buckle, Malthus, and Darwin all believed in the struggle for existence. William the Conqueror and his followers were a society of knightly adventurers: the English trading companies were similar; a late example was provided by the group of Englishmen who seized South Africa in the nineties. Complementary to the idea of the free and private individual was the idea of 'society', which was also in opposition to the state. Spengler admits that it signifies a sum of very positive ethical qualities, and that the ladies and gentlemen of fashionable English society have been united since 1750 by the same kind of feelings, thoughts, and behaviour. But they have always been dominated by feelings of success, of good fortune, and not—like the Prussians—of tasks to be performed; they were in reality Vikings returned home from plundering raids. Wealth along with noble blood have always been the conditions for belonging to English society. There was no German, no Prussian, society of this kind. In Prussia wealth was not decisive, but the work done. The captain stood above the lieutenant, even if the latter was a millionaire. Every Prussian officer, official, and workman felt that he was working for all, for the whole community, for the state. The English were a race of successful men; the Prussians a race of workers. A superficial

[1] *Mark* means first of all frontier, and then it comes to mean a frontier district or province; cf. die Mark Brandenburg, die Ostmark; cf. the Welsh Marches.

but not unimportant expression of these fundamental differences was provided by comparing 'men's fashions' in England with their counterpart the Prussian uniform. The one was the uniform of the private individual, the other signified public service. In a footnote Spengler pointed out that in the same way Frenchmen had discovered women's fashions. Instead of business (i.e. England) and service (i.e. Prussia)—*l'amour!*

It was part of the Prussian tradition that the will of the individual should surrender itself to the will of the community. Officers, officials, workers (Spengler's favourite way of dividing up German manhood), the German people in 1813, 1870, and 1914 (significant dates!) formed a unity, an entity, which was above the individual ['überpersönlich']. This was not the herd instinct ['Herdengefühl']; there was something infinitely strong and free in all this, which no-one who did not 'belong' would ever understand. An Englishman would never understand, indeed the whole world was unable to understand, that a deep and 'inner' sense of independence accompanied the 'Prussian style'. The 'practical' English freedom could only be achieved by the sacrifice of that 'inner' freedom. An Englishman was at bottom a slave—either as a Puritan, or a rationalist, or a sensualist, or a materialist! Every Englishman prided himself on being able to act for himself, but he did not think for himself. The same 'Weltanschauung'—with little or no real content, but with a slight theological tinge—had spread itself over all. Here if anywhere the term 'herd instinct' was applicable.

Spengler later compared Pietism and Puritanism.[1] He said— quite rightly—that Pietism had exercised a great influence on Prussian character. He told—with much justification—of the quiet faith without dogma, the genuine simplicity of heart, which characterized such Prussians as Queen Luise, William I, Bismarck, Moltke, Hindenburg. But he soon fell back into his exaggerations, his sweeping statements. He made Pietism identical with 'Prussianism', and asserted that Puritanism was its English antithesis; and he even put forward the theory that out of Puritanism developed Capitalism, and out of Pietism Socialism (Prussian Socialism, of course). Puritanism was further a from of Calvinism; it represented the idea of predestina-

[1] For a brief account of Pietism see pp. 195 ff. below.

tion and of the English as the chosen people; hence the self-confidence and lack of conscience in action which characterized and explained the rise of the English nation to power. Pietism was the spirit of community, the conception of one's whole life as service. A deep contempt of just being rich, of luxury, of indolence, of enjoyment, of 'good fortune' dominated both Pietism and Prussianism. But to an Englishman these things were gifts of God; 'comfort' was a proof of heavenly grace, reverently accepted. Work was to the Puritan the result of man's fall. To the Prussian it was the command of God. English people—and Americans—were only concerned with the results of work: success, money, wealth; and work was only the means to such ends. In order to achieve success a struggle with others was of course inevitable, but the Puritan conscience justified any and all means. Those who stood in the way were pushed aside: individuals, classes, and entire peoples; because God had willed it thus. Prussian, and Socialist, ethics said: This life is not concerned with happiness; simply do your duty, by working. English, and capitalistic, ethics said: Get rich, and then you do not need to work any longer. The one system was for a land without a state, for egoists, and for men who were by nature Vikings ['Wikingernaturen']: it was economic Darwinism. The other was Socialism in the fullest sense of the word: the desire to bring about the power and the happiness, not of the individual, but of the whole. 'Frederick William I and not Marx was in this sense the first conscious Socialist.' The world movement of Socialism started from him as its model personality. Kant expressed the movement in a formula with his categorical imperative of duty. Was one to prefer the categorical imperative of Kant: Act as if the maxim of thy action were to become a universal law; or the command of Bentham: Act so that you—achieve success? It was the struggle between the Viking and the Teutonic Knight; on the one hand the ethics of success, on the other the ethics of duty.

In dealing with questions of economics Spengler professed to find the same antithesis. The life of the settler in frontier districts, the colonizing activities of a knightly order, necessarily gave rise to the principle of the economic authority of the state. Duties and rights in the production and consumption of goods came to be divided equally. The aim was not the enrichment of the individual, but the prosperity of the whole. This was also the way in which Frederick William I and his successors colonized the marshes of the east. They regarded it as their mission; God had given them a task to perform. This was also how the genuine German workman thought of his work. But the island people, with their piratical instincts ['Seeräuberinstinkt'], regarded economic life quite differently. For them it was a question of a struggle for booty, and the share of individuals in that booty. The state created by the Normans rested entirely on such motives and principles: each of the lords was allowed to seize a piece of land and exploit it. And the successors of the Norman barons have never learned to look at the world in any other way. The aim had always been and was still to-day the production of wealth for the individual. The robber principle ['Räuberprinzip'] of free trade was typical of this 'Viking' system of economy. On the other hand, the Prussian, and therefore the Socialist, principle was state control of economic life for a higher purpose than the enrichment of the individual. Out of the Viking had developed the free trader, out of the Teutonic Knight the administrative official. With an ominous and obstinate pessimism that is so typical of the man, Spengler went on to declare that a reconciliation between the two types was impossible, that neither would be satisfied until the whole world was subject to his ideas, and that war would therefore continue until one of them had finally conquered. The spirit of the Viking and the spirit of the Teutonic Knight would continue to struggle to the end. 'Even if the world comes forth from the streams of blood of this century tired and broken.' Was world trade to be an exploitation of the world or an organization of the world? Was the world to be ruled by Capitalism or by Socialism? On the answer to these questions the fate of the world depended.

Spengler dealt next with the antagonism between England and Prussia in politics. He declared that the parliamentary system of government was a specifically English growth dependent on the Viking character of Englishmen and on England's insular position. It was impossible to imitate it. England had rendered powerless all those states to which it had given its own system of government—pretending that it was a medicine. The parliamentary system in Germany was nonsense—or treason. In England there was a free society of private individuals, who, because of England's insular position, had been able to do away with the state, and to maintain themselves—up to 1916—by means of a fleet manned by mercenary sailors and by an endless series of wars which they paid foreign statesmen and foreign peoples to conduct for them. The parliamentary system was also conditional on the existence of two parties of definite composition, interests, and principles. They were originally groups of the nobility, and came into being in 1642 and 1688. But the qualities of both were to be found in the old Vikings about whom the Icelandic Sagas tell. The Tories stood for pride in noble blood and in everything hereditary and legitimate, ownership of land, warlike undertakings, and bloody decisions. The Whigs took great joy in robbing and plundering, in easy successes, and in rich movable booty; they preferred cunning and daring to bodily strength. 'Whether Tories or Whigs are in power policy is simply a matter of business—in a piratical sense.' The members of these two parties were all gentlemen, belonged to the same fashionable society, and revealed an admirable unity in their mode of life. So that important matters could be settled in private conversation and in private correspondence, and much occurred which need only be admitted when success had justified the means. What happened openly and on the surface was only *fable convenue*. It was nonsense to say that the people had a share in the government. Only hopeless German Liberals believed this. Rule by the people was in reality impossible except in states the size of a few villages. The parliamentary system was entirely foreign to the nature of the Prussian and the German people; their indifference to elections and questions of franchise proved this.

Chapter 4 is entitled 'Marx'. Spengler here discovered that the ideas of Marx were typically English. For example, he declared that Marx must have got the idea of the class war from England, because only in England were the classes graded according to wealth. In Prussia, on the other hand, men and women were grouped according to the functions they performed, and according to the degree of command and obedience which their activities entailed. Spengler went on to assert that Marx's ethics also betrayed their English origin. Marx regarded work as a misfortune and preached contempt for work: an attitude which was absolutely in line with the English contempt for the manual worker! Here too was revealed the instinct of the Viking, whose job it was 'to capture booty and not to patch the sails'. English people had no conception of the dignity of hard work, which they regarded as incompatible with the name of 'gentleman'. The kernel of Marx's economics was the English idea of work as something to be bought and sold, whereas the Prussian idea was that work was a duty to the community, and no distinction was made as to the kind of work performed. That was Prussian democracy![1] The weapon of the strike, whereby the worker refused to sell his work except at a higher rate, was the most 'un-Socialistic' feature of Marxism and the most striking proof of its English origin. Marx was also English in that he left the state out of account. He did not understand the 'Prussian-Socialist State', which included the whole people and in which every employer and every worker had at bottom the character of an official ['Beamter']. 'Marxist, and therefore English', was also the idea of the free wage-struggle. The Prussian view was that wages of all kinds ought to be fixed impartially by the state, in accordance with the general economic position and in the interests of the entire people. One further point: Spengler denounced Marx's materialistic conception of history as English, and as the outlook of a people of uncontrolled Vikings and traders. Spengler felt sure in his own mind that the false Socialism of Marx would eventually be overcome by the genuine Socialism of Old Prussia.

In his conclusion Spengler declared that the great 'world question' of the age was the choice between the Prussian and the

---

[1] The Nazis were not slow to take over and exploit Spengler's assertions on the German and English attitude towards 'work', and such comparisons have been made repeatedly over the German wireless since war began. The following extracts from a talk (Deutschlandsender, German, 12.30, 6th May 1941) are typical: 'We Germans have always held work in high honour. . . . The unparalleled hard work of the Germans has always been feared and hated in England. In England it is regarded as unworthy of a gentleman to work himself. . . . Only coolies, only members of subject and therefore inferior nations, ought to work: that was always and is still to-day the real attitude of the ruling class in England and also in America. These plutocrats only recognize the honour of property, and regard work as something dishonourable.'

English 'ideas', between Socialism and Capitalism, between State and Parliament. And this decisive question must be settled in Germany for Europe and the whole world! Hitherto the 'Socialist workers' and the 'conservative elements' in Germany had misunderstood each other and had also misunderstood the true nature of Socialism. But to-day they must realize that their aims are identical. Prussianism and Socialism must stand together against 'the England within', against these foreign principles which had attacked the entire life of the German people, paralysing it and robbing it of its soul. The danger was tremendous. Woe to those Germans who out of self-seeking and lack of understanding were at this hour found wanting! The workers must free themselves from the illusions of Marxism, and realize that they had to choose between Prussian Socialism and no Socialism at all. The 'Conservatives' must free themselves of all thought of self, and realize that they had to choose between Socialism and destruction. All Germans must free themselves from English and French ideas of democracy, and realize that they had their own type of democracy.

At the end of his introduction Spengler appealed to German youth. 'I count in our struggle on that part of our youth which is deep enough to feel that Germany is strong and unconquered, and that the German path leads upwards in spite of everything, a youth Roman in its pride in service, not demanding rights from others but duties from itself.' At the end of the book his appeal was even more fervent and rhetorical. 'I turn to youth. I call upon all those who have marrow in their bones and blood in their veins. Educate yourselves! Become men! We don't want any more ideologists, no more talk about culture and world-citizenship and the spiritual mission of the Germans. We need hardness, a bold scepticism, a body of socialist supermen ['sozialistische Herrennaturen']. The path to power is clearly marked; the elect of the German workers together with the best representatives of the Old Prussian political spirit, both of them determined to create a truly Socialist state, a democracy in the Prussian sense, firmly united by a common sense of duty, by the consciousness of their great task, by the will to obey in order to rule, by the will to die in order to live, by the strength to make tremendous sacrifices in order to fulfil our destiny, to be what we are and what without us would be lacking altogether in the world. We are Socialists. We do not intend to have been Socialists in vain.'

English and American writers on Germany have often confessed themselves puzzled and not a little annoyed by the Nazi use of the word 'Socialism'. They claim to understand the 'Nationalism' in 'National Socialism', but they declare angrily that the 'Socialism' is not Socialism at all, and leave it at that. The solution to such difficulties and doubts is to be found in books like Spengler's *Preussentum und Sozialismus*, and by realizing that the Nazis have simply borrowed and developed the peculiar Prussian version of Socialism. It also becomes much more clear from a study of Moeller van den Bruck and Spengler how the combination of Nationalist and Socialist elements in Germany after the first Great War came about, and what exactly it involved. Thirdly, it is easy to see after reading these two outstanding Prussian writers where Hitler and the Nazis got their ideas about the 'pluto-democracies', and above all on England. It is for such reasons that we have given Moeller van den Bruck and Spengler pride of place and have dealt so fully with some of their works.

Chapter III

The Prussianism of Wilhelm Stapel

Wilhelm Stapel (born 1882) comes of an old Brandenburg family, a fact of which he is very proud. After studying at various universities, including Göttingen, München, and Berlin, he began to write, chiefly on art and literature. From 1911 to 1916 he was editor of the *Kunstwart*, a 'cultural' periodical of high repute, which had been founded as long ago as 1877. But like Moeller van den Bruck, he seems to have turned away from art and literature and culture under the pressure of events and particularly as a result of the Great War, and to have devoted himself primarily to politics. In 1919 he became editor of the periodical *Deutsches Volkstum*, which he made into one of the leading organs of young conservative nationalism. His book *The Fictions of the Weimar Constitution* (1927) attracted considerable attention. *Preussen muss sein* ['There must be a Prussia']—the book with which this chapter deals—was published in 1932. There can be little doubt that Stapel found his title in the peroration of Moeller van den Bruck's *Der preussische Stil*, an assumption borne out by the many striking similarities between the two works. Stapel's book has been chosen for special treatment because it proves that the ideas put forward by Moeller at the beginning of the Weimar period were still being fervently preached at the end, and right up to the time when the Nazis assumed power.

Stapel begins by raising such questions as: Does Prussia stand condemned by the outcome of the war? Does the breakdown of 1918 prove that Prussia was an 'error' in German history? Must Prussia be destroyed or split up? Has Prussia no longer a mission in Germany? What sort of people in Germany hate Prussia and why? He declares that the hatred of Prussia has four roots. Prussia is hated firstly by those Germans whose interpretation of recent German history is that the needy, ascetic, ambitious, military state of Prussia unhappily overcame the rich, mild, glorious imperial state of Austria, and robbed it of political leadership in Germany. Such opponents consider that since the Reformation, and above all since Frederick the Great triumphed over Maria Theresa, German history has developed on wrong lines, and that correction is urgently needed. Secondly, particularism is another source of opposition to Prussia. Every German state wishes to maintain its independence, and feels that this is endangered above all by Prussia. Thirdly, Prussia is hated for obvious reasons by Marxists and Social Democrats. Fourthly, there are many Roman Catholics who have not yet forgotten the religious persecutions under Bismarck ['Kulturkampf'].

In the second section—'Die preussische Situation'—Stapel asks what Prussia lost in November 1918. It lost first of all the Hohenzollern dynasty. Secondly, all weapons had to be handed over to the enemy. Stapel describes this as an 'un-Prussian act', for nothing is more shameful to a military state! And he supports this view by reminding his readers of what the Spartan mother said to her son: 'A soldier must not surrender his arms unless he surrenders himself.' Stapel admits that the disappearance of the Hohenzollerns and the disarming represent the loss of something specifically Prussian. To this he adds a third loss, namely, 'the occupation of the Prussian state by the Weimar coalition', asserting that, as a result of the parliamentary system, just those minds have come to rule in Prussia which Prussians reject. Prussia is now under the rule of its enemies, chief among which, of course, is Marxism, which Stapel describes as the great opponent, because Marxists interpret Prussianism as 'Junkerdom' and 'militarism'!

So much for the black side. Stapel is happy, however, to be able to inform his readers that a Prussian 'nucleus' remains, which may be expressed in these words: Hindenburg, the Army, and East Prussia.

Hindenburg, says Stapel, is a truly Prussian type; it is impossible not to recognize in him the spirit of the Prussian officer and of the Prussian nobility. 'And this Prussian is to-day the only man who holds the German Empire together, he is the cornerstone of the Empire, the only man in Germany who is absolutely indispensable.'

About the Army Stapel has little to say that is new. He deplores the change from 'an army of the people' ['Volksheer'] to a 'professional army' ['Berufsheer'], a play upon words with which Germans often expressed their chagrin at the limitation of the huge army based on conscription which had formerly been their pride. The depleted army nevertheless continues consciously to cherish and uphold the Prussian military tradition which extends from Frederick William I to Moltke and von Schlieffen.

His remarks on East Prussia are much more significant, and very Prussian. He argues that up to the Great War, Alsace, with the town of Strassburg, was the territory about which Germans were most concerned. But after the Great War, although France had remained the historic enemy, not Alsace but East Prussia was the land uppermost in German hearts and minds. The Romanticism of the Rhine had given way to the Romanticism of the Marienburg, Königsberg, Danzig. Just as in former times all Germans had shouted—in the words of the 'Watch on the Rhine':

Zum Rhein, zum Rhein, zum deutschen Rhein,
Wir alle wollen Hüter sein,

so to-day all Germans are eager and determined to guard East Prussia.

The third section is on the Prussian spirit, and the essence of 'Prussianism'. In words reminiscent of Moeller van den Bruck and Spengler he declares that to be a Prussian is not to belong to a Prussian tribe (Stamm), in the sense that a Suabian belongs to Suabia, and a Saxon to Saxony. A man is not Prussian by blood, but by 'Bekenntnis'. (This is an untranslatable word which means something like professing a faith, and living up to it.) A man cannot become a Saxon of his own will, but it is possible to become a Prussian in this way. Prussianism is the sum total of certain political qualities and virtues. It is as if the political strength of the German people had concentrated itself in Prus-

74

sia. In the Middle Ages the knights from all parts of Germany, filled with a mission and the will to conquer, found their way to Prussia. Later, the name of Frederick the Great attracted soldiers and politicians from all the German tribes. Scharnhorst, Gneisenau, Stein, Fichte, were not Prussians by birth but by conversion and affirmation ['Bekenntnispreussen']. What bound them together was the political law. They *became* Prussians, because in Prussia they could be politically active.

According to Stapel, the law of Prussia's being ['das preussische Gesetz'] has never been set forth in definite commands and prohibitions, but it has been embodied in three figures—the Great Elector, Frederick William I, and Frederick the Great. So much has been said already and is still to be said about the 'legends' attaching to these rulers that only one point from Stapel's very typical interpretation need be mentioned here. He admits that they belong to the age of baroque and rococo, but he hastens to add that baroque and rococo were in Prussia only a façade (cf. Moeller van den Bruck).

Like the Spartans and the Romans (again one is reminded of Moeller van den Bruck and Spengler), Prussia has produced no literature of the first rank, except political literature, for which Stapel instances Ernst Moritz Arndt and Heinrich von Kleist. In his *Hermannsschlacht* Kleist glorifies Prussia's German mission, and in his *Prinz von Homburg* he glorifies the Prussian 'law'. (Much more will be said about Kleist in Chapter XII.) These two plays are for Prussia what Virgil's *Æneid* was for the Romans! Prussia has no Homer, Dante, Shakespeare, or Goethe, but on the other hand Prussian philosophy is of the highest rank. Apart from the Greeks no nation has produced a philosophy to rank with that of Prussia. Kant, Fichte, Hegel—a Prussian by birth and two 'Prussians by conversion'—together represent German Idealism. Kant created the Prussian imperative, the theory of duty; Fichte created the theory of freedom, and Hegel the theory of the total state. Frederick William I declared: 'Eternal life is God's concern, everything else is my concern.' Stapel triumphantly points out that Hegel went beyond this, and made the state into something divine.

Stapel now tries to express 'the Prussian law' in a series of formulæ. He begins as follows: 'The king is the chief servant of the law. The life of every Prussian belongs to the king, who is the law. The king obeys the law, the Prussian obeys the king.' What at once strikes the reader is the prominent position here accorded to the 'king', and it is abundantly clear that up to 1932 good Prussians like Stapel had not given up hoping for the return of the Hohenzollern monarchy. Incidentally, this was all a wonderful preparation for the reign of Adolf Hitler, and the setting up of the 'principle of leadership' ['Führerprinzip']. But we must return to our 'Prussian formulæ'.

A Prussian is always a political person, for whom the state stands higher than home and family. The eye of the king is on every Prussian; the king sees everything a Prussian does. Therefore a Prussian has no private life. Family, home, and possessions are all subordinate to the state, they serve the state. The state does not exist for the sake of the family, home, and possessions. The 'estate' of the soldiers ['der Kriegerstand'] has first place in the state. What the soldiers wear is called the king's coat; and he who wears the king's coat must worthily represent the king in his conduct and actions. The second estate is that of the officials; they are soldiers in civilian clothes. Civilian clothes are, of course, always a little ridiculous, but they too are necessary. (This statement is so delightfully Prussian that it is perhaps worth while to quote the German original: 'Zivil ist freilich immer ein bisschen komisch, aber es muss das *auch* geben.') The third estate is that of the peasant. The peasants were there from the beginning of the world and have to work hard: therefore honour is due to them. The fourth estate consists of those who carry on trade and industry. They are important for the finances of the state, and one must therefore recognize their right to exist. Just as the king keeps his state in order, so must the peasant keep his farm, and the citizen his trade or business in order. Every button on the uniform must be faultlessly bright, and in the account books every Pfennig must be reckoned. (N.B. 100 Pfennigs equalled 1 shilling in 1932!) A torn dress must at once be neatly patched, a hole in a stocking must be darned without delay. For otherwise the king will be angry. Every Prussian must be able to obey, and able to command. And to be silent. When a Prussian has no-one to whom he can give commands, he at least gives them to his dog. (What Englishman would ever

think of his dog in this way?) Prussian women must also understand how to command. Therefore a Prussian and his wife must
always have clearly defined spheres of duty. But the eye of the
king penetrates into the kitchens and dairies also. It is this which
distinguishes Prussians from other people. Other people stand in
the presence of God, Prussians stand in the presence of their king
as well. In other words, all they do is related to the state.

Stapel declared that this Prussian State, which was at the
same time an 'order' like that of the Teutonic Knights, reached
maturity under the creative hands of Frederick the Great, and
was then ready for the great Germanic tasks it was destined to
perform. The first of these 'tasks' was the Wars of Liberation
which united the German people in a common cause; the second
was the foundation of the Empire of Bismarck, which raised
Germany to the status of a world power; and the third was the
Great War, in which Germany stood alone against the whole
world. Stapel's views on the Great War are typically Prussian—
and Nazi. 'The Prussians stood ten kilometres from Amiens—
another ten kilometres and the world would have lain at their
feet. But there the crash came, the most terrible crash that had
ever thundered through world history; Prussia broke down, the
hardest crystal in the world had cracked.' This feeling that they
had *almost* won the war, and the puzzled surprise as to why they
only just lost it, buoyed up many Prussians and Nazis and made
them quite eager to fight again, or as they preferred to think, to
continue a war which had not yet ended, and in which Adolf
Hitler would finally bring them revenge and victory.

The last section of Stapel's book is called 'The necessity of
Prussia' ['Die Notwendigkeit Preussens']. Prussia still has a mission to perform; the German Empire cannot become what it is
destined to become without Prussia; without Prussianism the
German destiny cannot be fulfilled; Prussia is not 'a four-hun-
dred-years-old-error' but a natural and organic growth in German history: Prussia is the political substance of Germany. In
his peroration Stapel declares that the eternal task for Germans
is the building up of the German Empire, and that any and every
German who supports the Empire must support Prussia.

Chapter IV

Three Prussian Officers of the First Great War

I now propose to discuss and compare the experiences of three young Prussian officers who fought in the Great War and the consequent effect on their characters and ideas. All three were writers of great power, and each found a large following among German youth in the post-war period. The first—Walter Flex—died fighting for his ideals, and his war story *Der Wanderer zwischen beiden Welten* ['The Wanderer between Two Worlds'] (1916) and his war poetry are a noble monument to his faith in Prussia. The second—Fritz von Unruh—survived; but the poems and stories and above all the plays which he wrote during and just after the war reveal how much the war changed him, until he finally became a convinced and bitter opponent of Prussia. The third—Ernst Jünger—also came through the war, and in the many books he wrote about it and in his essays on the science and philosophy of war he did much to maintain the Prussian military tradition, until it was taken over and exploited by the Nazis.

1. Walter Flex: the Prussian Ideal of Youth

Walter Flex was born at Eisenach in 1887. Two points about his life before the Great War may be stressed. The first is that Flex was for many years tutor to Bismarck's grand-children. He lived with the Bismarck family and was thus brought into contact with 'Prussianism' of a very old and very genuine kind. He was given access to the family library—at Friedrichsruh near Hamburg, and it was here that he was able to collect the material about the ancestors of the 'Iron Chancellor' which

THREE PRUSSIAN OFFICERS OF THE GREAT WAR

formed the basis of his short stories published under the title
Zwölf Bismarcks (1913), and of his drama *Klaus von Bismarck* (also
1913). The second point is that Flex played an active part in the
German Youth Movement [Wandervögel], which took its rise in
the early years of the twentieth century, went on from strength
to strength till 1914, and experienced a great revival after 1918.

When war broke out, it was natural and inevitable that Flex
should volunteer. In his novel *Der Wanderer*, which is written in
the first person and is a kind of war diary, he describes how he
served first of all as a private in the west, was selected for a commission and sent to a special training camp in the east, and
fought as a lieutenant against the Russians. To this brief survey
of the main facts of his life it is only necessary to add that Flex
was killed on the 15th October 1917, while taking part in an
attack on a Russian farm-house in Ösel, an island in the Baltic
at the entrance to the bay of Riga. He was thirty years of age.

Flex is one of the best-known of German war-poets. His first
collection of war-poetry appeared in 1915 under the title *Sonne
und Schild*, and contained many poems which later found their
way into anthologies and school-books. The first poem in this
collection is worthy of special treatment here, because it is such
a perfect expression of Flex's 'Prussianism'. It is called 'Preussischer Fahneneid' ['Oath to the Prussian Flag'], and in the
first two verses the poet describes how he and other faithful subjects have sworn to defend the King of Prussia now that he has
been attacked by enemies full of hate and cunning. The third
verse declares:

> *Von uns wird keiner die Treue brechen*
> *Und keiner den Eid.*
> *Wir wollen ihn schützen und wollen ihn rächen,*
> *Wir tragen sein Kleid.*
> *Wir sind dem König von Preussen verschworen*
> *Mit Leib und Seele, wie wir geboren.*
> *Wer auf die preussische Fahne schwört,*
> *Hat nichts mehr, was ihm selber gehört.*[1]

[1] 'Not one of us will break faith and the oath we swore. We are determined
to defend and avenge him; we wear the king's coat. We are bound body and
soul to the King of Prussia, with our whole lives. A man who swears an oath to
the Prussian flag has no longer anything which belongs personally to himself.'

There is here, first of all, an idea which is typically Prussian, namely, the idea of service to *the* King of Prussia, and not to a particular king. It is an idea specially associated with Frederick William I, who seems to have first given expression to it. Although king himself, he often talked of serving *the* King of Prussia, and demanded that his insubordinate son Fritz should prepare himself to do the same. The King of Prussia in this sense was always there; he never died, but went on and on; and with the help of this somewhat mysterious abstraction, Prussians long after Frederick William I symbolized their service to the Hohenzollern dynasty and the Prussian state. Secondly, there is mention of the 'king's coat' or uniform in an appropriate Prussian way. Thirdly, we may single out the idea of faithfulness ['Treue'], a virtue which Prussians and Germans like to regard as in some way particularly their own. Finally, there is the absolute denial and sacrifice of self expressed in the seventh and eighth lines. These two lines became so well known that they found their way into Büchmann's *Geflügelte Worte*, the best-known German collection of 'household words' and 'familiar quotations'. Not only is this an honour to Flex, because very few quotations from the poetry of the Great War achieved such a distinction, but it may be regarded as proof in a small way of the continuation after the Great War of the Prussian spirit and of Prussian ideals. Even more significant and very typical is the way in which this quotation has been exploited by the Nazis. Since 1933 the word 'preussisch' has been replaced by the word 'Hitler', so that it reads:

Wer auf die Hitlerfahne schwört,
Hat nichts mehr, was ihm selber gehört.

And as most Germans have forgotten, or never knew, where the quotation came from, once again Prussianism has been conveniently and swiftly transformed into Hitlerism and National Socialism.

But it is not so much for his war-poetry as for his war-novel, *Der Wanderer*, that Flex was chiefly remembered. It went through many editions and was probably the most popular of all the war books.[1] In many German families the confirmation of a son or

[1] The copy which I bought second-hand several years ago has on the title-page the note—'300.bis 341.Tausend'.

daughter is celebrated by restrained festivity and the giving of presents: for many years Flex's book was a favourite present, particularly for a boy.

The spirit and contents of the book may be summed up in the briefest terms by saying that it combines the two great factors in Flex's life: Prussia, and the Youth Movement. It is dedicated 'To the memory of my dear friend Ernst Wurche': Wurche is the hero of the book, and Flex describes how they met, how they became good comrades and friends, how they fought and talked together, and how Wurche was killed in battle and was buried. Photographs reveal that Flex was by no means handsome, and this perhaps explains in part his idealized picture of Wurche. Flex seems to have had a round, bullet-shaped head on a rather thick neck; he was almost bald; he had a somewhat fleshy nose and beady eyes, peering through spectacles; and his face was pock-marked. Wurche was twenty when Flex first saw him, that is to say, he was much younger than Flex. What impressed him first of all was Wurche's 'pure' or 'clear' eyes. Later he gives detailed and glowing descriptions of Wurche's appearance, stressing the beauty and strength of his slim form, his proud bearing, and imperious movements.

There are two passages in *Der Wanderer* which have again and again been singled out for quotation. The first occurs in a discussion in the train, when Flex and Wurche are on their way to the training camp for officers, and Flex puts into Wurche's mouth the words: 'To serve as a lieutenant means living as a model for one's men; to show them how to die is of course only a part of this model life.' ['Leutnantsdienst tun heisst seinen Leuten vor-eben, das Vorsterben ist dann wohl einmal ein Teil davon.'] Many German writers—particularly since 1933—have used these words to impress on German youth that they must readily accept death in the service of the Fatherland. But they seldom quote what comes immediately after: 'Many men are capable of showing others how to die—but it will always be a much finer achievement to show them how to live. It is also more difficult.' ['Vorzusterben verstehen viele—aber das Schönere bleibt das Vorleben. Es ist auch schwerer.'] Obviously, if the quotation is continued, the stress is on leading a 'model life' rather than dying a 'model death'. The second well-known quotation runs:

'How to remain pure and yet to grow to maturity—that is the finest and most difficult thing in the art of living.' ['Rein bleiben und reif werden—das ist schönste und schwerste Lebenskunst.'] This also has been given great prominence in books and pamphlets and speeches addressed to the Hitler Youth, but it is very seldom quoted with its context; nor is it explained that Wurche uttered these words at the end of a conversation about the spirit and aims of the Wandervögel. The Nazis have always tried to make their own youth movement appear unique and to minimize, if not to deny, any obligation to German youth movements in the past. After 1933, therefore, Flex and Wurche were interpreted simply as types of Hitler Youth, and not as Prussian Wandervögel.

One final point: Wurche carried in his knapsack a small volume of Goethe's poems, Nietzsche's *Zarathustra*, and the New Testament, all of them well-thumbed. He had intended to become a Protestant pastor, and had just begun his theological studies at a university when war broke out. This is worthy of mention because it shows that the Prussianism of Walter Flex did not exclude Christianity. On the contrary, a very definite and confident Christian piety was one of its main elements. The close connexion between Prussianism of the best kind and Protestantism has already been pointed out, and later, other notable examples, including Frederick William I, Hindenburg, Pastor Niemöller, and Ernst Wiechert will be cited. The fact is that it is wrong, and unjust to many of the finest and most genuine Prussian types, to regard Prussianism as a sweeping synonym for paganism and the denial of Christ.

2. Fritz von Unruh on the Prussian Idea of Duty

If there is one thing which more than any other characterizes the life of a Prussian, it is the idea of duty. It exists as a fixed and guiding star among all classes and ranks, and crops up under strange circumstances and in unexpected places. English people seldom talk about doing their duty; even in time of war the word is somehow taboo: which is perhaps the reason why on the few occasions in English history when an appeal to a sense of duty has been made the incidents stand out in high relief. Thus

Nelson's message at Trafalgar, 'England expects every man to do his duty', sounds somehow novel and startling in English ears. But in Germany the word has become through many decades of too frequent use a fetish, a talisman, a slogan for unscrupulous politicians, political opium for a long-suffering people. It has really been emptied of its ethical content and has come to mean blind obedience to the letter of the laws and to the commands issued by the state and those in authority. Significant also is the fact that duty in Prussia is often negative: Prussia is the classical land of prohibitions.

Now this is all very different from Kant, to whom lip-service is so regularly and unthinkingly paid as the creator of the Prussian idea of duty. Kant put forward his idea of duty as an integral part of a noble conception of man as an independent and autonomous being, possessed of a free will, a law unto himself, not governed in the last resort by his senses and emotions. And the famous 'categorical imperative' was simply the way in which Kant expressed and formulated this conception of moral autonomy; it was his rule for the achievement of a truly moral personality. 'Act only on that maxim whereby thou canst at the same time will that it should become a universal law.' Hundreds of German books and articles and speeches refer impressively to the categorical imperative, but it would be safe to say that the majority of those who use these magic words do not know what they really signify. It is futile to deny that Kant and his philosophy were Prussian by raising the quibble that Kant was really a Scotsman because of his ancestry, or by trying to prove that he was fundamentally opposed to the Prussian State of his day. The idea of duty and the categorical imperative are unmistakably and essentially Prussian—and in a very good sense. But Prussian, too, and in a bad sense, is the way they have been blandly and unquestioningly harnessed to the political machine and exploited in the service of the state. From the standpoint of the state and the government it is very useful to have to deal with citizens so ready to obey and to do what others tell them is their duty: especially in time of war. And there can be no doubt that much of the efficiency, thoroughness, and hard work for which the Prussians are rightly famous is due to the constant striving to do one's duty. But the tendency is to create human machines and political automata, rather than the free moral agents envisaged by Kant.

In the recent literature of Prussia the writer who stands out as a critic and opponent of the Prussian idea of duty is Fritz von Unruh. Unruh is chiefly known as one of the leading exponents of 'Expressionism', that short-lived and in many ways unwholesome literary movement which reached its climax in Germany in the years immediately after the Great War: but that is not our concern here. Born in 1885, he was the scion of an old Silesian noble family, many of whose members had been Prussian officers; and it is said that he went into the army not so much from inclination as from family tradition. During the Great War he was attached to General Headquarters, and spent some time in the entourage of the Crown Prince. His experiences filled him with an intense hatred of war, and drove him further and further towards cosmopolitan pacifism, until he came to reject in its entirety the Prussian military tradition in accordance with which he had been brought up and trained.

The idea of duty enters into practically all Unruh's works; it seems to have haunted him, and never to have let him go. Nor can it be said that this was due entirely to the horrors of the Great War—for duty is the central theme of the two plays he published before the War began: *Offiziere* (1911) and *Louis Ferdinand, Prinz von Preussen* (1913). German literary historians like Soergel and Naumann have pointed out that the mental and spiritual struggles of these plays are very reminiscent of Kleist's *Prinz von Homburg*, a play which will be discussed at some length in Chapter XII; suffice it to say here that the *Prinz von Homburg* is the best-known example of the 'drama of duty' ['Pflichtdrama'], and that it is concerned with the conflict between the political and military conception of duty and personal inclination and honour, between the laws of war and the state and those of free personal development. But whereas Kleist decided definitely in favour of the former, and thereby won the eternal gratitude of all Prussians (and Nazis!), Unruh admitted in his first play that there must be exceptions, and in his second play the question is left open.

Offiziere opens with scenes in the club-house where young officers spend much of their time and energy in drinking,

84

THREE PRUSSIAN OFFICERS OF THE GREAT WAR
gambling, and flirting, in a vain attempt to overcome the mono-
tony of their peace-time lives. But suddenly there is a call for service in South West Africa, to fight against the warlike tribe of
the Hereros. At the end of the third act they have already landed
in Africa, and the colonel is outlining his plans. Ernst von
Schlichting, the hero of the play, a young lieutenant who is
engaged to the colonel's daughter, is put in charge of a signalling station, and given strict orders not to release the signal for
attack until he is expressly told to do so. He strongly objects to
this kind of activity. Ernst (to the colonel): 'Why do you give
me a task like this?' Colonel: 'Is it usual to demand explanations from one's superiors?' Ernst explains that he is eager to
fight and to play his part as an officer, but the answer of the
colonel is simply: 'Then do your duty. Follow the straight path
of duty and do not stray from it.' The fourth act begins with a
thrilling scene in the signalling post up in the hills. Ernst's men
are almost mad and dying with thirst. Ernst finally declares that
he can wait no longer, and although the order has not arrived,
he gives the signal for the attack on the water-holes. Fully
realizing the responsibility he has taken upon himself, he decides
to ride as quickly as possible to headquarters, in order to explain.
A brother officer reminds him of the dangers of the ride, but
fails to dissuade him. He is seriously wounded. The colonel
receives him coldly, reproaches him for disobeying orders, and
without listening to his explanation dashes out to see if he can
'rectify the mistake'. Ernst dies. In the meantime a great victory has been won, and the colonel returns, overjoyed, eager to
congratulate Ernst. At first he does not realize that Ernst is
dead, and declares: 'So there are really cases when it is the duty
of an officer to act on his own responsibility! Schlichting, I have
done you wrong. I did not know the facts. Here it was your duty
to act on your own. I congratulate you.' To English readers
such a statement may seem almost a platitude and the whole
play much ado about nothing; but to Prussians such things are
of supreme importance, and Unruh stood condemned by the
purists in Prussian military circles from the very moment it became known that he had had the bad taste and the impertinence
to write such a play.

Louis Ferdinand, Prinz von Preussen, deals with the theme of duty
85

on a somewhat higher plane, and with a background of familiar personages and events in Prussian history. It would make an interesting study to trace the development of the 'legend' of Louis Ferdinand, and to compare the scant treatment which he has always been given in serious history books with his sudden rise to pride of place in several works of literature. In the second volume of Gebhardt's *Handbuch der deutschen Geschichte*, a standard work of over nine hundred large and closely written pages, he is only mentioned twice: once as the fiery prince who fell at Saalfeld on the 10th October 1806, in one of the preliminary encounters of the battle of Jena, and a second time as having led a party of Prussians who opposed Frederick William III's policy of tame submission to Napoleon. He was the son of Ferdinand, the youngest brother of Frederick the Great, and his real names were Friedrich Ludwig Christian. He seems to have been a Prussian Don Juan, and his illegitimate son Ludwig, by Henriette Fromm, one of his many loves, was ennobled in 1810 under the name Wildenbruch. For the literary historian it is of some interest to realize that the dramatist and novelist Ernst von Wildenbruch (1845–1909) was Louis Ferdinand's grandson.

Unruh's play describes how Louis Ferdinand finds himself opposed to the undignified and weak-kneed policy of Frederick William III, who is in the hands of incapable and treacherous ministers. The climax of the discussions and intrigues is a fiery scene in the royal council at which Louis Ferdinand declares that Prussia must fight to defend her honour in accordance with the glorious tradition of Frederick the Great. Then follows a scene in which Queen Luise reminds him of the commandment of duty. She says to him: 'It is wonderful to see a man who is conscious of his duty. Such a man is a tower of strength.' Louis Ferdinand replies: 'Duty is like an iron band placed round my burning temples!' The Queen: 'I could well sympathize, if I did not appreciate how sublime is the commandment of duty!' This then is the conflict: he cannot decide between his duty to the king and the state, and his own sense of honour. And in this uncertainty he dies fighting at Saalfeld.

Whenever war breaks out, it is the natural tendency for Prussians—even for the minority who have ventured to criticize and oppose in peace-time—to do their 'duty' blindly and tenaciously in defence of the Fatherland. (Hitler and the Nazis knew that war would give them an even greater hold of the German people than before; and anyone familiar with German, and particularly Prussian, character and psychology was convinced that the revolution, which many English people hoped for and expected at the outset of the second Great War, was a long time ahead, and that it would probably only come with military defeat.) Unruh provides a startling exception to the rule, as is clearly shown in his war-story *Opfergang* ['The Way of Sacrifice'], and his war-plays, *Ein Geschlecht* ['One Generation'], and *Platz* ['The Square'].

Opfergang, which mirrored the failure of the German offensive at Verdun in 1916, was written and printed in that year but could only appear after 1918. The following passage, which Unruh puts into the mouth of one of the soldiers, Clemens, shows that his rejection of the idea of duty has now taken on a very definite form. ' "Duty!" answered Clemens with emotion. "It is certainly a fine word and overcomes all personal feelings. But what lies behind it has degenerated. Duty is the cancer in the heart of the (German) people." ' ['der Krebs am Herzen des Volkes'].

Unruh began *Ein Geschlecht* in the summer of 1915, finished it in the autumn of 1916, and it was published in 1917; *Platz* was begun in 1917, finished in 1920, and published in that year. Both plays are 'Expressionist'; crowded with obscure symbols, bizarre visions, blood-curdling shouts, horrible murders, and sexual excesses; written for the most part in a nervous and hurried style, with occasionally a description or a metaphor of great beauty; on the whole confused, unpleasant, unwholesome. For several years Unruh had a large and enthusiastic following among the German theatre public, but it may be suspected that they applauded not so much because they understood the plays (I would defy anybody to do that!) or really appreciated their literary merits, but because they were revolutionary, attacked the authoritarian régime, and rejected the idea of duty and the Prussian spirit as a whole in favour of a humanitarian and cosmopolitan and Utopian political outlook. It is not difficult to understand why many ordinary decent Germans regarded these play with contempt and disgust, and it is in many ways unfortunate that the case against Prussianism should have found such an expression. For it only served to provide grist for the mills of the Prussian die-hards and Nazi demagogues.

The scene of *Ein Geschlecht* is laid in a churchyard on a hill; fighting is still going on in the valley below. The chief characters are the Mother, the Eldest Son, the Youngest Son, and the Daughter. At the beginning of the play the Mother and the Daughter and the Youngest Son are about to bury another son, the Mother's best-loved son, who has been killed in battle. The Eldest Son has fought bravely in the war, but his sufferings have resulted in a complete breakdown—physical, spiritual, and moral. He has been condemned to death for sexual crimes. He it is who embodies the spirit of revolt against the past and the present. He talks about 'der Götze Vaterland' ['the idol Father-land'] and declares:

> *Ich ducke mich nicht länger unter Tempel,*
> *die Vaterland um unsere Ohnmacht baut.*[1]

Towards the end of the play he commits suicide.

In the second play *Platz*, the Youngest Son in the first play re-appears under the name Dietrich; he is the new 'leader', the new 'Volkskönig' ['popular king']. The action takes place on or near a square surrounded by state buildings, with the idol of war and force ['der Platzgötze'] set up in the centre. It is Dietrich's avowed mission to lead the people away from the 'square', which is described as the 'Zuchthaushof der Seele' ['the prison yard of the soul'] and represents the *ancien régime*, and to teach them to form an ideal community based on peace and love, in which self-seeking and lust for power shall have no place. *Ein Geschlecht* was probably intended to symbolize the War, and *Platz* the Revolution which followed it. On one side stand the representatives of the old state and the old order: among them Graf Gutundblut [Count Wealth-and-Blood], the military commander, and Der Greis [the Old Man], the senior member of the Senate. They are opposed by Dietrich, who declares: 'Not another word about the war!' He denies the authority of the state; ridicules all heroic conceptions; and above all attacks the

---

[1] 'I am not going to bow down any longer in temples which the Father-land builds around our helplessness.'

idea of duty. The older generation try to force upon Dietrich their traditional appeal and command ,'Thou shalt'—to which Dietrich replies with his new principle, 'I will'. In the twelfth scene of the first act Dietrich declares:

> *'Du sollst' ist Zwang, schafft Zwang mir je Erlösung?*
> *Ist er nicht aller Qualen Wurzelstock?*
> *'Ich will' ist ruhiges Atmen, ist Natur!*
> *ist meiner Seele erstes Flügelbreiten!*[1]

Again in the twentieth scene the Old Man says to Dietrich: 'Du sollst uns Rede stehen!' Dietrich replies:

> *Du sollst? Du sollst?*
> *Ruf dir das Gestern wieder, Pfeif ihm doch,*
> *ob es noch einen Hasen apportiert?*
> *Das Heute leckt die Peitsche nicht mehr, Herren,*
> *mit der ihr unsern Willen niederschlagt.*[2]

The Old Man reminds Dietrich of the oath he had sworn, but Dietrich declares it is his task to free mankind from all such oaths.

Yet at times it would appear that Dietrich (and therefore Fritz von Unruh himself) is wavering, that he is longing for the comparative certainty of the regimented Prussian life in the past, and dubious as to the outcome of the new spirit and methods. Of this, the following passage from Act II, Scene 11, is a good example:

> *Und doch, seit ich mich losgelöst von dir,*
> *von dem Gesetz, was immer, seit ich's tat—*
> *gähnt überall der Willkür breiter Sumpf!*
> *Hier hatt ich Boden! Unter deinem Joch*
> *schlief ich, stand auf, gehorchte, schlief, stand auf,*
> *und alle Zweifeln trug für mich dein Buckel!*
> *Als ich im Stumpfsinn deinen Karren zog,*
> *da war Gesetz das Ziel,*

---

[1] " Thou shalt" is compulsion. Will compulsion ever bring me salvation? Is it not the root cause of all torments? "I will" is quiet breathing, it is nature! It is the first spreading of the wings of my soul!'

[2] 'Thou shalt explain! Thou shalt? Thou shalt? Call back yesterday, whistle to it, and see if it will still bring you a hare? Gentlemen, the present generation no longer lick the whip, with which you break down our wills.'

der Weg Erfüllung!
Jetzt ist der Weg betäubend, ist das Ziel
umnebelt von mir selben; tappe ich
auf schmalem Steg?[1]

With such uncertainties and doubts in the minds of his bitterest opponents, Hitler was bound to triumph. In their eager desire to be done with the uneasy flounderings in the sea of democracy which characterized the Weimar Republic, the German people rushed to place themselves under the yoke which Hitler held ready for them. The new régime was so very reminiscent of the familiar old Prussian yoke; they were happy to be reverting to type.

Unruh had planned to write a trilogy, but the third play—in which Dietrich was to set up his new order—was never written. One might suggest (unkindly) as a possible reason for Unruh's silence that his young hero Dietrich became a Nazi after all, and joined the S.S. (Hitler's Black Guards). The play *Stürme*, which was first performed in 1922, was a poor substitute for the crowning revelation which Unruh's admirers so eagerly awaited. He began to write it in 1913, but revised it later, and filled it with his new ideas. It is even more difficult to read and enjoy than the others: adultery and patricide prevail. For our purpose, however, it is of interest to note that the 'I will' of youth is again opposed to the 'Thou shalt' of the older generation. The play opens with the funeral service of a prince, and immediately afterwards his young successor says to his friend Count Stefan:

Als ich heute Nacht bei der Leiche wachte,
sank mir, höchst seltsam, das Gesetz der Väter
mit unters Sterbehemd. . . .
Ein eisern Joch fiel mit der Leiche ab.[2]

[1] 'And yet, ever since I freed myself from the law, no matter what I have done since I made myself free—everywhere the broad swamp of arbitrary action yawns before me. Here (i.e. on the basis of the law) I was on firm ground! Under thy (i.e. the law's) yoke I slept, got up, obeyed, slept, got up, and thy shoulders bore for me all doubts. As I pulled thy cart drearily along law was the goal, and the path itself was fulfilment! Now the path is benumbing, the goal is clouded over by my own actions; am I groping along a narrow bridge?'

[2] 'As I kept watch last night by the corpse it seemed to me as if the laws of our fathers disappeared with the shroud: a most strange thought. . . . An iron yoke fell off me when my father became a corpse.'

THREE PRUSSIAN OFFICERS OF THE GREAT WAR

The young prince is eager to try his strength in the open sea of action ['Meine Kraft will endlich in das freie Meer der Tat']. He speaks contemptuously of the people around him at his court as 'grunting animals in the cage of duty'.

It is hardly necessary to say that as soon as Hitler came to power Fritz von Unruh's day in Germany was done. He was already living abroad, and he stayed there. There is nothing deeper than the pit of oblivion into which the Nazis thrust their literary opponents; very few have so far emerged.

3. The Militarism of Ernst Jünger

Most writers of books on the Great War achieved fame—if at all—only for a brief period. This has not been the case with Ernst Jünger, whose fame has steadily increased. Many of them were only capable of writing one book on the War, but for Jünger the theme could apparently never be exhausted. When he had finished relating his war experiences in such books as *In Stahlgewittern* (1920) and *Wäldchen 125* (1925), he went on to develop his own philosophy of war in such works as *Feuer und Blut* (1925), *Der Kampf als inneres Erlebnis* (1929), and *Die totale Mobilmachung* (1931).[1] War is clearly in his blood; he is the born fighter, the kind of man who revels in war; war is the chief purpose and content of his existence. In this, as in many other ways, he represents a common Prussian type. This type is usually inarticulate; but Jünger is a master of language and certainly one of the greatest stylists in German literature of the past twenty years.

Born in March 1895, he was not yet twenty when war broke out; but he at once volunteered, and was soon made an officer. He was often wounded, some accounts say twelve times, others fourteen; but always on recovering he managed to land in the thick of the fighting, and to expose his charmed life to the greatest possible dangers. He distinguished himself particularly as a leader of 'shock troops' ['Stosstruppen'], and his war-books describe the development of a special type of soldier and a special

[1] 'In Storms of Steel'; 'Copse 125'; 'Fire and Blood'; 'War as an Experience of the Soul'; 'Total Mobilization'. An English translation of *In Stahlgewittern* was published by Chatto in 1929 under the title *The Storm of Steel*; this was followed in 1930 by a translation of *Wäldchen 125* under the title *Copse 125*.

technique for such attacks. Shortly before the end of the War he was awarded the *Pour le Mérite* order, a distinction which very few infantry officers obtained, and which was awarded far more sparingly than the Iron Crosses, which were showered on the German Army. Jünger remained in the army till 1923, when he took to writing, and quickly became one of the best-known members of the nationalist opposition. He was acclaimed as the mouth-piece of the 'Frontsoldaten', the soldiers who had fought at the front and in the trenches. Internationalism he met with nationalism, pacifism with 'heroic realism', the middle-class desire for security with the spirit of war and adventure.

In a typical passage in *Wäldchen 125* Jünger declared: 'The kind of patriotism which is carefully directed into certain channels by the authorities, as well as the forces which oppose patriotism, must be swallowed up by a belief in the Volk and the Fatherland which with demon-like power flares up from all classes of society; everybody who feels differently must be branded with the mark of the heretic and exterminated. We cannot possibly be nationalist enough. A revolution which inscribes this on its banners must and will always find us in its ranks. . . . The merging of all Germans into the great empire of a hundred millions which the future will bring—that is an aim for which it is worth while to die and to beat down all opposition.'[1] After reading such a passage, and it would be possible to fill pages with similar quotations, one realizes that the triumph of Adolf Hitler and National Socialism in 1933 was by no means so novel and unique as it appeared, and still appears, to many outsiders and foreign observers. Nor was it so novel and unique as the Nazis themselves would like people to think. The passage quoted above was published in 1925, that is to say, before *Mein Kampf*. Hitler could never have written these words, because his German style is far too coarse and complicated; but he and his

---

[1] 'Der behördlich wohl geregelte Patriotismus ebensowohl wie die Kräfte, die sich ihm gegenüberstellen, müssen von einem dämonisch aus allen Schichten auflodernden Glauben an Volk und Vaterland verschlungen werden, jeder anders Fühlende muss mit dem Brandmal des Ketzers behaftet und ausgerottet werden. Wir können gar nicht national genug sein. Eine Revolution, die das auf ihre Fahnen schreibt, soll uns stets in ihren Reihen finden. . . . Die Gliederung aller Deutschen in das grosse Hundertmillionenreich der Zukunft, das ist ein Ziel, für das es sich wohl zu sterben und jeden Widerstand niederzuschlagen lohnt.'

henchmen knew how to use such ideas and by constant repetition (*ad nauseam*) to make them generally accepted in Germany.

We now turn to Jünger's more philosophical writings, and particularly to the essays collected and published under the title *Blätter und Steine* ['Leaves and Stones'] (1935). In an essay entitled 'Feuer und Bewegung' ['Fire and Movement'] he declared that war was not simply one side or one part of life, but the expression of life as a whole and in its most powerful form: a view which is typically Prussian. Just how Prussian this is may be seen by remembering and comparing what Karl von Clausewitz (1780–1831), the most famous Prussian philosopher and theorist of war, wrote in his well-known work *Vom Kriege* ['On War']: 'War is nothing but a continuation of political relationships by the use of other means. . . . War is an instrument of politics.' ['Der Krieg ist nichts anderes als eine Fortsetzung des politischen Verkehrs mit Einmischung anderer Mitteln. . . . Der Krieg ist ein Instrument der Politik']. In both Clausewitz and Jünger there is, therefore, the same unhesitating acceptance of war as absolutely inevitable, as the most natural thing in the world; there is no thought of war as an unfortunate disease or ghastly crime which man in a more advanced and more perfect world will discipline himself to avoid.

The most important essay in the collection is that entitled 'Die totale Mobilmachung', which had already appeared as an independent work in 1931. Jünger's argument may be summarized as follows: The times are long past when it was sufficient to enrol a hundred thousand soldiers and send them under reliable leaders to the battlefields, as is described, for example, in Voltaire's *Candide*. But even as late as the second half of the nineteenth century wars could be prepared, waged, and won, which the elected representatives of the people could regard with indifference or even oppose: in other words, there was only partial mobilization. Gradually up to 1914 and very rapidly afterwards, however, war became a matter of gigantic industrial effort, as well as a fight with weapons of war. Alongside the armies which met on the battlefield there arose armies of a new kind—armies of transport, armies in the munition and armament factories, armies of those engaged in the production of foodstuffs and raw materials: in a word, the armies of the workers. Towards the end

of the Great War there was hardly a worker who was not caught
at least indirectly in the war-effort; even the woman sitting at
her sewing machine in her own home was included. It thus happened that, after the wars of the knights, of kings, and of citizens,
the wars of the workers followed. The countries waging war were
transformed into huge workshops, which produced armies and
weapons and supplies at the conveyor-belt, and sent them to the
battlefields, where mechanical weapons destroyed them at a
rapidly increasing rate. There was ever-increasing co-operation
between the General Staff and industry; merchant ships were
armed; civilians were compelled to do war work; the workers
were organized on a military basis. From now on war meant
that the entire population was involved—even babies in their
cradles. As Jünger points out: the squadron leader who orders his
men to drop their bombs at night and from a great height does
not distinguish between belligerents and non-belligerents; and
the deadly clouds of poison-gas spread over all living things
without distinction. Jünger maintains that by reason of these
tremendous changes, summed up in the phrase 'total mobilization', the Great War represents an historical phenomenon far
surpassing in importance the French Revolution.

There is one further point I wish to make about this essay.
In the preface to *Blätter und Steine* Jünger wrote with obvious
pride that the ideas he had expressed in 'Die totale Mobilmachung' and certain other writings had already entered into the
'general consciousness' of the German people. The essay first
appeared in 1931, and the preface to *Blätter und Steine* in 1935!
In a sense, therefore, Germany was better prepared than her
opponents for 'total mobilization' and 'total warfare'. Thanks
to men like Ernst Jünger, the continuance of Prussian militarism, and Nazi war ideology, the German people knew far more
what to expect and had been better organized and disciplined.
Whether this is better in the long run for a nation's morale—
to have everybody keyed up to war pitch from the commence-
ment of hostilities—is a doubtful point which only the outcome
of the war can decide.

Finally, brief reference must be made to a third essay in this
collection; it bears the title 'Über den Schmerz; ['On Pain'].
Jünger begins by saying that pain is the strongest trial in life.

'Tell me how you regard and bear pain, and I will tell you who you are!' Jünger notes the growing desire for possessions, the clamouring for luxuries, and the striving to make life more easy and convenient, all of which he sums up in the English word 'comfort'. (There is no exact German equivalent for our word; and to true Prussians like Spengler and Jünger both the word and the idea are anathema.) Jünger admits that in certain ways the advances of science and technology have diminished pain and increased comfort, for example, by the use of anæsthetics. But in spite of all this 'progress', he maintains that the total amount of pain in the world has not diminished. He apparently believes (somewhat naïvely) that there is a fixed quantum of pain to be borne, and that what human beings gain on the swings they lose on the roundabouts. For one thing, human sensibility has increased during the last one hundred and fifty years, and the balance is further restored by new kinds of pain, for example, nervous disorders, psychological and spiritual suffering, even boredom, which Jünger regards as a kind of pain. He also points out that technical methods and appliances are becoming more and more of a habit, and a protective covering to human susceptibilities. So that nobody troubles nowadays about a motor-accident or an explosion in a mine; and in modern warfare the armoured car gives those who are fighting in it a feeling of security, even when death is very near. 'Technology is our uniform' ['Die Technik ist unsere Uniform'].

What Jünger here writes about pain and about 'technology' is typically Prussian; and only a Prussian could have written it. The Prussian tradition has always stood—at any rate in theory —for a hard and ascetic mode of life, readiness to suffer without flinching or complaining, and little concern for the sufferings of others: in other words the cultivation of the 'heroic spirit'. And all this, particularly in its Nazi version, has often meant the suppression of personality, hypocritical bombast, inhuman cruelty, and deliberate ruthlessness. It is the search for Sparta and Rome, whereby Athens—and Nazareth—are usually forgotten. There is not the slightest need to doubt the sincerity or heroism of Ernst Jünger; but at the same time one must deplore and condemn the disastrous consequences of his militarism, and above all the exploitation of his views by the Nazis. From time to time there have been signs that Jünger was not exactly *persona grata* with the Nazis, and it would be easy to find many passages in his writings which run counter to accepted Nazi principles. For example, in the essay on pain he writes: 'It is impossible to create artificially a "heroic outlook on life". . . . The same applies to all questions of race.' But like many other good Prussians who in their heart of hearts are opposed to the Nazis, the outbreak of war in September 1939 found him once again fighting for the Fatherland. His last work, a fantastic novel, *Auf den Marmorklippen* ['On the Cliffs of Marble'] appeared at the end of 1939, and one reads on the title page: 'Begun February 1939, finished July 1939, revised in September 1939 in the army.'

Chapter V

The Captain of Köpenick

Everyone in Germany knows the story of the 'Captain of Köpenick', the cobbler and jailbird who on the 18th October 1906 appeared suddenly at the town hall of Köpenick, a Berlin suburb, dressed as an officer and at the head of some soldiers he had stopped and ordered to follow him, informed the Mayor and the other astonished officials that it was his painful duty to arrest them, and made off with the money in the Treasurer's office.

At the time of the incident Ludwig Thoma (1867–1921), whose contributions to the München weekly *Simplizissimus* had already won for him a great reputation as a humorist, was in prison at Stadelheim, serving a six weeks' sentence, to which he had been condemned for making insulting remarks about members of the Bavarian Morality Association. He was allowed to receive newspapers, and the notes in his prison diary (published under the title *Stadelheimer Tagebuch*) reveal with what relish and appreciation he read the accounts which they gave of the Köpenick affair. Under the date 19th October he wrote: 'I have read in the newspapers with much amusement the story of the Captain of Köpenick. It is wonderfully Prussian, and shows that Prussia stands to-day exactly where it stood in the year 1720, when King Frederick William I was in the habit of beating recruits with a stick. They would accept such treatment to-day just as they did then.' On the following day he continued his comments: 'The newspapers have much to say about the incident at Köpenick. The *Berliner Tageblatt* writes that humorists among the common people are making much of it. Of course

97

they are. Berlin people are famous for their humour, and in such moments as this it is up to them to prove that their humour really exists.' A week later (27th October) Thoma wrote: 'To-day I read in the *Münchener Neueste Nachrichten* the news that the so-called "Captain of Köpenick" has been caught. He is a cobbler called Voigt, fifty-nine years old, has already spent twenty-seven years in prison, and has never served in the army. His training was adequate for him to play the part of a Prussian captain.' The glee and the irony of these brief notes are pleasant to read. The next day Thoma continued: 'The papers are full of mockery about the solution of the riddle of Köpenick. That a cobbler should be able to make an officer of the reserve believe he is a captain, and in a train to make fun of civilians to another captain who really *was* a captain, and so forth—that is the most tremendous joke the world has ever known. Alongside this even the inventions of Shakespeare appear as nothing, and Falstaff becomes an everyday figure. The whole incident is a conse-quence of the Prussian system of education, and is therefore a most instructive satire. And ten volumes of *Simplizissimus* have not been able to show in a more splendid way how absurd mili-tarism is. The democratic parties ought to set up a monument to Wilhelm Voigt. The age of William II ought to remain for ever inextricably associated with this killing joke.'

Up to 1914 the incident was rather frowned on and hushed up as much as possible by the authorities, and it was only under the Weimar Republic that it really came into its own and was able to make its way into literature. In 1930 Carl Zuckmayer's play, *Der Hauptmann von Köpenick*, was performed for the first time, and published.[1] The play was an immediate and rousing success. It was performed all over Germany to large and enthusiastic audi-ences, and was hailed as one of the best light comedies in the whole of German literature, worthy to be set alongside Kleist's *Der zerbrochene Krug* and Hauptmann's *Biberpelz*. Significantly enough, it ceased to be performed as soon as the Nazis came to power. The fact that its author was a half-Jew is sufficient ex-planation of this, but no doubt there were other reasons as well. The Nazis never allowed a theatrical success of the Weimar period to be repeated if they could help it; and further they

[1] An English translation was published by Geoffrey Bles in 1932.

rejected any work of literature which was derogatory to the German, or rather Prussian, military tradition and to the 'heroic spirit'. As the play has disappeared from view in Germany and its author is exiled, there is all the more reason for giving a fairly detailed account of it here.

The first act takes place round about 1900, the second and third acts ten years later. The play opens in a tailor's shop in Potsdam. Uniforms and helmets are displayed everywhere. On the wall there is a picture of the Kaiser and his family, and there are also many signed photographs of officers in uniform—obviously satisfied customers. Captain von Schlettow is trying on a uniform, and making a great fuss about the buttons at the back. 'The regulation is that they must be six and a half centimetres apart. These are at least eight centimetres apart!' Wabschke, the assistant, begs to differ. So von Schlettow says to him: 'It is quite clear you haven't been in the army, you have no polish, no smartness, no bearing.' Wormser, the owner of the shop, and a Jew, now appears, and with his oily tongue flatters and pacifies the captain, promising to have the matter put right. He knows exactly how to deal with such a customer. When von Schlettow declares that one can always recognize the soldier at once by his attention to details, Wormser readily agrees, and adds: 'Old Fritz, the categorical imperative, and our Prussian drill—that's where we leave the others standing!' Towards the end of the scene, Wilhelm Voigt appears in the shop, apparently to ask for work, and is promptly and violently thrown out.

The second scene shows the interior of a police station in Potsdam. The windows are closed, and the air is stuffy. There are piles of official documents, and row upon row of files. On the wall hangs the inevitable portrait of the Kaiser. Voigt is there, arguing with a police officer, and trying to persuade him to give him a permit to live in Potsdam. (Anyone who has lived in Germany will recognize the system at once.) The officer cross-examines Voigt, who is forced to admit that he has spent many years in prison, including a sentence of fifteen years for forgery, passed on him when he was eighteen years old. He explains that he has been trying to get work as a cobbler, but that nobody will employ him unless he has a police permit to live in the area. The permit is finally refused, whereupon Voigt retorts: 'But this is a real roundabout. If I haven't a permit, I can't get a job. And if I haven't a job, I can't get a permit.' He then asks for a passport, explaining that he has already lived in Austria and is willing to return there. This too is refused, and Voigt sums up his unhappy position in the words: 'All I want is some kind of official document ['ein Papier']. I need that more than I need my daily bread.' (This too is a comment which only Germans and those who have lived in Germany can fully appreciate: Prussia has always been the land of officialdom and certificates.)

Scene 3 is in the Café National in the Friedrichstrasse. Von Schlettow is there in civilian clothes, and towards the end of the scene he tries to arrest a drunken private who is misbehaving. Voigt and a jailbird friend called Kalle look on at the scuffling with great interest. Von Schlettow tells the soldier he is a captain in the Guards, but the soldier replies: 'Anybody can say that! To me you are just a blinking civilian, like any other!' A policeman appears and arrests them both. 'You see, Kalle,' says Voigt, 'that's what I've always said. It's what a man looks like that decides how he is treated.'

The next scene finds Voigt in a queue in the office of a shoe-factory, again seeking work. The clerk asks each applicant: 'Have you been in the army? When? Where? How long?' And if the answer is in the affirmative, the man is given a job. When Voigt's turn comes he is turned down coldly and emphatically because he has not served in the army, and has no 'papers', i.e. no residence permit and no passport.

The last scene of the first act returns to Wormser's shop, where a certain Obermüller, who has just been made a captain in the reserve, is ordering his new uniform. He is very pleased with himself, and gladly allows Wormser to flatter him. 'Yes,' says Wormser, 'a man only begins to be somebody when he has got his commission. The Doctorate [i.e. the university degree] is the visiting card, but the commission is the open door. That's how one has to start.' A military march is heard outside, and this gives Wormser the opportunity for another patriotic observation. 'An old Prussian march like that is marvellous, isn't it? It makes a man pull himself together. One can feel it in one's very bones!'

THE CAPTAIN OF KÖPENICK

In the second act Voigt is back in prison: he had broken into the police station at Potsdam in order to steal a passport, and had been caught. The prison governor is giving some of the convicts 'patriotic instruction' ['vaterländischer Unterricht'], in celebration of the fortieth anniversary of the battle of Sedan. He is describing the battle to them, and his own glorious share in it, and in order to make things clear he divides his audience into cavalry, infantry, artillery, etc. The convicts have enjoyed so much 'instruction' of this kind and have so often participated in such 'celebrations' that many of them obviously know all there is to know about the constitution of the army, the commands, etc. Voigt in particular distinguishes himself, and shows he is able to lead a section of the troops quite independently. So much so that the governor finally exclaims: 'Bravo, Voigt! Where on earth did you learn all that?' And Voigt replies: 'A Prussian has this sort of thing in his blood, sir' ['Det hat n Preisse im Blut, Herr Direktor'].

After leaving prison Voigt goes to his sister and her husband, who treat him with great kindness. The husband, Hoprecht, is a clerk in a government department who talks enthusiastically with Voigt about the military training which like nearly all Germans he has to undergo. 'Soldiering is the best thing in life.' In another scene Voigt is sitting patiently with many others in the waiting-room of the local police station, where he has gone to make a last effort to get a residence permit. Suddenly a young lieutenant appears and is not kept waiting a moment. Voigt is impressed once again by the powerful effect of a uniform. As he is refused the permit he has to take leave of his sister and brother-in-law, and in a final discussion Hoprecht warns Voigt, who is now really desperate, not to try to do anything against the Prussian system. Hoprecht: 'Prussia is the land of order and discipline. Every German knows that, and every man must fit in and obey.' Voigt complains bitterly that he is not *allowed* to fit in and to obey. But Hoprecht refuses to listen to such complaints and blasphemies: 'I won't listen any longer, I *mustn't* listen any longer; I am a soldier and an official—with all my body and soul. You have never been in the army, Wilhelm. You don't know what it means—to obey. You have no sense of duty.'

In Scene 15, the first scene of the third act, Voigt buys a uniform at a second-hand clothes shop, pretending he wants it for a fancy-dress ball. It is the uniform which Obermüller bought from Wormser, and later discarded. A coincidence if you will, but it is by such coincidences and threads that Zuckmayer binds the play together. So far he has been preparing the ground step by step and above all creating a psychological background. In Scene 17 the dénouement begins. Two porters are standing on the platform of a Berlin station—just in front of a lavatory. One of them tries repeatedly to get in, knocks on the door, and makes loud and far from flattering remarks about the person who has been inside so long. Finally the door opens, and Voigt steps out transformed and resplendent in his captain's uniform; the public convenience has been his changing-room. The porter at once stops his cursing and involuntarily stands to attention. Voigt fixes him with a calm and confident gaze and asks: 'Have you been in the army?' 'Oh yes, Captain.' 'Then you have no doubt learnt how to control yourself. Which regiment were you in?' 'The Sixth Silesian Infantry, First Battalion, Third Company.' After this successful initiation into his role, Voigt calls a porter and gives him a parcel to carry to the left-luggage office. It contains his civilian clothes.

Things now move rapidly. Scene 18 reveals the entrance-hall and main staircase of the town-hall of Köpenick. Voigt's voice is heard from outside issuing commands to the soldiers he had 'requisitioned'. 'Halt! Eyes right! Eyes front! Fix bayonets!' etc. He now enters and strides swiftly to the policeman on duty, who at once springs to attention on seeing the captain approach. Voigt gives him various instructions, and then calls in his troops, some of whom he posts at the entrance, with strict orders that nobody is to be allowed to leave or enter the building without his express permission. He orders the others to follow him up the staircase.

The next scene takes place in the Mayor's room; and the Mayor is that same Obermüller whom we met at Wormser's and whose discarded uniform Voigt is wearing. When the scene opens Voigt is heard giving orders to some of his men outside, and as he enters one can see two soldiers standing outside with fixed bayonets. The Mayor, dumbfounded, slowly rises from his chair. Voigt: 'Are you the Mayor of Köpenick?' 'Yes.' Voigt clicks his heels and salutes. 'By command of his Majesty, the King-Emperor, I declare you arrested. I have orders to take you at once to the New Guard-House [Neue Wache] in Berlin. Get ready.' Mayor: 'But I don't understand. There must be some mistake.' 'How can there be a mistake?' retorts Voigt, pointing to the soldiers. 'Isn't that enough for you?' The Mayor continues to protest. Voigt: 'Have you been in the army?' 'Yes. I am a lieutenant-colonel in the Reserve.' 'Then you must know that resistance is useless. A command is a command.' Whereupon the Mayor gives in. Voigt then sends for the Town Treasurer, tells him he is arrested, and that he is to close his accounts as quickly as possible and hand over the account books and the money. Voigt then inquires where the passport department is, and learns to his dismay that there is no passport department at Köpenick, because it is not the chief town of the district. This is the point at which Voigt's well-laid and wonderfully executed plans miscarry, and on the very issue which was uppermost in his mind, and which had led him to such extreme and unprecedented action: how to get for himself some official document! But in spite of his great disappointment, he carries on and finishes the campaign. He graciously offers to allow the Mayor and the Treasurer to be taken to Berlin by the police instead of by a military guard, on condition that they give their word of honour not to attempt to escape. The Treasurer produces the money—4,042 marks and 50 pfennigs. 'Thank you,' says Voigt. 'I'll look after it for the present.' Glancing at the books he adds: 'Look here, the sum entered up is 4,042 marks and 90 pfennigs!' The Treasurer has to admit that the forty pfennigs are unhappily missing. 'All right,' says Voigt, 'I am not fussy. But I must of course make a note of it. Otherwise somebody might think I had put the forty pfennigs in my own pocket.' He laughs out loud at his own joke, and the others decorously laugh with him. Voigt then gives his final commands to the corporal: after half an hour he is to withdraw his men from their posts, march them to the station, go to Berlin and report at the New Guard-House that they have got back from Köpenick. 'Zu Befehl, Herr Hauptmann!' ['Very good, sir!'] says the corporal. Voigt gives him money for the railway journey, and money to buy a glass of beer and a sausage for each man at the station restaurant. The soldiers all stand stiffly to attention whilst the captain departs. The job at Köpenick has been completed.

Scene 20—Aschinger's Bierquelle, Friedrichstrasse; a well-known pub and restaurant in the centre of Berlin. It is early morning, but there are several people already there—a waiter, a charwoman, a taxi-driver, and so on; and Voigt, asleep on a bench in the background. Suddenly a man comes in waving a newspaper and roaring with laughter: in his rich Berlin dialect he tells them the story of the Captain of Köpenick. Of course by this time wonderful details have been added to what really happened. All the town council of Köpenick had been arrested and shut up in the cellar underneath the town hall, citizens had been driven handcuffed through the streets, fifty soldiers had been taken from the parade-ground, the whole town had been surrounded, and so on. Voigt buys a paper; at first he stares at it, motionless, and then he begins to read out in a low voice: '"And so this practical joker, about whom the whole world will be laughing to-day, is probably already in some safe place, where he can enjoy the fruits of his merry escapade." That's what *they* think! If they only knew!' And once again he lets his head sink wearily on to his arms.

In the last scene—a room in the Berlin police headquarters—we soon learn from the discussions of the police officers that Voigt has been arrested. He had apparently gone to a passport official and had said he would tell him who the Captain of Köpenick was, if he would promise to give him a passport. The official promised. Voigt: 'All right then, I'll call for the passport later; now arrest me; I am the Captain of Köpenick.' The police thought at first they had to do with a madman, but after they had obtained the captain's uniform from the left-luggage office of a Berlin station with the help of the ticket Voigt gave them, they realized that they had got their man, and were jubilant. The police inspector asked Voigt if it was his bad conscience that had compelled him to own up. 'By no means,' said Voigt. 'I did it to get a passport. There was not one to be had at Köpenick, and I simply had to have one. I know you will not let me go now. But once I am out again you can't refuse me the passport, because you've promised it me.' 'How old are you?' 'Fifty-six.' Voigt hands over the money, of which only eighty-three marks are missing. 'Why didn't you make off with it?' they ask him. 'As soon as I had spent it all I should have been in just the same old difficulty. I could have got across the frontier with the money, but without a passport I could never have come back, and I should have died in a foreign land and they would have buried me in foreign soil.' The police officers ask Voigt how on earth he had been able to carry it off, and Voigt explains how in prison the convicts had always been given as light reading in their leisure time the drill regulations and military service publications. He adds: 'Of course every child knows that in Prussia the military can do anything and everything they please.' They persuade him to put the uniform on, and Voigt at once falls into the role of captain, gives his orders, and they all address him as captain. Voigt asks for a mirror, looks at himself in it, begins to laugh, at first softly and then loudly. 'Impossible!' is his comment. Curtain.

The action and contents of this play have been reproduced at considerable length because they speak for themselves, and represent a first-hand and genuine German interpretation of Prussianism, of its virtues as well as its vices. The vices, and the unhappy consequences for individuals like Voigt and Hoprecht, stand of course condemned, but in a gay and humorous spirit, with hardly a trace of malice and bitterness. Such an attitude was possible under the Weimar Republic, because many Germans thought that the Prussian vices had been largely overcome and left behind. Anyone who saw the play performed in 1932 and heard the good-humoured laughter which greeted it was certainly not prepared for the revival of the very worst forms of Prussianism which began as soon as the Nazis came to power. But such was Germany's tragic fate. Zuckmayer and his play were soon to be banned.

Chapter VI

The Legend of Frederick the Great

One of the most striking manifestations of the Prussian spirit since 1914 has been the growth of the legend of Frederick the Great, until its volume and intensity and ramifications have become almost boundless. It would be very easy to write a book on this theme alone, and all that can be done here is to deal with a few selected examples from recent German literature, in order to illustrate this growth. As we proceed it will become clear that the word 'legend' is by no means a misnomer, for there is often surprisingly little connexion with authentic history. The attitude of many Germans towards Frederick the Great reveals, indeed, the fundamental romanticism of German character, their delight in creating a dream-world, and their never-ending search for the myth. At the same time the political consequences of the legend, that is to say, its translation into political activity and its influence on the general conduct of political affairs, have undoubtedly been very great, and on the whole disastrous.

The outbreak of war in 1914 seemed to have the effect of throwing Germans back upon themselves and of making them more egocentric and self-conscious than ever. Faced with a tremendous political and military struggle, many Germans turned instinctively to Prussia, which had risen to power and fame as the result of a long series of wars, and which, therefore, offered the greatest encouragement and the best hopes of success in this new and greatest of all wars. The Prussian spirit thrives on war, and Prussia in 1914 could claim to speak for Germany, and to be Germany, as never before. Strangely and yet significantly

enough, one of the first writers to give expression to this volun-
tary Prussianization was Thomas Mann, who later was to become one of the foremost opponents of Prussianism and Hitlerism. Towards the end of 1914 he published an essay of seventy
pages entitled 'Friedrich und die Grosse Koalition' ['Frederick
and the Great Coalition'], with the sub-title 'Ein Abriss für den
Tag und die Stunde' ['A sketch written for the day and the
hour']. There could be no better proof than this essay of the
strange attraction exercised by the Prussian spirit over Germans
who, by nature and cultural position, are far from being Prussian, and it is a telling example of the political dilemma in which
many great Germans find themselves, particularly in time of
war. Such Germans want to be patriotic and they want to
belong to a great and powerful political community, only they
must admit in their heart of hearts that the Prussian methods
are wrong. In peace-time they often have the courage to express
such unhappy doubts, but as soon as the cry of 'The Fatherland
in danger!' ['Das Vaterland in Gefahr!'] has been raised, the
voice of conscience and reason and humanity is drowned, and
they begin to search for explanations and excuses. It is clear
from many points in Thomas Mann's essay that he was not very
happy about his defence of Frederick the Great, although he
probably felt himself compelled to make it, in order to overcome
the qualms and forebodings as to Germany's political past, present, and future which even then tormented him, and in order to
gain something like peace of mind. He makes far too many ad-
missions and criticisms, of a kind which would at once rouse the
ire of a real Prussian, or of a Nazi. Thus he speaks at the outset
of the 'great mistrust of Frederick II of Prussia, the deep-seated
and, if we wish to be fair, the well-founded mistrust'; and proceeds calmly to admit that Frederick's claims on Silesia were
completely without foundation, at any rate, in any literal sense
and in view of solemn treaties! He also shakes his head at
Frederick's duplicity even as a young man by quoting a letter
which Frederick wrote to Algerotti, soon after his accession:
'Everything is prepared, it is only a question of carrying out the
plan which I have had in my head for a long time', and comparing this frank and rather boastful assurance with what
Frederick wrote about the same time in a letter to Voltaire: 'The

death of the Kaiser destroyed all my plans for peace.' Nor did Thomas Mann hesitate to repeat the 'blasphemy' that Frederick fled ingloriously and in great haste from the battlefield of Mollwitz in 1741, and left others to win the victory for him. But it is above all in his open discussion of certain sexual matters that he invited the wrath of Frederick's admirers. In his youth Frederick led a 'debauched and vicious life'. 'Then came a piece of bad luck; there were rumours of an operation—and from this time on there was something abnormal in his nature; he turned his back abruptly on voluptuousness; woman had played out her far from honourable role in his life. A deep hatred of women is henceforth inseparable from his being. . . . Sanssouci became like a monastery.'

Apart from such democratic and liberal indiscretions, as a Prussian or a Nazi might regard them, Thomas Mann succeeded surprisingly well (in view of the fact that he was Thomas Mann) in his attempts at glorifying and 'whitewashing' the greatest Prussian king. We read how the slack and pleasure-seeking young philosopher develops into the determined, self-confident ruler and passionate soldier the moment he comes to the throne. He puts on his uniform, which he had hitherto hated, and he hardly ever takes it off again. He is suddenly concerned to maintain 'the power of the state', which is an expression he uses in one of his first letters as king.

Thomas Mann also stresses Frederick's enormous capacity for hard work. 'His mode of life was strange. . . . In summer he got up at three o'clock. . . . He controlled everything—the army, justice, home and foreign affairs, the finances. His officials could never be sure that he would not interfere. . . . If one gets up at three o'clock and lives separated from one's wife it is possible to work like this. He showed the world what despotism really means.' Nor can he praise too highly Frederick's capabilities as a general. Frederick, we learn, despised the 'refined' methods of waging war which were typical of the century. He despised the entrenched position, which was held by others in such great honour. Compel the enemy to accept battle, no matter what the cost! Attack, attack! '*Attaquez donc toujours!*'

One of the most crucial and most illuminating passages is that in which Thomas Mann discusses whether the Seven Years War was a defensive or an offensive war. He is here obviously clutching at historical straws in order to justify Germany's action in 1914. That Frederick began the war in 1756 does not disprove the view that it was a war of defence (cf. Germany's invasion of Belgium); for he was hemmed in on all sides and would possibly have been attacked in the following spring (cf. the 'encirclement' of Germany in 1914 and also in 1939?). But did he really want war? Thomas Mann's considered opinion is that 'he realized quite early that he would have to want it and so he had malice and pride enough to want it of his own free will.' 'In the whole world he had not a single moral support. It is difficult to imagine the noise which arose in Europe about this unheard-of breach of the peace and of the law of nations. Or perhaps one ought to say that recent events have made one able once again to imagine the noise.' Here then is the rub! Was Frederick right in 1756? Was Germany right in 1914? And Thomas Mann answered both questions in the affirmative by flopping down the following tremendous and so typically German bucket of whitewash on his hero's head: 'His right was the right of a rising power, a problematical, still unheard-of right, which had to be fought for, which had to be created. If he were beaten, then he would be regarded as a miserable adventurer. Only if success showed that he was commissioned by fate to act in this way, only then could he claim to be in the right.' It is strange to think that this splendid example of Prussian and Nazi apologetics comes from the pen of such a great democrat and liberal!

As in most other versions of the legend, it is the old king, Old Fritz ['der Alte Fritz'], the suffering and untiring hero of the Seven Years War, and to a less degree, the queer yet lovable philosopher of Sanssouci, who dominates Thomas Mann's mild panegyric. For seven years, we are reminded, Frederick marched from place to place, and fought battles, first against one enemy and then against another, was defeated and almost destroyed. He was always in his shabby uniform, with cocked hat, high boots and spurs; year in and year out among his soldiers, in an atmosphere of sweat, leather, blood, and gun-powder. But in the interval between two battles, between a sorry defeat and an incredible triumph, he played his flute, scribbled French verses, or argued in letters to Voltaire. He always carried poison with him. Under these terrible ardours and as a result of the never-ending tension he rapidly became old, his teeth fell out, his hair turned grey, his back was bent, his body became gouty and shrank. And even after the Seven Years War, according to Thomas Mann, Frederick continued to work hard and unceasingly in order to restore agriculture, the finances, industry. He never spared himself. His sense of duty amounted to a kind of 'possessed state' ['Besessenheit']. What is the key to all this? How can one explain it? Thomas Mann puts forward the theory, often exploited since, that Frederick the Great was a sacrifice ['Opfer'], and the instrument of a higher will. This conception of a secret instinct, of a demon-like element which was superior to all his personal feelings and desires ['überpersönlich'], of the dictates of fate, and of the spirit of history, is in Mann's view (vintage 1914!) something especially German. 'He was a sacrifice. He thought of course that he had sacrificed himself, his youth to his father, his later years to the state. But he was wrong if he believed that he might have been allowed to act differently. He was compelled to commit wrongs and to lead a life in opposition to things of the mind, so that the mission of a great people on this earth could be fulfilled.'

Now that we have become fairly and squarely involved in this question of Thomas Mann's Prussian leanings in the past, we may as well draw attention to some of the views he expressed in the collection of miscellaneous writings entitled *Betrachtungen eines Unpolitischen*, although these 'Thoughts of One who is not a Politician' are not directly concerned with Frederick the Great. Perhaps we ought to stress once again that our motive and aim is not so much to remind Thomas Mann of things he might prefer to forget, but rather to make clear the attractions of the Prussian spirit even for the most democratic and liberal of Germans, and the dilemma in which they consequently often find themselves. The 'Thoughts' were written in 1915, 1916, and 1917. Here are first of all some interesting and typical passages from the preface. 'I confess I am deeply convinced that the German people will never be able to love political democracy, for the simple reason that it cannot love politics, and that the much-condemned authoritarian state ['Obrigkeitsstaat'] is and remains the kind of state which suits it, which is its due, and which at bottom it wishes to have.' 'Historical research will reveal what part international enlightenment and world freemasonry played in the preparation and bringing about of the war of "civilization" against Germany.' 'Germany's enemy in the most spiritual, most instinctive, most poisonous, most deadly sense is the pacifist, virtuous, republican, bourgeois demagogue and son of the French Revolution.' Like so many other Germans Mann had nothing but scorn for the ideas of 'civilization' and 'progress'; and in the essay called 'Der Zivilisationsliterat' he painted a lurid picture of the Europe which would result from a victory of these ideas: 'a little ridiculous, a little platitudinously humanitarian, trivial and demoralized, with a feminine elegance, a Europe far too "humane", too much given up to press-bandits, democracy of the big-mouth, a Europe of tango and two-step morals, a Europe of big business and pleasure, literary in the sense in which a Parisian prostitute is literary.' A few pages later he asked: What does this 'progress' mean for Germany? And he replied that it was a question of making Germany excessively political, literary, intellectual, and radical, of turning Germany into a democracy, in a word, of robbing Germany of its most German qualities ['Entdeutschung']. In the essay on 'Politik' he declared scornfully: 'The masses are now of age ['mündig']? A childish dream!' Towards the end of the book he cast his mind back longingly to 1876, declaring, oddly enough (Nietzsche, for example, would have profoundly disagreed!) that the German nation then stood at the height of its creative powers ['auf dem Gipfel ihrer Fruchtbarkeit'], led by such men as Bismarck, Moltke, Helmholtz, Nietzsche, Wagner, Fontane. The most significant point about this list of heroes is that the first three and the last were Prussians of the Prussians. Mann asks with a sigh: 'What have we to-day?' And he replies: 'Mediocrity and democracy. The process of making Germany humane, literary and democratic has been going on with great speed for nearly twenty years. Is it not time we had a little conservatism?' Dr. Goebbels might indeed do worse than turn to these writings of Thomas Mann and twist them into propaganda!

Such Prussianism, conservatism, nationalism, hatred of democracy, and so forth make a strange contrast with Thomas Mann's utterances and writings after the Weimar revolution: for example, his speech 'Von deutscher Republik' ['On the German Republic'], delivered, in honour of Gerhart Hauptmann's sixtieth birthday (15.11.1922) at the University of Frankfurt-am-Main, and printed in the November number—the special Hauptmann number—of the well-known liberal and democratic literary periodical *Die Neue Rundschau*. After making some graceful references to the presence of Gerhart Hauptmann and the President of the Reich, Ebert, in his audience, Thomas Mann tried to make an impassioned appeal to youth to support the republic and its ideals. But it is obvious that he was not quite comfortable, and thought it necessary to explain and defend his new position. 'How does the word "republic" strike you, falling from my lips?' he asked. 'My resolve is, I declare frankly, to win support for the republic and for what is called democracy, and what I call humanitarianism.' 'I hear you say: And what about your book? Your anti-political, anti-democratic thoughts of the year 1918? Renegade! Turncoat! Unprincipled adventurer! My dear friends, I stand my ground. . . . I withdraw nothing. . . . I might very well say *Et nos mutamur in illis!* But I can only reply that I am in fact a conservative, whose task is to preserve and not to revolutionize.' And so on. But many Germans did not want to hear about democracy and humanitarianism from such an amateur man-of-letters-turned-politician. They preferred to listen to Prussians like Moeller van den Bruck and Spengler, and later to that even more downright and truculent demagogue, Adolf Hitler. The Weimar Republic failed partly because of its defenders and friends, who, in spite of worthy motives, could not but make it appear helpless and ridiculous. The path of that king of agitators, Hitler, could hardly have been made more easy and more smooth!

In order to counter the possible objection that Thomas Mann is an isolated case of a very special kind, I wish to discuss briefly another instance of a well-known liberal and democrat who unexpectedly reveals pronounced Prussian tendencies: Ludwig Thoma. We have already encountered him in connexion with the 'Captain of Köpenick' episode. His prison diary, which has already been quoted, contained some very contemptuous criti-

cisms of William II's published speeches, and indeed a great
deal of what he wrote before 1914, particularly his contributions
to the humorous München weekly, *Simplizissimus*, stamped him
as an ardent Bavarian, and a determined opponent of Prussia
and the Hohenzollerns and all their works. Yet after August
1914 one finds Ludwig Thoma writing the most fiery patriotic
verses, of which the following, taken from a poem entitled 'Am
ersten August, 1914' ['The First of August 1914'] are typical:

> *Auf zu den Waffen,*
> *Die Wehr zur Hand,*
> *Und schützt das Vaterland!*
> *Auf springt das Volk, es reckt die Glieder,*
> *Und keine Sorge drückt uns nieder.*
> *Komm, was es sei....*
> *Hurra, Du Mutter uns—Germania.*[1]

In another poem, John Bull is ordered to put down his trousers
and receive the thrashing he had long deserved. A third poem
celebrates the victory at Tannenberg. But perhaps even more
surprising are the confessions Ludwig Thoma saw fit to make in
his memoirs ['Erinnerungen'], which were published after the
War. Describing his first visit to Berlin in the spring of 1901, he
wrote: 'As a convinced admirer of Frederick the Great ['als
eingefleischter Friederizianer'] I spent a wonderful day at Potsdam, where much still points to the spirit, knowledge, and character of a great man, in a way which is scarcely possible in any
other place.' He then defended 'Potsdamismus' as the happiest
combination of cleverness and a firm will, with the result that a
mighty state had been created out of a land that was originally
small and poor. Later he discussed in a somewhat unhappy
fashion the reproaches which he admitted had been made against
him, to the effect that he had changed his views since 1914.
There can be no doubt that Ludwig Thoma was sincere, but he
was carried away in 1914, refused to admit Germany's defeat in
1918, and could not reconcile himself to the Weimar Republic,
although it ostensibly embodied many of the ideals and prin-

[1] 'To arms, take up your arms, and defend the Fatherland! The people leaps
up, it stretches its limbs, and no cares depress us. Come what may. . . .
Hurrah, our mother, Germany!'

ciples and methods for which he had fought and dared previous to 1914. In all this he was not alone. His tragedy was the tragedy of many good Germans, and thus the way was prepared for the tragedy of a great people.

I turn now to a very different writer—Paul Ernst, who, apart from certain youthful dabblings in Socialism, strove throughout his life to foster German nationalism of a most pronounced and uncompromising kind. He came into his own, so to speak, after the Nazi triumph in January 1933, and would certainly have garnered even greater praise and honour if he had not died a few months later (15th May). It is significant that in one of the most typical of Nazi treatises on modern German literature—Hellmuth Langenbucher's *Volkhafte Dichtung der Zeit* (1937)—he was given pride of place. His importance has of course been greatly exaggerated by the Nazis for political reasons, and it is interesting to compare Langenbucher's panegyrics with the verdict of that sturdy old nationalist and anti-Semitic freebooter of a literary historian, Adolf Bartels, who, in the latest edition of his *Geschichte der deutschen Literatur* (16th edition, 1937), declared (p. 659): 'Now that he is dead some people would like to prove that Paul Ernst is a great writer, but it can't be done: he lacks the elements of genius.'

On the 27th January 1915[1] Paul Ernst's *Preussengeist* ['The Prussian Spirit'], a drama in three acts, was performed for the first time in Weimar. There can be no doubt that, like Thomas Mann's essay on Frederick the Great, it was written specially 'for the day and for the hour', and represented Paul Ernst's first reactions to the War. Like so many other Germans in the early days of the first Great War, Paul Ernst found himself more 'Prussian' than ever before, filled with an intensified admiration for the Prussian virtues, and convinced that only Prussianism could ensure success in the great struggle. The play is in brief a glorification of the Prussian ideas of duty and self-sacrifice. It idealizes Frederick William I and Frederick the Great, and provides a novel portrait of Katte, the young officer who was executed for taking part in Frederick's attempted flight.

[1] Incidentally, it was surely deliberate that the date chosen for the first performance was the Kaiser's birthday, a day celebrated with much ceremony in the Second Empire.

Katte, according to Paul Ernst, does not share Frederick's love of pleasure and of the arts; on the contrary, he is dominated by the same strict idea of duty as the king, and, therefore, only accompanies Frederick on his flight in order to save him from worse things; and by the heroic sacrifice of his own life, he leads Frederick to his true self, to the spirit of genuine leadership and service to the state. For the young lieutenant Katte, just as for Frederick William, life does not mean beauty and enjoyment, but duty and sacrifice and hard work. 'Happy the man who is given the opportunity for sacrifice,' says Katte. 'To be a German means to do one's duty,' says the king. Or: 'Happiness is for us work and worship of God.' At the opening of the play there is a discussion between the king and the queen about young Frederick, in which the queen appeals to Frederick William's feelings as a father. The king replies that Frederick is not so much their son as the future king of Prussia. In a conversation between Frederick and Katte, the latter says that his greatest sorrow is the enmity between father and son, and that his greatest joy would be to see them united. In the second act, Frederick and Katte are brought in as prisoners. The king says to Katte: 'I alone have the power to pardon you, for I am responsible only to God, who gave me the crown. Speak, Katte, is it right for me to pardon you?, Katte replies: 'No.'

In a later scene in the second act three judges appear and declare Katte guilty of attempted desertion but recommend life imprisonment. The king rejects their verdict and condemns Katte to death. In accordance with the Prussian spirit Katte asks that he may die as an honourable soldier, that is to say, he asks if he may be shot, with his sword at his side. In the third act Katte tells Frederick, who visits him in prison: 'I am a soldier, my life is not my own'; which is again a sentiment calculated to warm the hearts of all Prussians. In an impossible, far-fetched, and most unconvincing scene, Frederick stands alone at the window of his cell, describes the execution of his friend, and decides that he too will make sacrifices. The king enters, and Frederick tells him of his change of heart. 'Now I say: Let me live, your Majesty, for I belong to my Fatherland.' The king: 'I thank thee, God, that Thou hast helped me, and hast given me back my son. The blood that has flowed in the courtyard flows for the Fatherland.' The king now knows that his son will be a worthy king of Prussia. 'He will be the servant of his people and do what is right.' All this is incredibly bad drama but wonderful Prussian politics and propaganda. As in Thomas Mann's essay there is the idea of Frederick the Great as a sacrifice, although it is differently expressed. The logic of the interpretation is obvious: the greatest Prussian king sacrificed himself, his whole life and being, to the state, and all the more humble Prussians, and Germans, must do likewise. The value of such a legend to those in authority in Germany can hardly be exaggerated.

I propose now to discuss the interpretation of Frederick the Great provided by a literary historian of pronounced nationalist tendencies and reputation: Friedrich Lienhard. His brief history of German literature in the popular series 'Aus Geist und Wissen' (published by Quelle and Meyer), contains a section on Frederick the Great. Lienhard declares that a history of German literature would not be complete if it did not include some treatment of Frederick; and in support of this view he quotes Goethe. Goethe, he says, several times testified to the great effect which the battles of the Seven Years War, particularly Rossbach and Leuthen, had on the imagination of contemporary Germans. Frederick became a model for others and thus came to exert a powerful educative influence: he was—in Goethe's words—a pole-star ['ein Polarstern']. Then Lienhard makes the surprising assertion that dramas like Goethe's *Götz von Berlichingen* or Schiller's *Die Räuber*, with their intense desire for freedom and their emphasis on the value of human personality, could hardly have been written without Frederick the Great's 'shining example of heroic activity' ['leuchtendes Beispiel heroischer Tatkraft']; these and other plays of the time declare war on despotism in favour of a free and pure humanity. As if Frederick the Great was not one of the greatest despots of all times! Such a view is, however, according to Lienhard, absolutely false. He roundly denies that 'the enlightened philosopher of Sanssouci' was a tyrant: on the contrary, he was the 'first servant of the state', who proudly placed upon himself the heaviest of burdens. Of course, he also put heavy burdens on his subjects, but not for any selfish reasons! Then comes the familiar picture of Old Fritz in the Seven Years War, hemmed in on all sides, but bearing himself nobly and determined to fight on, in order to win for his beloved Prussia a larger sphere of activity. He felt himself to be the champion of the Protestant North, but in religious matters he was a model of tolerance, as is shown by his dictum: 'Let everybody in my land seek salvation in his own way' ['Jeder soll in meinem Lande nach seiner Façon selig werden']. 'It is a lofty conception of the state, of duty, of kingship, of the profession of soldier and official, which dominates this witty and strong-willed king.' Naturally such an idealized portrait would not be complete without some account of Frederick's daily life and work. 'He gets up at four o'clock, in two minutes his hair and his plait are in order, the inevitable top-boots are put on. He possesses neither slippers nor dressing-gown. Even when he is ill he usually keeps his hat on his head and his boots on his feet. He works all day until evening. His great relaxation is the daily concert, when he plays the flute.' Lienhard's triumphant conclusion is that Frederick the Great was a wonderful example of the heroic spirit ['ein Vertreter des Heroismus'].

Lienhard's book on 'Das klassische Weimar' also contains a section on Frederick the Great. After the usual references to Goethe, some extracts from the German translations of Frederick's French 'poems' are solemnly quoted and appraised. And then Lienhard proceeds to explain away Frederick's attitude to German literature as expressed in his well-known essay, 'De la littérature allemande' (1780). Lienhard admits that his hero knew nothing of Klopstock, Lessing, Herder, Wieland, Winckelmann; that he was unable to appreciate Shakespeare, and that he was equally repelled by Goethe, whose *Götz* he described as 'a detestable imitation of those bad English plays and full of insipid platitudes'. He nevertheless declares that the essay shows Frederick's touching solicitude for Germany's literary and cultural progress, and is finally very happy with the excuses supplied him by Frederick's prophetic utterances about the future greatness of Germany in these fields. 'We shall have our classical writers: everyone will be glad to read them in order to learn from them. These great days in our literature have not yet come, but they are approaching: I announce their approach to you. I am like Moses: I see from afar the promised land, but I shall not set foot in it.' Noble sentiments! But the fact remains that

Frederick's ideas on literature were but a distorted echo of the classicism of Voltaire, and that he did not have enough contact with his own people or enough perspicacity to see what great things were being done under his very nose by some of the greatest writers of all time.

The objection might perhaps be raised that writers like Thomas Mann, Paul Ernst, and Friedrich Lienhard were all 'highbrows' with little or no popular appeal, and that, therefore, what they wrote about Frederick the Great only reached a minority of the German people. This is, of course, to a certain extent true; but there are many other writers whose treatment of Frederick the Great did undoubtedly reach the masses, and thus contributed far more to the spreading and deepening of the legend. One of these writers was Walter von Molo (born 1880), whose novel *Fridericus* (copyright 1918) soon proved to be a best-seller, and was read by thousands of Germans, young and old, in the years just after the Great War. It was the first novel of a trilogy, *Ein Volk wacht auf* [A People Awakes], of which the second, *Luise*, appeared in 1919, and the third, *Das Volk wacht auf*, in 1921. We are only concerned with the first novel here.

It is significant that one of the most popular books in Germany during the dismal years of defeat and inflation should have been a glorification of the greatest Prussian king. The critics were from the first enthusiastic. Even the *Vossische Zeitung*, left-wing and liberal and democratic in a staid and rather refined way, thought fit to praise it. 'Frederick, the man, the king, the general, the hero, is here formed into a wonderful synthesis; this is what we imagined him to be, this is the idea we had of his tragic personality. The whole life, the whole personality, and the whole soul of the great king is mirrored in this novel. This work proves that our love for Frederick was well-founded.' Such a tribute of praise from one of the chief organs and defenders of the new régime makes strange reading indeed. From patriotic Prussian periodicals like *Die Wartburg* one would naturally expect high tribute: 'It does one good to read this book in the difficult times through which our nation is passing. It came just at the right hour, and brought with it much comfort. One reads the book with bated breath. Here is artistic talent of the most mature kind.'

THE LEGEND OF FREDERICK THE GREAT

The novel is one day in Frederick's life, and what a day! Walter von Molo seems to have collected all the facts and stories and features of the legend, and to have splashed them all on to his narrow canvas. It is portmanteau historical romance; all the titbits in one huge pie. During the course of the novel one is often reminded of the battle of Torgau, for example, by the attack on a much larger Austrian army entrenched in a favourable position on a hill. But the scene of the novel is Silesia, and Torgau is in Saxony. Further, Torgau was fought on the 3rd November 1760, and during the night Frederick is informed of the death of his favourite sister, Wilhelmine, who died on the 14th October 1758; yet the novel ends with the news of the death of the Empress Elizabeth of Russia, who died on the 5th January 1762! Poetic licence, if you will. But it is often so in Germany; the cautious, painstaking, and conscientious citizen throws historical truth to the winds as soon as an appeal is made to his patriotism.

It is impossible to give more than an impression of all the varied incidents of this 'day' of over four hundred pages. Frederick receives humble petitioners: a wife pleading for the life of her husband who has been condemned to death for desertion; merchants, who beg him to foster trade. He arranges for a soldier with a false message to fall into the hands of the enemy. He plays with his favourite greyhound, and gives her pieces of sugar. He suffers great pain, but refuses to give in. When finally he lies down to rest in his humble headquarters—of course still fully dressed—he has terrible and wonderful dreams, which allow Walter von Molo to bring in all kinds of exciting and significant episodes from Frederick's early life. He dreams, for example, that he is once again witnessing the execution of his friend Katte; that his father is beating him; that he is happy in Rheinsberg. When he wakes up his brother Wilhelm appears and begs him to make peace. Frederick of course refuses. This gives him an opportunity to profess his love of peace (cf. Hitler): 'I hate war no less than you. I know war better than you. And better than everybody else! I don't want war; I am extremely unhappy about it. But it can't be avoided, fate wills it!' And why? 'They want to *destroy* Prussia!' 'So now it is a question of holding out until our fortunes change, or until I and Prussia are dead. Prussia has a right to exist, to rise. Hitherto the others have refused to admit that Prussia has a mission to perform in Europe. Prussia *will* become great. . . . I must perform my mission to the end. Austria, from whom I took Silesia, has out of revenge forged the ring of enemies around me! No state ever became great without conquests, and I bear all the responsibility. What took place is my will! In everything I do I am only concerned to promote the interests of my people. The petty morals of a private citizen are not seemly for a man who is responsible for the welfare of millions. In the struggle between nations, nothing but force decides the issue. Peace can only come if we are granted the right to develop in freedom. If I am wrong, then Prussia will go under.' Frederick paused, and drew himself up: 'Prussia will not go under!' This Prussian speechifying is so reminiscent of Hitler that it is surely not necessary to do more than draw attention to the parallels.

The climax and grand finale of the novel is a detailed and picturesque description of Frederick's glorious participation in the battle. Several horses were shot under him! He rode straight at the Austrian batteries at the head of his troops! 'Legs flew, and arms!' Once he seized hold of the flag of a regiment, and 'the unfurled eagle of Brandenburg fluttered wildly in the breeze!' Later he rode on his favourite white horse right into the centre of the murderous fight! Finally the victory was won, and the soldiers could sing Luther's hymn 'A safe stronghold our God is still' and cry 'Vivat Fridericus! Vivat Fridericus!'

But the very best proof of the way in which the legend of Frederick the Great penetrated to the masses of the German people, and took firm root in their minds and lives, is probably to be found in the collection of stories, anecdotes, myths, and visions which Josef Winckler (born 1881) first published in Low German [Plattdeutsch] in 1927 under the title *De Olle Fritz* [Old Fritz]. A High German (i.e. standard German) version entitled *Der alte Fritz* appeared in 1934. This is one of the best and most amusing books of its kind that have appeared since the Great War, and worthy to be placed alongside *Der Hauptmann von Köpenick*. Josef Winckler explained in the preface to the second edition (1935) that he had heard many of these stories as a boy, and that he had been collecting them from the peasants of his native Westphalia ever since. He described how in this part of Germany one frequently finds Frederick the Great painted on dishes and tiles, moulded in iron and wax, carved on chests, cupboards, and wardrobes, and how the stories serve as a complement to such visible expressions of the legend. Even as a boy, he declared, he preferred them to the stories about the gods of the ancient world: 'For I felt here the breath of my own people and the smell of my mother earth.' Incidentally it is all the more striking and significant to find the legend so widespread and firmly rooted in Westphalia, because Westphalia was not joined to Prussia till 1815, and it may be assumed that Frederick the Great never set foot in most of the villages where these stories were collected.

Naturally one suspects that Josef Winckler has put a great deal of his own admiration for Frederick the Great into the work, together with a great deal of his own literary imagination and skill of presentation. But at the same time, it would be impossible for anyone to invent such stories out of thin air, and there is about most of them a genuine ring which overcomes all doubts and carries the reader along. The book is, in a word, Frederick the Great as seen by generations of Westphalian peasants. The life at Sanssouci is described just as if it were a large and prosperous Westphalian farm. There is a Westphalian cook called Kathrin, who 'mothers' the king, and Westphalian menservants. Many of the chapters describe visits which Frederick is supposed to have paid to Westphalia; how he drank with the peasants, took part in their festivities, talked with children in a school, sat in judgement over lazy and inefficient peasants, and rewarded those who were thrifty and hard working. A poor widow finds him one night in the cowshed milking a cow he had brought her. One Sunday morning he went to church, and disgusted with the smug and wishy-washy sermon, which had quickly sent the peasants to sleep, he got up in the pulpit himself, and gave them a sermon which ended: 'Ihr saudumme, stinkende, krokodilgemeine Höllenäster, Amen'—which is very difficult to translate, but means something like: 'You idiotic, stinking, low-down collection of crocodiles and sons of hell!' Perhaps best of all is the story of how he tries to persuade the sly, cunning, but narrow-minded and conservative Westphalian peasants to grow—and eat—potatoes. It is of course true that Frederick the Great did much to popularize the potato, and if he had not done so, it is highly probable that contemporary Prussians and most certainly later generations of Germans would not have been able to stand the strain of the frequent wars put upon them by their rulers. The story tells how Old Fritz appeared in a Westphalian village, accompanied by two servants carrying a sack of potatoes; and how he took the potatoes out of the sack with his own hands, and placed them in the furrow. Each peasant was given a hatful, and told to plant them in the best soil he had, and the peasant who grew the largest potatoes was to be hailed as the cleverest of them all.[1] But the peasants did nothing about it, so the following year Old Fritz appeared again, and this time he invited them all to a huge 'potato-feast' ['Kartoffelessen']. The peasants partook heartily of the beef, venison, and fish, but they left the potatoes on their plates, or dropped them on the floor, and none of them ever dreamt of planting potatoes. The third year Old Fritz invited them to taste some 'Schnaps' (a kind of gin) which had been made from potatoes, and pointed out they could drink several times as much if they made their Schnaps from potatoes instead of from corn. That settled it, and the Westphalian peasants took up the cultivation of potatoes with enthusiasm.

The thread running right through the book is provided by the visions which some of the Westphalian peasants had of the 'little yellow man' ['das gelbe Männchen'], who would one day appear at the coffin of Frederick the Great in a 'pointed little hat', at a time 'when the queen and her children have to flee'. The little yellow man in the cocked hat is, of course, Napoleon, who did actually stand in the days of his triumph over Prussia at Frederick the Great's coffin, and the queen is Luise, who had to flee to East Prussia. Frederick heard of these visions, and that explains partly his visits to Westphalia; he wanted to hear more. The 'prophecy' filled him with anxiety and dread, and that is why, according to the Westphalian legend, he worked so hard, even after the Seven Years War: all the time he was

[1] This, by the way, is just the opposite of the proverbial saying in Germany to-day: 'The stupidest peasant always grows the largest potatoes!' ['Der dümmste Bauer hat immer die dicksten Kartoffeln.']

preparing his beloved Prussia to withstand the terrible visitations which he believed were to come upon her. According to the legend, he died muttering something about the 'yellow man'!

One final story: Old Fritz died, went to Heaven, and knocked at the door. Saint Peter opened, and told him there was no place in Heaven for such a dangerous fellow. So Old Fritz asked if he might have a word with God Himself, who happened to be engaged near by in plucking some 'paradise apples' for the little angels. God also told him he was far too wild for Heaven, and that he had better get out. Whereupon Old Fritz slowly put his hat on, clicked his heels, and shouted: 'Attention! The whole battalion, about turn, quick march!' And what do you think? All the Prussians in Heaven goose-stepped past God and out through the door. 'Stop! Stop!' shouted God. 'You're taking the very best people out of Heaven! Sit down at once, please sit down!' 'Now you know who I am?' said Old Fritz with a smile. This piece of Prussian blasphemy surely requires no comment.

Josef Winckler's concluding chapter is entitled 'Old Fritz as a Ghost' ['Der Alte spukt']. He declared that Old Fritz never died. Like Frederick Barbarossa, he lived on, ready to come to the help of the German Empire in its hour of need. 'And he was greater and more famous than Barbarossa!' He helped to overthrow Napoleon; and would he not come again, now that Germany had lost the Great War? And thus—significantly enough —the century-old legend of Frederick Barbarossa of Hohenstaufen came to be ousted and replaced by the upstart legend of Frederick the Great of Hohenzollern.[1] A new age and a changed people demanded new heroes and new myths.

[1] One of the best-known expressions in German literature of this romantic belief that Frederick Barbarossa never died, but in a magic sleep awaits the call to sally forth and restore the German Empire, is the poem by Rückert (1788–1866) which begins: 'Der alte Barbarossa, der Kaiser Friederich.'

Lord Bryce dealt with the legend of Barbarossa in his *Holy Roman Empire*: it is one of those fine, rich passages of English prose, which one reads once and never forgets. 'To the south-west of the green plain that girdles the rock of Salzburg, the gigantic mass of Untersberg frowns over the road which winds up a long defile to the glen and lake of Berchtesgaden. There, far up among its limestone crags, in a spot scarcely accessible to human feet, the peasants of the valley point out to the traveller the black mouth of a cavern, and tell him that within the red-bearded Emperor lies amid his knights in enchanted sleep, waiting the hour when ravens shall cease to hover round the

WEIMAR AND POTSDAM, 1919-1933

In the preface to *Der Alte Fritz* Josef Winckler declared (November 1934): 'The national revolution has made hundreds of thousands aware once again of the significance of Old Fritz.' This was by no means a misstatement or an exaggeration; only it must be stressed that hundreds of thousands of Germans, and above all Prussians, had already become intensely conscious of the importance of Old Fritz during the years of the Weimar Republic, and that the surprising growth of the legend of Frederick the Great was a wonderful preparation—psychologically and spiritually—for the meteoric rise of Adolf Hitler and the triumph of National Socialism.

peak, and the pear-trees blossom in the valley, to descend with his crusaders and bring back to Germany the golden age of peace and strength and unity.' It was probably coincidence rather than the influence of the legend which led Adolf Hitler to choose Berchtesgaden for his personal and private abode: coincidence directed partly by a desire to be near (but not too near) München, the city in which the Nazi movement took its rise, and also by the urge to be as near as possible to the Austrian frontier, so as to be able to hop over it quickly, if things got too hot for him in the Reich. But it is nevertheless a sad if intriguing thought that the cavern where Frederick Barbarossa slept and waited for so long has now been replaced in the imagination of the German people by Haus Wachenfeld on the Obersalzberg, and that the picturesque and symbolical red beard of the medieval Emperor has degenerated into the Charlie Chaplin moustache of the Führer. *Sic transit gloria mundi.*

Chapter VII

Anti-Frederick

The legend of Frederick the Great was one of the chief forms of expression and one of the main pillars of the Prussian and nationalist revival which merged into National Socialism after 1933. But such a political legend naturally calls forth opposition, and in this case the rival spirit of Weimar made opposition inevitable. The strange thing is that the opposition should have remained so much in the background, and have proved so ineffective; but the reason is surely that the Prussian spirit maintained its power after 1919, and that the Weimar Revolution was in this as in most other respects far from being a complete break with the past. Indeed, the new rulers of Germany showed themselves quite eager to share in the 'glories' of the Prussian past; so that Frederick the Great was still officially recognized and continued to appear in school-books as one of the great German 'heroes'.

As far as literature is concerned, the chief evidence of an 'anti-Frederick' reaction is Werner Hegemann's monumental work (782 pages!) entitled *Fridericus oder das Königsopfer* [Fridericus, or the Royal Victim]. This is undoubtedly one of the most interesting and thought-provoking books published in Germany since the first Great War; not only for its interpretation of Frederick the Great, but also for its views on all kinds of things literary, historical, religious, including Goethe, Voltaire, Louis XIV, and Christianity. It is worthy of separate treatment and detailed analysis, as an expression of a German cultural attitude which is the very antithesis of Prussianism, but which unhappily seems doomed to disappear.

125

Werner Hegemann was born in Mannheim in 1881, studied at various universities and technical colleges, and took his Doctorate in Politics. He spent many years in the United States, where he learnt a great deal about architecture and town-planning, and where his aversion to the political structure and spirit of Imperial Germany was greatly strengthened. Returning to Germany, Hegemann made a reputation for himself as an architect; he wrote several books on architecture and town-planning; and in 1924 he became editor of a leading architectural monthly, *Wasmuths Monatshefte für Baukunst und Städtebau*. His book on Frederick the Great came as a surprise even to his friends, and created a great stir. The first edition appeared in 1924; the fourth, revised and enlarged, in 1925. A good English translation was published in 1929 under the title *Frederick the Great*, but it is unfortunately far from being complete. It is the fourth German edition to which I here refer.

The book is in the form of seven long 'discussions' ['Sieben Gespräche'] between a certain Manfred Maria Ellis and some of his great European contemporaries, including Rudolf Steiner, Rudolf Borchard, Hugo von Hofmannsthal, Georg Brandes, Thomas Mann, Pierre Lièvre, Lytton Strachey, and G. B. Shaw. Ellis, who probably never existed, is supposed to have an American father and a German mother; he was sent to a German school and studied at various German universities. Hegemann solemnly explains that he made his acquaintance at Boston in 1909, and that the discussions took place in 1913 in the Villa Boccanera in Naples, where Ellis had gone to live, in order to be near 'the great Benedetto Croce', to enjoy his society and that of other old friends of all nationalities, whom he gladly welcomed as his guests. In the Appendix to the first edition Hegemann explains that Manfred was never heard of again after the disappearance without a trace of the liner *Alsatia*, on which he had sailed from America in 1916 in order to serve in the German-American Red Cross. Hegemann declares: 'I regarded it as my duty to tell my countrymen of the doubts expressed by Manfred about the legend of Frederick the Great.' Researches into the truth of all this must be postponed to a later date: but one may assume that Manfred and his discussions were purely imaginary, and the products of Hegemann's fruitful brain, and that they represent a skilful and entertaining, if sometimes long-winded, way of 'getting his ideas across'.

In the preface Hegemann explains his sub-title—'The Royal Victim'—by pointing out that the murder of a tyrant or the sacrifice of a king was on several occasions regarded by Athenians and Romans, the Swiss and the English, the French and the Americans, as an indispensable act in the struggle for political freedom. But in Germany few men have shown themselves strong enough or courageous enough to undertake the bloody slaughter of tyrants and Cæsars, either by assassination or on the solemn scaffold. Hegemann hazards what is no doubt very true, namely, that the great majority of Germans were happy and thankful that William II quietly disappeared and thus saved the German people from such unpleasant things as court-martial, execution, and tyrannicide. He continues: But if it is true that political freedom must be bought by the 'sacrifice of kings', then 'the nation of poets and thinkers' (i.e. the Germans) may achieve its freedom by a royal sacrifice much more serious and much more spiritual than the shedding of blood. As long as Prussians and Germans continue to believe in their 'Great King' ['der Grosse König', i.e. Frederick the Great], then the monarchy stands firm in German hearts and minds. Other peoples have learnt to thrive politically without 'Great Kings', but the Germans have not yet learnt this. On the other hand, if it is the spirit of Frederick the Great which can save Germany in her present distress, then nothing deserves more serious research than this spirit. Later in the book Hegemann writes: 'False political legends are dangerous, and it seems to me that the legend of Frederick the Great is one of the most dangerous.'

If other contemporary writers were doing all they could to idealize and glorify Frederick the Great, Hegemann certainly succeeded in damning him with faint praise and in painting him blacker than had ever been done before. He says that there wer always two kinds of Fredericks alongside each other: the willing pupil of Parisian philosophy and the unwilling Prussian task-master. But if one scratches a little of the 'Voltaire varnish' from him one finds underneath the noisy and uncouth Frederick William I. Hegemann makes no bones about discussing Frederick's homosexual and sodomite tendencies, although in doing so he is careful to cite the most accepted and unimpeachable authorities. Frederick is also portrayed as a tyrant of a most cruel and capricious kind: his treatment of Major Trenck, for example, is described in great and convincing detail. Apparently Trenck and Frederick's sister Amalie fell in love, and as a result Trenck soon found himself in prison. In a letter (29th April 1755) to his chief jailer Frederick gave orders that he was to be fastened by chains on his hands and feet to a wall, so that he could not get near a window or a door. Hegemann flatly denies the accepted version that Frederick abolished torture soon after coming to the throne, pointing out that a certain General Walrave was tortured in 1748 because he was suspected of maintaining contact with Austria. Nor will he allow the equally well-worn theory that Frederick was one of the great exponents of religious toleration, in spite of his oft-quoted saying: 'Let everybody in my country seek salvation in his own way.' He favoured the Jesuits at a time when in other countries they were being persecuted—only because he thought they brought him money! On the other hand, he drove out several Roman Catholic professors, and he also drove out many Jews (cf. Hitler), for example, four thousand at one stroke from West Prussia. In the course of the discussions Hegemann also succeeds in introducing all kinds of minor points, which help to make Frederick look ridiculous, and petty, or worse. For example, that it was one of his favourite amusements to mock at the Bible; that he thought it funny to give his dogs Holy Communion; that he once introduced his wife to a guest as 'my old cow'; and that in many of his letters to his favourite valet Fredersdorf, he wrote at length about their common misfortune —piles.

With regard to Frederick's fame as a statesman and political leader, and above all his claims to be one of the chief founders and creators of the modern German Empire, Hegemann is chiefly concerned to show that his policy was anything but German, or in the best interests of Germany as a whole, and that it was narrowly Prussian and dynastic, and hopelessly misguided. Frederick's reign of forty-six years, we are told, was fundamentally one long rebellion, open or veiled, against that great and noble lady, the Empress Maria Theresa, who often referred to Frederick as 'that bad man'. He it was who caused the civil war, the struggles of Germans with Germans, Hohenzollern against Habsburg. Frederick was always opposed to the idea of strengthening the German Empire: he only saw in this a danger for Prussia and humiliation for himself and his house. Thus he tried several times to bribe the Turks to make fresh inroads into the Empire; on the 27th August 1757 he told the English ambassador that a Prussian agent had spent £50,000 on inciting the Turks to make war. Hegemann also quotes very effectively from Frederick's *Testament* of 1752, stressing that Bismarck had written on the back, 'Always to be kept secret' ['Dauernd zu sekretieren'], and that only the downfall and disappearance of the Hohenzollern dynasty in 1918 had brought this extremely important document to light. In the chapter on 'Foreign Policy' Frederick wrote: 'Our interests demand that we remain in alliance with France. Silesia and Lorraine are two sisters of whom the elder has married Prussia and the younger France. These marriages compel us to pursue the same policy. Prussia cannot allow France to lose Alsace and Lorraine.' Hegemann asserts that such a policy can only be understood from the narrow Prussian standpoint, and that Frederick's whole life must be regarded as a continuous plot against Germany as a great power. In support of this very drastic condemnation he makes Manfred quote the great German patriot of the Wars of Liberation, Ernst Moritz Arndt. 'Frederick the Great never thought of grouping the German nation round his eagles and protecting it. Nothing is more ridiculous than to attribute to him patriotic German ideas' (*Geist der Zeit*, 1805). After he had read out the quotation from Arndt, Manfred said: But just listen to what the chief of the 'intellectual bodyguard of the Hohenzollerns',[1] the historian Ranke, has to say on this point. 'The idea which Frederick the Great had in his mind from the beginning of his reign, but which he had not carried out, namely, to unite the great interests of the German Empire with the maintenance and growth of his state—

[1] This is a reference to the proud statement of Professor Du Bois-Raymond in a speech on the 3rd August 1870: 'The University of Berlin, with its quarters opposite the palace of the king, is the intellectual bodyguard of the house of Hohenzollern' ['Die Berliner Universität, dem Palaste des Königs gegenüber einquartiert, ist das geistige Leibregiment des Hauses Hohenzollern'].

this idea now became (in 1784) possible and urgent for both parties.' Ranke was here dealing with the League of Princes [Fürstenbund], which Arndt declared was only a political trick aimed against Austria, and the very reverse of patriotic enthusiasm for the German Fatherland. Hegemann's comment is crushing: 'That great bookworm, Ranke, suffered from the unpardonable disease of blindness.'

The book also contains on page after page similar downright denials of Frederick's greatness as a general. Thomas Mann is supposed to take part in one of the discussions and praise Frederick's revolutionary methods of conducting war. As a matter of fact Hegemann is simply quoting whole passages of Thomas Mann's essay on 'Friedrich und die Grosse Koalition', which we have already discussed in the previous chapter. In Hegemann's opinion (and he cleverly supports it by facts and figures, and by statements from accepted Prussian historians like Professor Hans Delbrück, Treitschke's successor in the Chair of History at the University of Berlin), Frederick won his victories not because of his superior generalship, but because of his superior army, and by sheer good luck. Even so he only won half the battles he fought. He often made wonderful plans, but he was seldom able to carry them out; for example, his attempt to capture the whole of the Austrian army in Prague in the first winter campaign of the Seven Years War. Similarly Hegemann declares that it was unwarranted and foolhardy to attack an army twice the size of his own and occupying a very favourable position, as he did at Kolin (1757). Even the victory of Torgau (1760) was dearly bought, and in reality it was only a sham victory. And if Frederick had not fought the battles of Prague, Kolin, and later Zorndorf (1758) and Kunersdorf (1759), he would have been able to last out the war much better. Napoleon criticized him for not concentrating more men at Kunersdorf, and allowing himself to be beaten at a very critical juncture, just because he used only half his army. And so on and so forth! Nor is much left of Frederick's reputation for personal bravery. It is stressed that Frederick fled from the battle of Mollwitz in 1741, and that both Prince Heinrich and Prince August Wilhelm (his brothers) wrote accounts of his flight from the battle of Lobositz in 1756. Declaring roundly that most of the anecdotes about

Frederick the Great are inventions, Hegemann makes short work of the story according to which some of Frederick's soldiers, sitting round the bivouac fire on the eve of the battle of Torgau, were greatly moved when they saw the poisoned pills roll out of his pocket. Unfortunately for the effectiveness of the story it can be proved that Frederick had shown these pills to several other people, including his secretary De Catt, and that although he had threatened suicide on and off for three years previously, he had somehow managed to survive such humiliations as the defeats of Hochkirch, Kunersdorf, and Maxen. In a word, Hegemann dismisses the story simply as proof of Frederick's love of the theatrical and the sentimental.

So much for Frederick's fame as a statesman and a general. Thirdly, his management of the finances. Hegemann challenges the verdict of the economic historian, Gustav Schmoller (1838–1917), in whose eyes Frederick's organization of the finances was 'exemplary', by quoting from an article in the *Handwörterbuch der Staatswissenschaften* [Dictionary of Political Science]: 'Frederick the Great was an old miser, who, out of malice against his heirs, deliberately and arbitrarily veiled the true state of the finances, buried ingots of gold, or hid money in a stocking, or sewed a roll of thalers into a mattress. After his death it took years before it was possible to get anything like a final settlement.' It is also stressed that immediately after the Seven Years War Frederick began to build his New Palace in Potsdam, for which there was absolutely no need, and which, according to competent authorities, cost at least fifty million marks in present-day currency. Yet Frederick repeatedly complained that he had no money to give to the ravaged towns and villages, or for the care of disabled soldiers! Incidentally, Hegemann quotes competent authorities on architecture in order to disparage and ridicule the buildings erected under Frederick's patronage and direction. And it is abundantly clear that Hegemann, who, as a successful architect and a well-known authority on architecture is well qualified to judge, has no use for the 'Prussian style' so much praised by Moeller van den Bruck. For example, he declares that the proportions of the Neues Palais are wrong, and that there is far too much ornamentation. Sanssouci ought to have been built higher; the architect Knobelsdorff planned it so, and he was heart-broken when his lord and master inter-fered, and did not allow him to move the main building nearer to the front of the terrace, and to make it a few steps higher. 'To-day the south side rises up like an Egyptian temple which has sunk into the mud of the Nile.'

Fourthly, Hegemann disposes of Frederick the Great as the 'philosopher of Sanssouci' and the apostle of culture. He once again attacks Schmoller—this time for declaring: 'Frederick the Great placed all the power and organization of the state in the service of a wonderful cultural development.' On the contrary, says Hegemann, it was in spite of Frederick, and thanks to his death, and thanks to Klopstock, who abhorred him, and to Goethe, whose *Götz* he despised, and the other great names of the German Classical Period, that such a wonderful cultural development took place. Could anything be more ridiculous, Hegemann asks, than the attempts of Erich Schmidt (1850-1912)—for many years Professor of German Literature at Berlin, and author of the standard biography of Lessing and many other important works—to excuse or even to justify Frederick's attitude to German literature? Erich Schmidt described Freder-ick's confession that he could only speak German 'like a coach-man' ['wie ein Kutscher'] as 'humorous', to which Hegemann replies that a king must have the intelligence of a coachman if he cannot learn the language of his people better. It is also pointed out that Frederick made the Prussian Academy entirely French, and even ordered it to publish only in French, although its found-er, the great philosopher Leibniz (1646-1716), had expressly recommended its members to cultivate the German language.

Hegemann is also able to show how many of the great Ger-man writers of the time turned away from and against Frederick the Great. In a letter which he wrote in 1763 Winckelmann declared: 'I shudder from top to toe when I think of the Prus-sian despotism and the oppressor of peoples. I would rather be a Turkish eunuch than a Prussian.' Lessing refused the Chair of Rhetoric at Königsberg chiefly because the professor had to make a panegyric once a year on the Prussian king. And in a letter which he wrote in 1767 to Gleim, the author of the *War Songs of a Prussian Grenadier*, and an abject admirer of Frederick the Great, Lessing asked: 'Why should I think of becoming a

miserable galley-slave in Berlin?' Schiller planned for a time to
write an epic on Frederick the Great, but was finally compelled
to admit—in a letter to Körner (the father of Theodor Körner,
the young poet of the Wars of Liberation): 'Frederick II is not a
subject for me. I cannot make myself like this figure; he does not
fill me with sufficient enthusiasm for me to undertake the huge
task of idealizing him.' The question of Goethe's attitude to
Frederick the Great is given the special attention which it
deserves. Thomas Mann is supposed to say in one of the discussions what he had written in the essay on 'Friedrich und die
Grosse Koalition': It was none other than Goethe who said of
Frederick the Great that his deeds 'had given to German poetry
for the first time contact with real life in a true and higher
sense.' This and the other familiar quotations from Goethe's
Dichtung und Wahrheit are skilfully brought in, and Hegemann's
reply is that such statements must not be separated from their
context, and must not be considered without reference to later
passages in which Goethe condemned Frederick the Great.
Hegemann then quotes a long passage in which Goethe described how surprised he was to find on his arrival in Leipzig in
1765 that the citizens had but scant praise for the Prussian king.
They refused to admit that he was in any way a great man.
They said it was no great feat to achieve small successes ['einiges
zu leisten'], if one had the means at one's disposal and if one
was not sparing of 'countries, money, and blood' (cf. Hitler).
But Frederick had not shown himself to be great in any of his
plans, and if one went through the Seven Years War step by
step, one would find that he had sacrificed his splendid army
quite unnecessarily, and that he was himself to blame that the
disastrous struggle has lasted so long. 'A truly great man and
general would have finished off his enemies much quicker. In
support of these views they [the people of Leipzig] were able to
give innumerable details, which I was unable to deny. And
gradually I felt the unconditional veneration with which I had
regarded this prince from my youth up, grow cold.'[1]

[1] 'Ein wahrhaft grosser Mann und Heerführer wäre mit seinen Feinden viel
geschwinder fertig geworden. Sie hatten, um diese Gesinnungen zu behaup-
ten, ein unendliches Detail anzuführen, welches ich nicht zu leugnen wusste
und nach und nach die unbedingte Verehrung erkalten fühlte, die ich diesem
merkwürdigen Fürsten von Jugend auf gewidmet hatte.'

WEIMAR AND POTSDAM, 1919–1933

One of Hegemann's final blows is to prove that in the familiar portraits and statues Frederick's features have been greatly idealized, and that even the well-known and much admired death-mask was touched up; it was only 'eine Überarbeitung', that is to say, it was really a falsification of the genuine death-mask. Nor were Frederick's eyes at all as large and piercing as painters and writers love to depict them.

It can well be imagined that Hegemann's book raised a storm of protest in Prussian and nationalist circles. Hegemann deals with some of the criticisms in the appendix to the fourth edition. Some writers had accused him of being an Austrian, or a Saxon. Others tried to make it appear that he had used 'well-known libellous authorities' ['bekannte Schmähliteratur']. A certain Professor Helmholt wrote a long review (*Literarische Wochenschrift*, 10th October 1925), in which he spoke of the tendentious and provocative character of the book, and of its seditious contents. Professor Erich Marcks, the author of many important works on German, and particularly Prussian, history, described the book as 'dangerous', because Germany had so few great political figures, and because Germans would find it difficult to do without their belief in their 'Great King'! Wilhelm Boehm declared (*Deutsche Rundschau*, May 1926): 'One must not allow oneself to be convinced in any way by Hegemann. This book is not compatible with an aspiring political consciousness.' But perhaps the most typical and most revealing cry from a Prussian heart was that of General von Zwehl, who declared in an article entitled 'Slanders on the Great King' ['Schmähungen des Grossen Königs'] in a leading military weekly (*Militärwochenblatt*, 30th November 1925): 'Things must once again become as they were in the past. Fridericus Rex, our old Fritz, was a symbol of his time, to which after more than one hundred and fifty years we also look up with admiring enthusiasm.'[1]

'So wie es damals war, muss es wieder werden.' As it was in the Prussian past, is now, and ever shall be, (the German) world without end, Amen! Such was the constant prayer and longing

[1] 'So wie es damals war, muss es wieder werden. Fridericus Rex, unser alter Fritz, war ein Symbol seiner Zeit, auf das auch wir nach mehr als hundertfünfzig Jahren mit bewundernder Begeisterung blicken.'

of thousands of ardent Prussians and nationalists during the years of the Weimar Republic. And many of them thought their prayer had been answered with the advent of the new political Messiah, Adolf Hitler.

Chapter VIII

Adolf Hitler and Alfred Rosenberg: in Praise of Prussia

As final proof of the continued activity of the spirit of Potsdam in the period of the Weimar Republic, I now wish to draw attention to the eulogies of Prussia contained in the writings of Hitler and Rosenberg. Here first of all are a few quotations from *Mein Kampf*. 'Prussia is an ideal political creation.' 'The history of Prussia shows, in a manner particularly clear and distinct, that it is out of the moral virtues of a people and not from their economic circumstances that a State is formed.' 'Prussia, which was the germ-cell of the German Empire, was created by brilliant heroic deeds and not by a financial or commercial compact.' The greatest tribute to Prussia comes, however, towards the end of *Mein Kampf*, in Hitler's summary of 'German political history of a thousand years.' He declares that if one examines the chain of political vicissitudes through which the German people has passed during this period, only three great and lasting achievements stand out in the field of politics and foreign policy. (1) The colonization of the Eastern Mark (i.e. Austria); (2) The conquest and settlement of the territory east of the Elbe; (3) The establishment of the Prussian State and the development of a particular conception of the nature and functions of the state. Hitler dwells lovingly on this third great achievement and declares that it would be impossible to over-estimate its importance.

This praise of Prussia is all the more striking because of Hitler's biting scorn and rage at his native Austria and at the

136

separatist dreams of other states like Bavaria. It is in this connexion that he expresses himself at greatest length about Prussia,
and it is here above all that his 'Prussianism' (by adoption) is
revealed. Quite early in *Mein Kampf* he describes how in the
summer of 1915 the first enemy leaflets were dropped on the
German trenches, and that one of the striking features of this
propaganda was that in sections of the front where Bavarian
troops were stationed, every effort was made by the enemy to
stir up feeling against the Prussians. Hitler was in a Bavarian
regiment; and the memory of this propaganda filled him with
fury. But he is forced to admit that it began to achieve success
from 1916 onwards, and that the feeling against Prussia grew
quite noticeably among the Bavarian troops. He accuses those
in authority at the time of doing nothing to counteract it. 'This
was something more than a mere crime of omission, for sooner
or later not only the Prussians would have to suffer severely for
it, but the whole German nation, including the Bavarians.' In
most typical fashion Hitler blames the Jews for carrying on this
propaganda at home. 'While Jewry was busy despoiling the
nation and tightening the screws of its despotism, the work of
inciting the people (in Bavaria) against the Prussians increased.'
It was all 'a clever Jewish trick for diverting public attention
from themselves to others'. 'While Prussians and Bavarians
were squabbling, the Jews were taking the sustenance of both
from under their very noses. While Prussians were being abused
in Bavaria the Jews organized the revolution, and with one
stroke smashed both Prussia and Bavaria.' Later in the book,
when he describes his first ventures into politics, Hitler tells of a
political meeting at which a 'professor' recommended his hearers
to work for the secession of Bavaria from Prussia: 'At this juncture I felt bound to ask for permission to speak and to tell the
learned gentleman what I thought. The result was that the
honourable gentleman slipped away, like a whipped cur.' In
tones of righteous (if somewhat snarling) indignation Hitler
describes how at some of these great public meetings in München hatred against Prussia was roused to such a pitch that a
North German would have risked his life by attending one of
them. They often ended in wild shouts: 'Away from Prussia!'
'Down with the Prussians!' 'War against Prussia!' There can

be no doubt that Hitler's sympathies at this critical period, as later in his political career, were with Prussia, and against the separatists.

Careful reading of *Mein Kampf* also provides abundant evidence of Hitler's admiration for Frederick the Great, to whom he several times refers as a 'brilliant hero'. The following passage may be quoted as typical. 'As long as the historical memory of Frederick the Great lives, Friedrich Ebert (the first President of the Weimar Republic) can arouse only a problematic admiration. The relationship of the hero of Sanssouci to the former publican of Bremen[1] may be compared with that of the sun to the moon; for the moon can shine only after the direct rays of the sun have left the earth.'

A few examples will suffice to show that Hitler's admiration for Frederick the Great increased rather than diminished after 1933. Composite photographs and etchings appeared all over the place—in shop windows, schools, and restaurants—showing the profiles of Frederick the Great, Bismarck, and Hitler. Photographs of Hitler's sanctum in the new Chancellery which he caused to be built in Berlin revealed most fittingly the presence of two busts: Frederick the Great and Napoleon. And it is reported on good authority that in his private room in the Braune Haus at München, the headquarters of the Nazi Party, two portraits of Frederick the Great adorn the walls and that the famous death-mask of the greatest Prussian king stands on the Führer's desk. On the 20th April 1939, Hitler's birthday, Rosenberg presented him with the original manuscripts of some of the comparatively few letters which Frederick the Great wrote in German, a gift which, according to the Nazi press, filled Hitler with much emotion and joy. On the 24th January 1930, the 228th anniversary of the birth of Frederick the Great, Hitler made a speech to army and air force cadets, in which he advised them 'always to follow the example of Frederick the Great, who had set a high standard of soldierly virtue.'

As final evidence for Hitler's Prussianism a speech by his chief

[1] This is one of the few cases in which the complete and unexpurgated English translation of *Mein Kampf*, published by Hurst and Blackett in 1939, is at fault. It speaks of 'the former republican of Bremen' (p. 220). The German word is *Gastwirt*. Probably this was first of all translated by 'publican' and then 'corrected' into 'republican'.

henchman Göring may be quoted. On the 18th June 1934 Göring addressed the Prussian State Council and explained the new position of Prussia. He declared: 'It is clearly apparent that the old Prussian concept of the state has already merged into the Reich, that is to say, that Prussia no longer has any tasks to perform as a sovereign state as formerly. But the eternal ethics of Prussianism remain. . . . Prussia is known as a country that has produced fewer artists; but it has given the German Reich the statesmen who were necessary in order to create the conditions that to-day at last enable an Adolf Hitler to satisfy the longing of the German people. . . . I know of no more genuine Prussian than the Führer.' This was of course in part a piece of skilful propaganda, an attempt by Göring to influence the Prussians in Hitler's favour. But even so, there is a solid kernel of truth in what at first sight seems a surprising statement. And most of the Prussians were only too eager at that time to agree.

If Hitler's *Mein Kampf* may be described as the first 'Bible' of the Nazis, Rosenberg's *Mythus des 20. Jahrhunderts* (1930) is certainly the second. And here also one finds great tributes of respect to Prussia, for example, in Rosenberg's comparison between the Prussian soldier and the Jesuit. The Jesuit sacrificed to his order independent thought, individual personality, human dignity, and ultimately, all his racial and spiritual values ['sein rassisch-seelisches Wesen']. The Prussian soldier is also a member of an order, and superficially and technically he is subject to stern discipline, but in his heart and mind he is free. Whereas the Jesuit system has no place at all for the idea of honour, the Prussian system centres *only* round this idea. The first system has always been and still is a parasitic fungus in the German national life, a disintegrating acid sapping all the strength and greatness of Germany's most precious past. But the second system is the germ-cell (cf. Hitler, page 136 above) round which Germany's whole life has been built up, a force effective ever since the days of the Vikings and the early Germanic tribes, in whose day it first appeared. Rosenberg's mention of the Vikings in this connexion may be taken as proof that he had learnt and borrowed a great deal from Spengler's *Preussentum und Sozialismus*, although like most Nazis he was slow to admit his obligations, and on occasions bitterly attacked Spengler's interpretation of history because it was too pessimistic, neglected the determination and will-power of the German people, and did not pay sufficient attention to questions of race and the influence of race on culture.

There can be no doubt about the strong Prussian bias of Rosenberg's conception of modern German history. The following summary is typical. In the Thirty Years War two-thirds of the German people were extirpated, the towns were in ruins and farms deserted; art and culture had disappeared. 'And in spite of all this, the German blood (Rosenberg is fond of blood) roused itself to oppose the sloppy degeneracy ['Verlotterung'] of the Habsburgs and to oppose French threats. The trumpets of Fehrbellin still sound in our ears even to-day and fill us with hope and we still hear the voice of the Great Elector from whose deeds Germany's resurrection, salvation, and rebirth took their rise. One may find fault with Prussia as much as one pleases: but this primitive rescue of the essential features of German life remains for ever its special glory; without this there would be no German culture, no German "Volk" whatever, but, at the most, millions to be exploited by neighbours greedy for plunder, and by avaricious princes of the church.'

It is, therefore, quite in keeping and not in the least surprising to find Rosenberg indulging in a tremendous panegyric of Frederick the Great. 'It is not a matter of chance that above all to-day, in the midst of a new and terrible fall into the abyss (Rosenberg was writing at the end of the twenties), the figure of Frederick the Great appears in dazzling brightness, for in him are united without a doubt—in spite of his human weaknesses— all those qualities of character for the supremacy of which the best of the German people are once again to-day eagerly striving: personal daring, unhesitating resolve, consciousness of responsibility, penetrating sagacity, and an appreciation of what is meant by honour.' Then follow suitable quotations from Frederick's works and correspondence: 'If I had more than one life, I would sacrifice it to the Fatherland'; 'I do not think of fame, but of the state'; 'You must know that I am not concerned about my life, but about the performance of my duty'; 'I would never allow myself to conclude a disadvantageous peace'; 'Either I shall be buried under the ruins of my Fatherland or I shall make an end to my life. I have always allowed myself to be led by this inner voice and by the demands of honour in my actions, and intend to do this in the future as well.' Rosenberg concluded that Frederick the Great was thus the symbol of everything heroic; he was indeed Frederick the One and Only ['Friedrich der Einzige']. Had Rosenberg ever read Hegemann, and the other 'calumniators' of his hero? No doubt he had, and probably it was the thought of such 'blasphemies' which made him declare: 'He who attempts to falsify the figure of Frederick the Great with malicious comments must appear to us to-day as a truly pitiful scoundrel.'

It is not to be wondered at, therefore, if thousands of Prussians quickly 'fell' for Hitler and Rosenberg, in whom they saw at the very least spiritual and political allies. Even before 1933 many Prussians left the parties of the Right and threw in their lot with the Nazis, because the latter seemed to offer the best guarantee of a large-scale and really successful Prussian revival. The Nazis were always very glad to welcome such recruits, provided they allowed themselves to be absorbed completely into the new party and the new faith.

PART II

Prussia and the Third Empire
1933–1940

Prussia and the Third Empire, 1933–1940

The National Socialist revolution of 1933 was a revolution of a new kind; it was largely a revolution of propaganda, made possible by the advances in communications, and in the dissemination of ideas and news. It was a long-drawn-out revolution and superficially peaceful. There was little violence or bloodshed; no storming of 'Bastilles', no barricades, and very little street-fighting. In most places the Storm Troopers simply marched to the key-buildings, took over, and hoisted the swastika flag! The Nazis often boasted in the early days of their triumph that they had only used 'political' and 'legal' methods to attain their ends. A favourite assertion was that 'Not a hair on the head of a single Jew has been tweaked'; and in a sense this was true.[1] Only gradually did the majority of the German people come to realize the nature and scope of the changes which were taking place, and that the hair of a rapidly increasing number of Jews, as well as Communists, Social Democrats, Liberals, Pacifists, and 'Reactionaries' was being more than tweaked.

One might compare the German body politic early in 1933 with a sick man who had been prepared by months of threats and agitation for a serious and drastic operation. The anæs-

[1] Hitler declared in his speech to German workers in a Berlin armaments factory on the 10th December 1940: 'I did not want to destroy anything in Germany. I have always proceeded cautiously, and it is my pride that the German revolution of 1933 took place without even the shattering of a window-pane.' This seems to have become one of Hitler's *idées fixes*, for he used almost identical words in his speech on the 30th January 1941: 'It was my pride to carry through this revolution without one single window-pane in Germany being broken.'

thetic was administered—but in small doses, so that it left him dully awake; and then he was punctured all over with a surgical needle, starting first in the regions of the heart and the head. If the Nazi specialists had tried to use the knife at the outset, the patient would probably have kicked them all to blazes. But by the time they had finished their treatment, he had little fight left in him, and the state of coma had become more or less permanent. Meanwhile, there was a disgraceful and unholy haste among many non-Nazis, and above all among Prussians, to be received into the brotherhood and the faith, so much so that the term ' Märzgefallene' was coined for those who 'fell' on the political battlefield and became Nazis as late as March 1933. The main driving force behind these rapid and wholesale conversions was undoubtedly fear, and fear of a new and Nazi kind: fear of being spat upon and cast out, of losing one's job or one's pension, one's home-life or one's security, fear of the Secret State Police (Geheime Staatspolizei—soon abbreviated to Gestapo), and of the concentration camp. But it would be unfair and inaccurate to ignore the great and strong feelings of sincere patriotism, self-sacrificing idealism, and new-born hope which took possession of many Germans. There was indeed a remarkable change in the political temper of the German people. Even among those Germans who did not want or were not allowed to join the Party there was an astonishing wave of nationalism. Those who had won Iron Crosses or other decorations in the War put them on and wore them constantly. (This was particularly the case with the dark and swarthy types of 'pure-blooded' Germans, so that they should not be mistaken for Jews.) Military topics began to dominate conversation, and the many bands and orchestras discovered that their repertoire contained more Prussian marches than pieces by classical composers.

How is one to account for the peaceful nature of the revolution, the drugged and passive attitude of the German people, the readiness for conversion, and the almost entire absence of articulate and organized opposition? This is the great riddle of 1933, and it has remained a riddle ever since. It is of course possible to stress the personality of Hitler, the cunning and ruthlessness of the Nazi leaders, the perfection of their revolutionary technique as shown in their propaganda methods and their policies of infiltration and disintegration. But such factors alone do not offer an adequate explanation or solution. More important is the realization that the great majority of Germans could not make up their minds in 1933, and they have not made them up since; they have always regarded National Socialism as good in parts; they have changed their attitude from day to day, often from hour to hour and according to their mood or the company they were in. This uncertainty and vacillation on the part of the people as a whole to canalize, organize, and make effective the tremendous forces antagonistic to Hitlerism, which have all along been lying latent and scattered, is an outstanding feature of Nazi Germany; it is the main cause of Hitler's initial triumph and his continuance in power. And one of the chief reasons for this great national dilemma is surely the continued effectiveness of the Prussian spirit from 1919 to 1933, which the foregoing chapters have attempted to illustrate. Because of this, the majority of Germans were wonderfully well prepared for National Socialism. Hitler appealed directly and powerfully to the Prussianism in the German people, and in the first glow of enthusiasm many Prussians, at any rate, thought they were getting what they wanted and hastened to acclaim it; only gradually did it dawn on the best of them that they and their Prussianism were being corrupted and exploited, and that National Socialism was a perverted Prussianism, combined with certain new and even more deplorable vices and failings. Even so, most of them could not tear themselves away from Hitler; and so they continued, as if hypnotized and paralysed, to worship the Nazi gods, while suffering intermittently torments of doubt and remorse. Only a few had the courage to make their disappointment and disillusion known. The worst of the Prussians, on the other hand, were happy; the great reversion to type had begun; they had found their way back to their true selves.

In the chapters which follow an attempt is made to show, firstly, how the Prussians, headed by Hindenburg and by men like Carl Dyrssen, Friedrich Schinkel, and August Winnig, let the Nazis in and welcomed them; secondly, how the Nazis did all they could to exploit the Prussian spirit and the Prussian past; and finally, how some of the best and most genuine Prussians expressed their opposition.

147

Chapter IX

Hindenburg and the Day of Potsdam

In the Great War a favourite and successful way of raising money in Germany was to erect huge wooden statues of Hindenburg in public places and to invite the patriotic populace to drive nails into them, of course at a fee which was graduated according to the kind of nail. There was always something truly monumental about Hindenburg, and this giant of a man cast his shadow protectingly over Germany through many sad and difficult years. He typified Prussia, and was in many ways an embodiment of 'Prussianism' in the best sense of the word: in his simplicity, honesty, piety, patriotism, and devotion to duty. In 1933 he was a tired old man, still eager to serve the Fatherland and to do his duty, but also longing to be at rest. He it was who finally opened the flood-gates, and allowed the dark waters of Hitlerism to swirl over Germany.

Hindenburg's autobiography, *Aus meinem Leben* (1920),[1] is one of the most Prussian books ever written. We learn from it that he was born in 1847 at Posen, the chief town of the district which from 1919 to 1939 formed the 'Polish Corridor' to the Baltic, and that at the time of his birth his father was a lieutenant in the army, stationed at Posen. Some of the happiest and most lasting recollections of his childhood centred round the family estate of Neudeck in East Prussia, where he was taken every year in the summer, and where after his grandparents died his father and

---

[1] An English translation was published by Cassell in 1920 under the title *Out of My Life.*

mother settled in 1863. This is how Hindenburg writes about his family: 'The simple, and indeed hard, life of a Prussian land-owner and nobleman who was also an officer, and who lived in a modest way, finding in work and in the fulfilment of his duty the main features of his life, gave our family its stamp. . . . My father and mother endeavoured to fit us for life's struggle by giving us healthy bodies and a strong will for the active fulfilment of our duties, but also a trusting belief in our Lord God and a bound-less love of the Fatherland and of what they recognized as the strongest support of the Fatherland, namely, our Prussian royal house.' The ideas of doing one's duty to God and one's duty to the Fatherland occur again and again in Hindenburg's writings and speeches and are the ideas which dominated his long life. It would be futile to cast doubts on his straightforward and un-flinching patriotism, and it would similarly be futile to call in question his simple and earnest piety. His motto, which often accompanied reproductions of his coat of arms, was a quotation from Psalm 62, v.1—'My soul truly waiteth still upon God, from whom cometh my salvation.' (The German words are even more beautiful and more adequate than the English, because they are so compact and yet they make it clear at a glance that our word 'still' means 'quiet': 'Meine Seele ist stille zu Gott, der mir hilft.')

Hindenburg was always intensely proud of his Prussian an-cestry and upbringing: 'No matter where my profession led me, I always felt myself to be an Old Prussian ['Altpreusse'].' He went to school at Posen, Graudenz, Glogau, garrison towns in the east of Germany where his father was stationed in turn, and when he was old enough he was sent to the well-known military academy at Walstatt, near Liegnitz in Silesia. He fought as a lieutenant at the Battle of Königgrätz in 1866, and was wounded while leading an attack on an Austrian battery: 'It was a proud feeling, as I stood among the cannon I had captured, bleeding from a slight wound in the head.' He took part in the Franco-Prussian War of 1870–1, and was present as the representative of his regiment at the proclamation of William I as Emperor of Germany at Versailles on the 18th January 1871. He describes with pride how he stood with other officers in the guard of honour at the coffin of William I in Berlin Cathedral: 'On my writing desk lies a block of grey marble. It came from the old cathedral, and from the spot on which the coffin of my Emperor stood. It would be impossible to make me any present I should value more highly.' In 1911 Hindenburg fell under official displeasure and was put on the retired list, but a few days after the Great War began he was recalled and given command of the armies in the east. At the end of August 1914 these armies won the great and decisive victory at Tannenberg, in which thousands of Russians were trapped and slaughtered among the lakes and swamps of Masuren in East Prussia. Soon afterwards he was given supreme command of all the German forces, and for the rest of the War he was chiefly concerned with the struggle on the Western Front. His account of how the end came is typical of the man and typically Prussian. He admits that the fighting strength of the German army decreased, and that the only hope lay in immediate support from home and in a *levée en masse*, a united effort of soldiers, politicians, and civilians. But in his view the politicians and civilians unhappily did not rise to the occasion and play their part. 'An English general said quite rightly: The German army has been stabbed from behind.' (Who this mysterious English general was is not stated; but if an English general did really present German 'patriots' with this Heaven-sent excuse and priceless weapon of propaganda, it is perhaps better that he should remain undiscovered.) Hindenburg opposed the signing of the Treaty of Versailles, and although he had to admit that the prospects of success were very slight, he advised a resumption of hostilities, declaring that as a soldier he would prefer to die fighting rather than agree to such shameful terms. Immediately after they had been accepted by the Weimar government he resigned and retired to Neudeck, where for a man accustomed to wield the sword and not the pen he wrote his memoirs in a remarkably short space of time. It is difficult to understand why this frank glorification of everything Prussian and more particularly of the Hohenzollern dynasty was allowed to appear in 1920, so soon after the Revolution and the creation of the new order. And it offers striking proof of the desire of the Weimar Republic to compromise with the old order rather than to destroy it. So Hindenburg's star began once again to shine, and it shone ever more brightly until he was elected President of the Reich in 1925. By coming out of his retirement Hindenburg admittedly helped the Weimar Republic to overcome an awkward political dilemma, which had arisen out of the party struggle. In the first election the Conservatives and nationalists [die Deutschnationalen] had as their candidate Jarrés, the Lord Mayor [Oberbürgermeister] of Berlin; the Centre Party its leader Marx; the Bavarian People's Party the head of the Bavarian Government Held; the Democrats the President of Baden, Hellpach; the Social Democrats the head of the Prussian Government, Braun; the Communists Thälmann; and the Nazis Ludendorff. The result was indecisive, and as it seemed very unlikely that their candidate would get the absolute majority necessary for election, the Conservatives and nationalists turned to Hindenburg, who in the second election triumphed over Marx and Thälmann. In a letter accepting the candidature Hindenburg insisted that he was not standing for a single party, but as the representative of all nationally minded [nationalgesinnte] Germans. In his speech on taking office (12th May 1925) he declared he was ready as always to serve the nation and the Fatherland to the best of his ability, and he spoke of the principles he had learned in that great school of duty, the German army; principles which culminated in the idea that duty comes before privileges or rights, and that the individual must subordinate himself to the community, above all in times of stress. In the spring of 1932 he was persuaded to offer himself once again for election. This time he was opposed by Düsterberg as candidate of the Deutschnationalen, Thälmann for the Communists, and Adolf Hitler for the Nazis. Once again he triumphed, but his triumph was short-lived. Germany was in the throes of economic depression, with well over six million unemployed; the Nazis were rapidly increasing in numbers, volubility, and insolence; great pressure was brought to bear on the tired old man and all kinds of intrigues were started, in which Hindenburg's friend and counsellor Franz von Papen played a sinister but decisive role. Finally, on the 30th January 1933, Hindenburg gave up the unequal struggle and called upon Hitler to form a government. From now on he was a mere figurehead, a puzzled spectator of events over which he had not the slightest control. The story went the rounds at this time that

Hindenburg once dropped his handkerchief and that his secretary Meissner stooped to pick it up. 'Leave it, leave it,' said the old man testily, 'it's the only thing I am allowed to put my nose into these days.'

The Nazi showmen were not slow to make use of Hindenburg for purposes of advertisement and propaganda, and he was dragged round from one 'circus' to another. One of the earliest and cleverest and most successful of these was the solemn opening of the German Parliament (Reichstag) in the Garrison Church at Potsdam on the 21st March 1933. (The Reichstag building had been conveniently and theoretically 'burnt' by the Communists, and so Parliament simply had to meet elsewhere.) The whole performance was indeed a brain-wave and a masterstroke. For one thing it was the first day of spring, the end of winter-gloom and the re-birth of the year, the triumph of light over darkness, and Germans have always shown a hankering after 'nature myths' far more persistent and primitive than other civilized and Christian countries. But more important was the fact that it either won over or silenced the Conservatives and nationalists and all those who were in any way 'Prussian' in sympathy and outlook; it linked up the Nazi revolution with the most popular period of Prussian history; it satisfied the romantic longings of the great mass of the German people for political power and a national revival; and it allowed Adolf Hitler to stand forth as the representative and embodiment of the Prussian spirit, the successor and heir of Frederick William I and Frederick the Great. Hindenburg appeared dressed in his field-marshal's uniform, carrying his baton and wearing his medals; Adolf Hitler greeted him outside the church, dressed in a frock coat just to show how harmless and normal and even good middle-class [gutbürgerlich] he was; and the two were photographed shaking hands, Hindenburg, grave as ever, leaning only very slightly forward, and Hitler, probably for the first and last time in his political career, bowing very low in an effort to express deference. It was a touching scene and a wonderful photograph, over which many German eyes filled with thankful tears (Germans *are* sentimental!): the old and glorious Germany of Prussia and Hohenzollern meeting the new and even more glorious Germany of National Socialism and the Third Empire;

and on the more personal side, the unknown but brave (Iron Cross, First Class) corporal of the Great War standing before his former Commander-in-Chief.

Poor old Hindenburg did not enjoy for long the bitter-sweet joys of the new empire of a thousand years; and on the day of his death (the 2nd August 1934) the Deputy Leader of the Nazi Party, Rudolf Hess, spoke the following message over all German wireless stations and it was printed in all German newspapers: 'Hindenburg is dead. Hindenburg lives on in our hearts as the symbol of glorious German history, as the father of a great people. Hindenburg summoned the Führer, and Hindenburg inaugurated thereby a new period of German history. Hindenburg's living legacy for Germany is the Führer. Loyalty to Hindenburg is loyalty to the Führer, means loyalty to Germany. We brace ourselves to continue the struggle for the future of our people!' In this brief but very skilful appeal one can sense the Nazi uncertainty and apprehension. Hindenburg had had a large personal following, and many important individuals and sections of the people had given their support to Hitler only indirectly out of loyalty to Hindenburg; many of them had seen in Hindenburg a necessary check and a pledge of decency. Would they now continue their support? Further, Hindenburg's death had created an awkward constitutional difficulty: could Hitler become President of the Reich [Reichspräsident] and be head of the Reich government [Reichskanzler] as well, and if Hitler did not become President, who else was there? The problem was settled with typical Nazi speed and by a typical Nazi trick. Hitler declared that Hindenburg had so hallowed the office of President that it would be sacrilege to appoint another to fill it. Let Hindenburg remain the first and only President of the new Germany. He—Hitler—would continue as Chancellor, and would also become titular head of the state by assuming officially the title of 'Führer'. The Nazis then staged a grandiose and martial funeral service at Tannenberg, where Hindenburg was buried in one of the towers of the tremendous war memorial which had been built in the form of a fort on the battlefield. Hitler's long speech on this occasion ended with the words: 'Dead General, enter now into Valhalla!'

Chapter X

Prussia Welcomes Hitler

---

1. Carl Dyrssen and the 'Schlesische Zeitung'

Several of the books we have discussed, for example, Moeller van den Bruck's *Der preussische Stil* and *Das dritte Reich*, Spengler's *Preussentum und Sozialismus*, were published by Wilhelm Gottlieb Korn of Breslau. In addition to publishing books this firm owns the *Schlesische Zeitung*, one of the best-known daily newspapers of south-east Germany, and a recognized organ of Prussianism, Protestantism, Junkerdom, anti-Catholic and anti-Polish feeling. The paper has been in the hands of the Korn family ever since the days of Frederick the Great, and is one of the few family concerns of this kind remaining in Germany. An interesting summary of the spirit and traditions of the firm and the paper is provided by the introduction to a special number published in 1935 with the title 'Three Centuries of Silesian History Mirrored in the *Schlesische Zeitung*.' This introduction is also an illustration of the way in which good Prussians welcomed Hitler, and of how they saw in him the fulfilment of Prussian ideas. 'A newspaper is an educational institution for adults. It does not exist simply for the bald recital of news, but has an essential part to play in the education of the people. These principles, which have now been expressed in the form of laws (i.e. the Nazi press laws), were laid down and tried out for the first time in the age of Frederick the Great. That great king, who in decisive hours himself wrote the reports published in the newspapers (the forerunner of Goebbels?), demanded from his Prussian journalists unconditional loyalty and devotion to the state. He gave the right to publish a newspaper only to men whose integrity had been tested and proved. For this reason he deprived the publisher of the *Nouvellen-Courier* (the predecessor of the *Schlesische Zeitung*) of the right to publish a newspaper in Silesia and conferred it upon the bookseller Johann Jacob Korn, who had gone over to the side of the king immediately after Prussian troops marched into Silesia. In this way the *Schlesische Zeitung* was given a definite task to perform from the day it was founded, namely, the education of the people of Silesia to serve the Prussian State ['die Erziehung des Schlesiers zum preussischen Staate'].'

Early in 1933 Carl Dyrssen, the editor of the *Schlesische Zeitung*, published a book entitled *Die Botschaft des Ostens: Fascismus, Nationalsozialismus und Preussentum* [The Message of the East]. Dyrssen declared in his preface, which was dated Autumn 1932, that his book was intended as a cry of warning; its aim was not to promote peace and quietness, but to rouse people. Above all, it was a demand for a Prussian revival. It is full of ideas we have already encountered in Moeller van den Bruck and Spengler, although Spengler is attacked for his theories about the 'Decline of the West', which Dyrssen described as a fairy-tale, and pure nonsense, only accepted by men who were too weak to overcome the 'so-called misfortune' of the Great War. Like Moeller he declared that Germany ought to be thankful for the War, which for the healthy and strong nations was not an end, but a beginning. But it smacks more of Spengler than Moeller when he raves against the capitalistic domination of the world and the sins of economic individualism. Like both writers he is strongly opposed to Marxism and the 'pseudo-Socialism' of the Social Democrats, demanding instead a return to the genuine Socialism of Old Prussia. He declares that Germans have always been 'revolutionary Socialists', ever since they appeared armed on the 'Thingplatz' ['the tribal meeting place']! 'To be a German and a revolutionary Socialist is one and the same thing.' When Frederick the Great said (oh, blessed quotation!): 'The king is the first servant of the state,' he was simply expressing in a new way a very old and very German idea—the idea of true Socialism. The Socialism of the class war declares that property is theft; the Prussian answer is that property is duty. Dyrssen's ideal man is the armed peasant-farmer of eastern Germany ['der wehrhafte Bauer des deutschen Ostens']; he calls him the primary German ['der primäre Deutsche'], and like Moeller van den Bruck and other good Prussians he is convinced that the fate of Germany will be decided in the east. ['Der Osten ist der deutsche Schicksalsraum'].

In Dyrssen's opinion it was desirable and even imperative that National Socialism should now turn from South Germany and Austria, and concern itself more with North Germany and Prussia. Everything pointed to Prussia. German history showed that the German Empire must be dominated by a North German spirit, and by Protestantism. Only Old Prussia had produced a truly aristocratic and military society which was at the same time truly Socialist. The German people must be led back to its soldierly nucleus, namely, Prussia. The Storm Troopers, the Black Guards and the Steel Helmets[1] had the task of providing the military scaffolding ['das soldatische Gerüst'] for the new state which would take its rise after the defeat of the capitalist democracy of Weimar. This new state must be fundamentally Prussian in character, that is to say, soldierly and Socialist. National Socialism must be welcomed and accepted by the German people because it represented Prussianism in its most authentic form. 'Nationalsozialismus ist die Urform des Preussentums': these are the words—in large print—with which the book ends.

2. *Friedrich Schinkel on Prussian Socialism*

Another ardent Prussian patriot who greeted the triumph of Hitler with much jubilation was Friedrich Schinkel, whose book *Preussischer Sozialismus* was published in 1934, again by Wilhelm Gottlieb Korn of Breslau. Even more than Carl Dyrssen, Schinkel felt himself to be continuing the work of Moeller van den Bruck and Spengler, and he was far more frank than Dyrssen in expressing his obligations to them, particularly to the latter.

[1] The Steel Helmets (*Stahlhelmer*) were members of an organization of war-veterans which was always closely associated with the parties of the Right.

In the preface he declared with obvious satisfaction that although in the years immediately after the Great War even conservative circles in Germany turned away from Prussia, the word Prussia had recently become a political and literary fashion. Nor was it a matter of chance that the Prussian 'idea' had once again won such topical importance. For the National Socialist revolution had without doubt much more in common with the Old Prussian era than with that of Bismarck or William II! The Prussian task to-day consisted in uniting Conservative and Socialist principles. This was a process which began in the Prussia of Frederick the Great, continued intermittently throughout the nineteenth century, and reached its climax in the National Socialist revolution.

Spengler's treatment of the subject was rather abstract and speculative, whereas what Schinkel tried to do was to supply the historical background, by tracing the socialistic elements in Prussian politics from Frederick the Great to Adolf Hitler. It is not possible to deal here with each of the periods in turn as Schinkel does, and I propose only to take the beginning and the end of his story: Prussian Mercantilism in the eighteenth century and Prussian Socialism in the Third Empire.

If one considers the economic development of the last few decades, says Schinkel, one realizes that the period of liberal free trade is at an end and that we are approaching once again an economic system like that which characterized the absolutist states of the eighteenth century. Most countries have by now introduced measures controlling immigration, exports and imports, the exchange of goods and money. Such measures cannot be reconciled with liberal principles, and have indeed much more in common with the so-called mercantile system, or Mercantilism, which was developed in a more complete form in the Prussia of Frederick the Great than in any other state. Frederick William I was the real founder of Prussian Mercantilism: he it was who began the concentration of all the forces of the state in the service of foreign policy, as a necessary preparation for the political and military offensive. This policy was continued and developed by Frederick the Great. The army, the officials, the finances were thoroughly organized; nobility, peasants, weavers, merchants—all had their part to play, and all were controlled by the state. Within the Prussian boundaries self-sufficiency, or 'autarky', of a far-reaching nature was achieved, and Frederick the Great planned, according to Schinkel, to extend the autarkic economic area under Prussian control by the inclusion of Saxony and Poland. (Shades of the 'Customs Union' of 1834, and even more of the Nazi ideas of 'living space'!) All private interests and rights were subordinated to the welfare of the whole community. The system was indeed—so Schinkel gravely asserts—Socialism in a very true sense.

In the chapters which follow Schinkel gives a comprehensive survey of German economic policy in the nineteenth century, noting all the time with regret the growth of Liberal Capitalism, and the retreat from the principles of Prussian Mercantilism. And he proves to his own satisfaction that the Weimar revolution did not result in real Socialism but in plutocracy.

The final chapter is entitled 'Nationalsozialismus und Preussentum'. Early in the chapter Schinkel repeats much he had already said in his preface. With the downfall of the monarchy and the triumph of Marxism and kindred forces after the Great War, the fate of Prussia seemed sealed. But the Prussian revival came; and as in the years after the breakdown at Jena in 1806, it was above all due to the activities of 'Wahl-Preussen' rather than 'Geburts-Preussen', that is to say, men who were not born Prussians but had become Prussians of their own free will, by adopting the Prussian outlook and mode of life, and by assimilating themselves to the Prussian State and the Prussian tradition. Moeller van den Bruck and Spengler were men of this type, and they gave to the movement for national regeneration its spiritual direction and its theoretical form, above all by striving to bring about the union of nationalist and Socialist principles. For several years the situation in Germany had seemed hopeless, and the dreams of Moeller van den Bruck and Spengler unlikely of fulfilment: until Adolf Hitler and National Socialism appeared, and transformed into political realities what had hitherto been preached as romantic Utopias. Then follow certain statements which are so interesting as to warrant an exact translation: 'If Prussianism had once sacrificed its own political and social life for the sake of the Second Empire (we have already encountered this idea in Moeller van den Bruck's

Der preussische Stil—see page 54), the new Germany found its way back to Prussianism by the creation of the Third Empire. And the important point was this: that the impulse to this rebirth of the Prussian idea did not start in Prussia itself but in the South, which had always hitherto opposed Prussianization. The subordination of the Reich to the social and political law of Prussia, which Bismarck had struggled in vain to achieve, now took place automatically, as a result of the National Socialist victory, and indeed on a scale which it would never have been possible to achieve with Prussian means alone.' There could be no more definite expression than this of the conviction held by many good Prussians—and others—that National Socialism was a continuation, a new form, an intensification of 'Prussianism'.

Like his chief founts of inspiration, Moeller van den Bruck and Spengler, Schinkel declared that only Prussian Socialism could be regarded as genuine Socialism, and he went on to prove triumphantly that National Socialism was its heir and its heritage, its climax and its fulfilment. He quoted a speech by Göring, delivered apparently in the early days of the revolution to representatives of the workers. 'We should like to stress once again that this is a nationalist *and* a Socialist revolution, and that it is not correct to speak only of a nationalist revolution. For not only German nationalism helped to achieve victory, but—and this makes us particularly happy—German Socialism has triumphed as well. And he who stands for German Socialism is truly nationalist.' The power of the state, said Schinkel, was no longer dependent on parties and vested interests and other organizations within the state, as it had been in the Weimar Republic, and the state could now assert itself and take the lead —as was only right and proper—in the large-scale planning and ordering of economic policy. Further, what the Prussian State had tried in vain for nearly a century to achieve, namely, the 'nationalization of the workers', was now an accomplished fact. The German words he used were 'die Nationalisierung der Arbeiterschaft', and he meant that the workers had become nationalist and patriotic.

3. *August Winnig and the German Workers*

Discussion of the works of Moeller van den Bruck, Spengler, Ernst Jünger, and Friedrich Schinkel has shown that they all realized the decisive importance of the political outlook and activity of the German workers, and hoped to win them for the cause of nationalism. But none of these writers was, or had been, a worker himself, or a member of a workers' organization; and they were therefore less qualified to speak for the workers than August Winnig, to whose book *Vom Proletariat zum Arbeitertum* we now turn. It is impossible to translate this title adequately, but the main idea behind it is that the German workers were in danger of becoming a proletariat, in the sense of Marx and Communism, and that they were preserved from this fate and raised to the higher level of a nationalist spirit and a nationalist organization, chiefly because of the noble efforts of Adolf Hitler.

August Winnig (born 1878) learnt the trade of a mason [Maurer] and followed it for many years. He played a leading part in the organization of a trade union for masons and others engaged in the building trade. In 1905 he became editor of the union's periodical *Der Grundstein* ['The Foundation Stone'], and in 1913 he was elected president. In July 1919 his services to the workers' organizations and the Social Democrat Party were suitably recognized by his appointment as head of the provincial administration in East Prussia [Oberpräsident]; but in March 1920 he was relieved of his office and expelled from the Social Democrat Party for taking part in the abortive nationalist rising known as the Kapp Putsch.

Vom Proletariat zum Arbeitertum first appeared in 1930, but in the preface Winnig was at great pains to point out that he had formulated and expressed the ideas it contained as early as 1924 in an essay printed in the December number of the *Süddeutsche Monatshefte*, a nationalist monthly. The book is really an account of the German Labour movement, from a Prussian and national-ist standpoint. It is opposed to Marxism and to the class war, to the abolition of property and to social revolution; it denies that the economic factor is decisive in human affairs, and condemns materialism as the lowest form of Weltanschauung. On the other hand it stresses the value of community life, above all for

160

the workers. The advent of factories and towns destroyed the medieval communities of craftsmen and merchants, and created the proletariat. The great task of the present and near future is to organize the proletariat into communities. The worker is the bearer of a destiny and has a mission to perform, just like the nobility, and later the middle classes, in days gone by. The proletariat is destined to become a new 'estate', to create values and ideals of its own, to rejuvenate the old social forms and not to destroy them.

Winnig declares that in order to fulfil such a destiny and to find his true self, the German worker must be freed from Marx. Marx was the first Jew to interfere in the German workers' movement, but a long line of Jews came after him. His presence at the birth and baptism of the movement, and the influence he was able to exercise on its later development, was the most ominous factor and the most terrible feature not only in the history of the movement but in German history as a whole since that day. Marx was inspired by a hatred of all authority, including the state and religion, a hatred which cannot be explained without reference to his Jewish origin. For the Jew is always in favour of 'progress' and 'freedom', that is to say, in favour of the loosening of bonds, and the destruction of the political and social life of the people among whom he is in reality only a guest. As a result of this alien spirit, this shadow over Germany, the workers lost all connexion with the state, and were led to regard it in a negative and hostile way. The German workers' movement thus became unfitted to perform its historic mission, namely, the regeneration of the state. When Wilhelm Liebknecht and August Bebel opposed in the Parliament of the North German Confederation the granting of credits for the Franco-Prussian War of 1870–1, the policy of the Social Democrat Party was fixed for a long time to come. This was a crime because it interfered with the achievement of that unity which the German people had so long desired, and also with Germany's struggle to become a great power. An improvement in the standard of life of the worker was made possible by the expansion of German industry after 1870, but this was clearly connected with Germany's rise to political power. The mass of the German workers still stood outside politics, and most of their leaders did not truly represent them, but some of them—including presumably Winnig himself—began to realize that the welfare of the workers was inextricably bound up with the maintenance of Germany's position among the Great Powers. Proof of this growing insight and change of heart was given when the trade-union leaders decided on the 1st August 1914 for participation in the national front, without even waiting for the decision of the Social Democrat Party. When the party met on the 4th August, only fourteen Members of Parliament out of one hundred and ten voted against support for the war. Winnig is therefore able to portray in glowing terms what he calls the outburst of national community feeling at the beginning of the war; but his enthusiasm wanes when he goes on to describe how later in the war overwork and nervous strain and hunger, but above all lying and treasonable propaganda, broke the spirit of the workers and led them to betray the nation and themselves. Like most other German 'patriots' he accepts gladly as the explanation of Germany's defeat in 1918 the theory of defection on the home front, and the 'stab in the back' which paralysed the glorious and undefeated German army; and then he takes a grim and melancholy delight in castigating the Jewish 'intellectuals', who came to dominate the Communist and Social Democrat Parties, the trade unions, and the left-wing press. Under the leadership and influence of such 'aliens', men who were naturally opposed to everything national and to all really German ideas of state and society, the workers threatened to degenerate into a proletariat, an uncontrolled and disorganized mass. They had lost all conception of the historic state, which they no longer regarded as the highest embodiment of the idea of community, but simply as the plaything of parties. Hence, says Winnig, the political weakness of Germany, and also the economic distress (*quod erat demonstrandum?*).

When Winnig was writing his book in 1930 he had obviously pinned his faith to the Christian and National Trade Unions ['die Christlich-Nationalen Gewerkschaften'], although they had only just over a million members compared with the five million workers in the Socialist organizations. They alone were fitted, in Winnig's opinion, to oppose Marxism, and lead the German workers from the chaotic swamps of proletarian degeneracy to the sublime heights of purposeful and self-redeeming nationalism. But by the time Winnig came to prepare the 1933 edition of his book, the political situation in Germany had fundamentally changed, and Winnig's opinions had changed accordingly. So in order to do himself—and others—justice, he added a graceful postscript, a kind of political *apologia pro vita sua*. Writing in August 1933, almost exactly three years after penning the preface to the first edition, he described the false and vain hopes he had placed in Dr. Brüning, one of the leaders of the Christian and National Trade Unions, who became head of the Reich Government [Reichskanzler] early in 1930. In March 1930 Winnig told a meeting of the Christian and National Trade Unions that if they did not rise to the occasion, seize their opportunities, and take over the leadership of the 'nationalist' workers, then the initiative and the power would pass to the National Socialists. Now that his prophetic utterance had so swiftly become reality, he apparently felt justified in jubilating over the victory of Adolf Hitler and National Socialism. It was a victory for youth and for the German worker; a new period had begun; the ban of Marxism had been broken. Adolf Hitler had created a mighty national movement, and had succeeded not only in uniting the upper classes and the workers, but all Germans. In one glorious word, he had set up the 'Volksgemeinschaft', the community of the German people. The state had now a greater prestige and a deeper significance than ever before, and in this new state the workers would play their full part, and fulfil their national destiny. They would become the basis of the state, and carry the new empire, the Third Empire. 'Heil dem Volkskanzler, Adolf Hitler!' ['Hail to the Chancellor of the Volk, Adolf Hitler!'] It was with such ecstasies that Winnig ended the topical supplement to his book, and one cannot help wondering how long this mood remained, when he observed how the Nazis proceeded step by step to exploit the workers, robbed them of the rights for which they had fought so long, forced down their standard of life, and harnessed them to the war-machine. But as we have seen in other cases, disillusionment seems to increase rather than to break down the self-discipline of the Prussian, and to make him passive rather than active. Besides, it was too late, and of little use to kick against

163

the pricks. So August Winnig sank into discreet retirement like all the other labour leaders of the pre-Nazi period who were spared death, exile, and the concentration camp; and the stage was left entirely free for the disgusting antics of Dr. Ley and his satellites.

Chapter XI

The Nazi Exploitation of Prussia

1. Kleist and Fichte in Nazi Dress

One of the most interesting proofs and illustrations of the Nazi exploitation of Prussia is the way in which they have taken the great Prussian writers of the past, put their own interpretation on their works, and used them, or rather, misused them, for their own political ends. Two of the greatest of these writers have been selected for special treatment: Kleist and Fichte.

In his *History of German Literature* Professor Robertson described Kleist as an 'enigmatic, even an unsympathetic figure'. Many English students of German literature would agree that the first adjective is certainly appropriate, and that there is little reason for quarrelling with the second. In accordance with family tradition, Kleist became an officer, but dissatisfied with this career and with life as a whole, he soon left the army, spent some time in Paris and in Switzerland, and finally returned to Germany, where he began to write. After Prussia's defeat in 1806 he became a member of a Berlin circle of patriots who were united in their opposition to Napoleon. Kleist's works found little approval among his contemporaries; even his comedy *Der zerbrochene Krug* (1808), later to be regarded as one of the greatest comedies in German literature, was a failure. His *Käthchen von Heilbronn* (1810) achieved a certain success, but the dramas by which he is chiefly remembered—*Die Hermannsschlacht*, written in 1808, and *Der Prinz von Homburg*, written in 1810— were not even published, let alone performed, during his lifetime. Embittered by these failures and by the seemingly hopeless political situation, he committed suicide in 1811, and thus brought to a fitting end a life of brooding, disappointment, and unhappiness.

In order to make clear to English readers what it is exactly in Kleist's *Hermannsschlacht*, and above all, in his *Prinz von Homburg*, which appeals so much to Prussians and Nazis, it is necessary to give a brief account of their contents. The hero of the *Hermannsschlacht* is Hermann, or Arminius, the chieftain of the Cherusker tribe, who in A.D. 9 defeated the Roman legions under Quintilius Varus in the battle of the Teutoburger Wald. But it is clear that in the play Rome represents France, and Hermann and his fighters represent the Prussian and German opponents of Napoleon. The play was first performed in Dresden in 1861, but it was not until after the Franco-Prussian war of 1870–1 that it achieved real success. In the first volume of his *Deutsche Geschichte im 19. Jahrhundert* (1879) Treitschke described it as 'a lofty song of revenge, a mighty poem of the lust of reprisal', and that is how it has been regarded ever since.

Kleist's *Prinz von Homburg* is a play about the battle of Fehrbellin. On the night before the battle, the Prince, who is to command the cavalry, is told in no uncertain language that he is not to attack until expressly ordered to do so, and that the Great Elector's plan is not to give the order until the Swedes have been attacked in the rear and the bridges over the River Rhyn have been captured, so as to prevent them from retreating. The second scene of the second act, one of the most famous battle scenes in German literature, shows the Prince on a hill overlooking the battlefield; he sees that the Swedes are already giving way, and although the order to attack has not yet come, he is unable to hold back any longer. His brother officers try in vain to prevent him. A glorious victory is won, the Swedes are severely defeated; but because Homburg attacked before the bridges over the Rhyn could be seized, part of the Swedish army escaped. Homburg, in spite of his great bravery and decisive share in the victory, is arrested, brought before a court-martial, and condemned to death. The idea of death fills him with horror, and the last scene of the third act finds him entirely desperate and broken; he is ready to renounce honour, career, love, indeed everything,

THE NAZI EXPLOITATION OF PRUSSIA

if only the Great Elector will grant him his life. The Elector, representing the hard Prussian conception of law ['das Gesetz'] refuses to listen, not only to the intercession of his niece, Natalie, who loves the Prince, but even to the pleas and protests of the army. He tells Natalie that it is impossible for him to go against the verdict of the court: 'What would be the consequences if I did?' Natalie, who does not understand, asks: 'The consequences for you?' And the Great Elector replies:

> *Für mich? nein!—Was? Für mich!*
> *Kennst du nichts Höh'res, Jungfrau, als nur mich?*
> *Ist dir ein Heiligtum ganz unbekannt,*
> *Das, in dem Lager, Vaterland sich nennt?*[1]

To Kottwitz and the other officers he declares that he scorns a victory won by chance, and that he is determined to uphold the 'law', which he describes as 'the mother of the Prussian crown' ['die Mutter meiner Krone'].

He decides to place the decision in the Prince's hands by sending him a letter, explaining that when he ordered him to be arrested he believed he was simply doing his duty, and that he had expected the Prince would entirely approve his action—but if he did not approve, it was only necessary for him to say so, and he would at once be set free. The effect on the Prince is that he regains his old courage and his sense of honour; in a moment of revelation he sees that the Elector was right in acting as he did, and that he too must do his duty. He declares he is ready to accept sentence of death, the penalty of his disobedience and self-will, the necessary sacrifice to the 'law' which he had transgressed. In this way he will set a glorious example, and help to overcome an enemy far more dangerous than the Swedes, namely, the enemy within, the enemy which lies hidden in the personal feelings and desires, the individual self-assertion, the tendency towards insubordination of Prussian subjects, not only in his own day, but in days to come. He thus wins the Elector's pardon.

The play embodies, therefore, in a perfection of form which

---

[1] 'For me? no!—What do you mean? For me! Don't you know something higher, my girl, than only me? Don't you know anything at all about the sacred treasure which soldiers call the Fatherland?'

no other work in German literature has excelled, the idea of strict and merciless discipline, the idea of duty to the law of war and to the law of the state. From the Prussian standpoint the Prince is a model character. He develops from an irresponsible youth into a man and a hero. He learns to suppress his own personality and to think only of the state.

The Nazis were not slow to recognize the propaganda values in all this, and very soon they had taken over Kleist, lock, stock, and barrel. In November 1933 the 'Kleist-Gesellschaft' was reorganized. Professor Oskar Walzel, who had been president from 1930, was replaced, no doubt partly because he was non-Aryan, and the 'nationalist' Minde-Pouet and Professor Julius Petersen became editors of the Year Book of the Society. Articles on Kleist began to appear in all the Nazi newspapers and periodicals; extracts from his works and talks about him were frequently heard on the wireless; professors and students at the universities busied themselves with him as never before, and discovered that he still provided lots of good subjects for lectures, 'Seminars', and theses [Doktorarbeiten]. His *Prinz von Homburg* became a safe and favourite piece in the repertoire of many theatres. But one of the literary climaxes of this Nazi exploitation of Kleist came with the publication in 1935 of a short study of Kleist by Walther Linden, one of the best-known of the 'nationalist' and Nazi historians of literature. The title of Linden's book—*Heinrich von Kleist, der Dichter der völkischen Gemeinschaft*—in itself speaks volumes to those who are familiar with Nazi Germany. In his introduction, Linden asked: 'What is Kleist to us?' And his answer ran: 'We see in Kleist not a "poet" [Dichter] in the old sense, that is to say, a man who creates beautiful literary forms and is concerned only with individual questions of life, but also a man who discovered the pulsating reality of the community, and thus came to foresee and to mould those questions which are fundamental for the existence of the German people.' (Admittedly this does not impress, and indeed fails to make much sense, when translated into English; but it is typical of the airy 'blurb' served out regularly by Nazi mouthpieces as an unheard-of and simply awe-inspiring political philosophy.) The most important thing about Kleist, said Linden, is that he was a solitary forerunner and prophet of that tre-

mendous transformation in thought and life which had culminated in the Nazi revolution of 1933. Kleist discovered the community of the people ['die völkische Gemeinschaft'] not as an
abstract community of language and culture, but as a living
organism, dependent on blood-relationship. Kleist is the poet of
this community life ['ein Gemeinschaftsdichter'], who realized
himself, and made others realize, that fate demanded from the
German people the most determined concentration of effort,
and a soldierly and heroic readiness for sacrifice. 'Kleist gets to
the very heart of our own time!' ['Kleist greift an das innerste
Wesen unserer Zeit.'] The logic and inference of all this is
obvious, namely, that everything the Nazis said and did had the
authority and blessing of the great and popular dramatist,
Heinrich von Kleist. From this standpoint it is surely not without significance that one of the outstanding theatrical successes
in Berlin's first winter of war (1939–40) was the new production
of Kleist's *Prinz von Homburg* at the Schiller-Theatre, with Nazi
Germany's best-known actor, Heinrich George, in the role of
the Great Elector.

For the purposes of this whole inquiry, Linden's conclusion,
with its stress on Kleist's Prussianism and the identity of such
Prussianism with National Socialism, is of great interest and importance. Kleist, he said, is above all a 'Prussian' poet; not only
because of the subject matter of his works, but because of the
nature of his heart and mind. 'For there lives in him the spirit of
the German East, and of those who conquered and colonized it.
There lives in him the hardness, the sobriety and resolution, the
fighting efficiency, the heroic will-power, but also the dark tendency towards things mystical and demoniacal which are to be
found in the German East. Just as Kant is the philosopher of the
German East, so Kleist is its greatest poet, the poet of Prussianism ['der Dichter des Preussentums']. Thereby and at the same
time, he is for all Germans the poet of the revival of those heroic
powers of will and those values of community life, which are
stored up in Prussianism.'

Before describing how the Nazis seized upon Fichte, certain
reasons may be suggested to explain why they have always
fought rather shy of that even greater Prussian philosopher,
Kant. Of course, many of them have paid lip-service to him,

just as Walther Linden did at the end of his book on Kleist; they have described him as the greatest Prussian philosopher, and referred gracefully but vaguely to the categorical imperative and the idea of duty, and so on. But it would be true to say that officially the Nazis have made very little of Kant, almost to the point of ignoring him altogether. One reason may be that even the Nazis realized the disparity and indeed the unbridgeable gulf between their own philosophy and methods and Kant's categorical imperative. But we are concerned with literature and politics, and not with moral philosophy, and must, therefore, pass on quickly to another reason, namely, Kant's views on international affairs, as expressed in his work *Zum ewigen Frieden* ['On Perpetual Peace'] (1795). These views were given considerable prominence by some of the leaders of the Weimar Republic, who were not slow to point out their bearing on the attempts to create and work satisfactorily a League of Nations. The first section of Kant's essay, which is written in the form of a treaty between states, contains what he calls the preliminary articles for the achievement of perpetual peace. Article 2 reads: 'It shall not be possible for any state (whether great or small, that is all the same here), to pass into the possession of another state whether by inheritance, exchange, purchase, or gift.' Article 3: 'Standing armies (miles perpetuus) shall in time cease to exist entirely.' Article 5: 'No state shall interfere by force in the constitution and government of another state.' These few quotations are surely sufficient; it is clear that the Nazis could have nothing to do with weak-kneed pacifist nonsense of this kind!

Fichte was, superficially at any rate, free from such blemishes. He was a popular figure, because of the part he had played in stirring up Prussians and other Germans to revolt against Napoleon; and his *Reden an die deutsche Nation* ['Speeches to the German Nation'] (1807), which gave expression to this spirit of revolt, were well known and simple enough to be read in abbreviated and selected form by ordinary people and school-children. After the Nazis came to power many books and booklets appeared on Fichte; one by Ernst Bergmann, Professor at the University of Leipzig, entitled *Fichte und der Nationalsozialismus* (published in 1933), may be selected as typical. In his introduction Professor Bergmann referred with feeling to those leading personalities in German history who in the new dawn are rising up once again, at the head of them all—Frederick the Great. And alongside the great national heroes like Frederick the Great appeared also the great spiritual leaders, above all Fichte. Professor Bergmann was not content to describe Fichte as a great forerunner of National Socialism; he declared that Fichte *was* a National Socialist! So much for the introduction. Later Professor Bergmann analysed Fichte's character, teaching, and achievements from the Nazi standpoint. Like so many other great Nazis, including Adolf Hitler, Fichte was a man of the people and came from the people. His father was a poor linenweaver in Saxony, and in his early days Fichte looked after geese and worked at the loom. Then followed a section dealing with Fichte's fighting spirit ['Kämpfernatur']; and a section on Fichte as an orator, in which stress was laid above all on the *Speeches*, and how they filled Germans with a consciousness of unity and the will to achieve it, and how they inspired a lofty love of the Fatherland. Fichte realized the sacredness and the blessings of work; he held that the Church could not be responsible for national education, but only the state; he believed that the Germans were a chosen people, and the 'salt of the earth'. (Whether Fichte really made assertions of this kind might very well be called in question, but that is not the point here.) The booklet concludes: 'And so the call goes out to every German teacher: Discover the eternal Fichte in thy bosom, rise up, and enter into our Teachers' Association.'

What Professor Bergmann and other Nazi admirers of Fichte rather conveniently forgot was that Fichte in his early works (e.g. *Beiträge zur Berichtigung der Urteile des Publikums über die französische Revolution*, 1793) had ardently defended the French Revolution (anathema to the Nazis), and that, like Kant, he had continued to regard it as an event of outstanding importance.[1] They also forgot that as late as 1804, when Fichte delivered his first series of lectures at Berlin on the 'Grundzüge des gegenwärtigen Zeitalters' ['Fundamentals of the Present Epoch'], his out-

---

[1] In this persistently positive attitude towards the French Revolution Fichte and Kant provide a contrast to the poet Klopstock, who, rather like Wordsworth, recanted his initial enthusiasm, and in his ode 'Mein Irrtum' ['My Error'] (1793) confessed that 'the delight of the golden dream has disappeared'—'des goldenen Traumes Wonne ist dahin'.

look was still in the main cosmopolitan, and that it was rather pressure of circumstances, his love of freedom and his hatred of tyranny, which turned the 'citizen of the world' ['Weltbürger'] into the Prussian and German patriot of 1807. Further, one might remind the Nazi admirers of Fichte that the *Speeches* were among those works forbidden by the Prussian censorship authorities when they took stern measures against 'liberals' and 'democrats' after the murder of Kotzebue in 1819, and that in 1824 the publisher Georg Reimer was refused permission for a second edition. Indeed, with the help of inquiries which have already been made into Fichte's political philosophy, it would be possible to argue that many of his ideas were the very opposite of Prussianism and Hitlerism. Joseph Nadler wrote in his monumental *Literaturgeschichte der deutschen Stämme und Landschaften* ['Literary History of the German Tribes and Provinces']: 'The state was for Fichte only a subordinate means. The only goal which he always had in mind was the (individual) human being.' And in one of the best biographies of Fichte ever written, Fritz Medicus spoke of the *Speeches* as 'the noblest expression of Fichte's democratic mind'; but that was in 1922, and the spirit of Weimar may be held responsible for such an exaggeration. Nor would I go quite as far as a recent English writer (H. T. Betteridge: 'Fichte's Political Ideas, a Retrospect,' *German Life and Letters*, July 1937): 'To sum up, we may say that Fichte was a liberal democrat in the case of the superior citizens in any state, and for all mankind in the ideal future society. For the existing masses, he was an authoritarian socialist. Ideally he was a pacifist and an internationalist, but he welcomed and encouraged nationalism in Germany.' But at all events, enough has been said to show that the Prussian and Nazi claims to Fichte are not at all as solid and comprehensive as they would wish them to be. In one point, however, the Prussian and Nazi appropriation of Fichte is practically unassailable, and that is with reference to his Socialism. And here Mr. Betteridge would seem to be definitely on the wrong path. He wrote: 'Interest began to be taken in Fichte as a political thinker when socialistic ideas started to spread; he then became a philosopher of Socialism. Since 1930 he has attracted the attention of the opposite school of thought and to-day he is generally accepted as the intellectual founder of

National Socialism.' But Fichte's Socialism, as expressed chiefly in his work *Der geschlossene Handelsstaat* ['The Self-contained Economic State'] (1804), was that Prussian kind of authoritarian and state Socialism which writers like Spengler and Friedrich Schinkel preached after the Great War, and which was largely taken over by the Nazis. And if Fichte is to be regarded as the first and greatest philosopher of 'Prussian Socialism', then it is no opposite school of thought, but a continuation of that school of thought which made him so popular in this respect since 1930, or rather since 1933.

2. *Nazi Writers exploit the Prussian Past*

I now wish to illustrate, by discussing the works of four Nazi writers, how the Prussian past entered into German literature from 1933 to 1939. The first writer I have chosen is Anne Marie Koeppen, a high priestess of the Nazi faith if ever there was one. Her novels and poems are entertaining examples of what normal and intelligent Germans call 'nationaler Kitsch', which means something like 'patriotic rubbish'; and if they were not so typical and so widely read and accepted, one could simply laugh at them or ignore them altogether. Her best-known work is *Das Erbe der Wallmodens* ['The Heritage of the Wallmodens'], a model of what a Nazi 'Blood and Soil' ['Blut und Boden'] novel should be. It is the story of a North German family, or rather, clan (naturally the fashionable word 'Sippe' is used). The heroine bears the name Haseltrud, which sounds delightfully Nordic; her eyes are, of course, bright blue ['hellblau'], and when her hair is not 'wheat-blond' ['weizenblond'] then it is 'yellow-like-the-lime-tree-blossom' ['lindenblütengelb']. She could often hear the voices of her ancestors murmuring in her blood: the voice of the blood. The novel contains a strong element of Germanic paganism, and there is a great deal about the old Germanic gods.

This is what goes through Haseltrud's mind when she is eating an apple. 'Ah, the apples of one's homeland! What could taste better? What are the most wonderful fruits of foreign lands compared with the rosy-cheeked juicy apples which ripen in our gardens and in whose spicy freshness all strength and all wealth seems to be hidden?' (This reminds one of the story about the patriotic German lady who asked the Berlin market woman if she was absolutely sure the apples she was offering for sale were German. 'Why?' asked the market woman. 'Do you want to talk with them?') As one would naturally expect from a girl whose name begins with 'Hazel', our heroine is very fond of nuts. 'Many a hard brown nut had she cracked between her white teeth, and the sweet kernel had tasted more delicious than the most toothsome sweetmeats which her father regularly brought her back from the town.'

One of the novel's main themes is the struggle between the old simple life of peasant farmers, deeply rooted in the soil, and modern ideas of comfortable living and how to make money. There are frequent ecstasies like the following: 'Where is our Mother Earth happiest? On the spot where a man builds a house, and together with his wife, kindles a fire on the hearth. Where children are born and cattle and corn thrive. Where a capable farmer sets his hand to the plough . . . and where he scatters the holy seed over the soil.' We learn that it is a tradition in the Wallmoden clan never to allow a Jew to set foot on their land. But the eldest son allows Abram Löwy to appear, and then bad luck begins. There is also a struggle between Protestantism and Catholicism; of course to the discomfiture of the latter. Rudolf von Lage, a young blue-blooded Junker whom Haseltrud loves, is on the point of becoming a monk, but he is happily prevented from this unfortunate step by seeing Haseltrud holding up a hazel twig (how appropriate!), which suddenly brings to his disturbed mind all the life of nature and the powers of the soil which he will be renouncing and betraying if he carries out his threat. At the end of the novel Rudolf von Lage and Haseltrud marry, and on the very last page a son is born to them. (It is a sign of God's favour when a son is born, and a sign of displeasure if it is a girl!)

Anne Marie Koeppen's poems, collected under the title *Wir trugen die Fahne* ['We Carried the Flag'] and dedicated to 'My Führer', are even more strikingly Nazi than her novel, and it is here above all that the combination and interplay of Nazi and Prussian elements reveals itself. It is a volume of one hundred and eighty pages; the first half is entitled 'Volk und Führer'

['Nation and Führer'] and the second 'Heimat und Glaube' ['Homeland and Faith']. The first poem is addressed to Hitler and reads as follows:

> Du bist im Wachsen der Ähren,
> Du bist in der Kinder Gesang.
> Du bist im Schürfen des Pfluges
> Und in der Sensen Klang.
> Im Brausen der Räder und Wellen,
> Im dröhnenden Hammerschlag.
> In den ruhenden Ackerschollen,
> Im Bergwerk, tief unter Tag.
> Wo immer Deutsche schaffen,
> Da klingt auch dein Name dazu.
> Gott rief eines Volkes Seele,
> Und diese Seele bist du.[1]

In a poem entitled 'Die deutsche Frau an Adolf Hitler' ['The German Woman to Adolf Hitler'] there is a verse which runs:

> Wenn unsre Kinder deinen Namen nennen,
> Dann klingt es wie ein frohes Lerchenlied.
> Ein Jubel ist's. Ein dankbares Bekennen,
> Das durch die jungen, reinen Seelen zieht.
> Du hast ihr Herz in deine Hand genommen,
> Und formst es nun mit echter Meisterschaft.[2]

In another poem a sick child wakes up so happy—

> Du Mutter, denk, ich hab so schön geträumt,
> Der Hitler ist an meinem Bett gewesen.[3]

[1] 'Thou art in the growth of the ears of corn, in the song of the children, in the movement of the plough, and in the sound of the scythes. Thou art in the noise of the wheels and the turning axles, and in the resounding hammer blows; in the resting clods of the fields; in the mine, deep under the ground. Wherever Germans are working, thy name is to be heard. God summoned the soul of a people, and thou art this soul.'

[2] 'When our children utter thy name, it sounds like the merry song of the lark. It is full of jubilation. It is a grateful cry of allegiance which runs through the young and pure souls. Thou hast taken their hearts into thy hand, and thou mouldest them with genuine mastery.'

[3] 'Oh Mother, just think, I have had such a beautiful dream. I dreamt that Hitler had stood near my bed.'

Another poem tells how the Führer goes through the towns and villages:

> *Und junge, reine Kinderhände schmiegen*
> *Sich weich in seine starke, feste Hand,*
> *Vertrauend, wie das ganze weite Land.*[1]

But at night the Führer looks up at the stars, overcome with the thought of the sufferings of the German people, and says: 'Oh God, let me bear their sufferings!' Other poems attack the Treaty of Versailles, or deal with such themes as the 'crusade' for the Third Empire, the marching Storm Troopers, Horst Wessel's fight and self-sacrifice.

But mingled with all these typical Nazi poems, there are many poems about the Prussian past. For example, a poem called 'Fridericus-Tag' ['The Day of Frederick the Great'], written on the anniversary of his birthday (24th January 1933), contains such lines as:

> *Preussen! Alarm! Fridericus-Tag! . . .*
> *Preussen-Deutschland will auferstehen! . . .*
> *Ganz Preussen muss mit! Ganz Deutschland muss mit!*
> *Der König steht auf und hebt die Hand*
> *Und zeigt mit dem Krückstock weit in das Land.*[2]

From a thousand throats the cry is heard:

> *Kein Unglück ist ewig. Preussen wird frei.*
> *Der König lächelt. Weit leuchtet sein Blick.*
> *Er weiss, dieses Preussen weicht niemehr zurück.*[3]

Then the poetess declares:

> *Du bist nicht gestorben, König Fritz.*
> *Du lebst! Und dein Blick hat uns alle durchglüht.*
> *Du gibst unsrem Führer den Krückstock zur Hand:*

[1] 'And young and pure hands of children nestle softly in his strong firm hand: full of confidence, like the whole, wide-spreading land.'

[2] 'Prussia! Awake! It is Frederick's Day! . . . Prussia-Germany is eager to rise up! . . . The whole of Prussia must join in! The whole of Germany must join in! The king rises up (out of his grave) and lifts his hand, and points with his crooked stick far into the land.'

[3] 'No misfortune lasts for ever. Prussia will become free. The king smiles. His eyes gleam, and look far into the distance. He knows that this Prussia will never give way.'

'Da, mach Er mir Ordnung im Preussenland.
Er kann's! Von allen nur Er allein.
Er soll meines Willens Vollstrecker sein.'
Fern wirbelt rauschender Trommelschlag
Empor in den klaren Wintertag.
Wir bau'n dir dein Preussen wieder auf!
Fridericus, mein König, verlass dich darauf.[1]

Another poem entitled 'Potsdam' has very much the same theme. The first two verses describe the flags in the Garrison Church. The third verse contains the lines:

Hier, an seines Grabes Schwelle,
Hier schlägt uns das Gewissen der Nation.[2]

In the fourth verse we learn that in Potsdam there lives on what the world regarded as dead and what even many Germans no longer wished to believe in, namely, German honour and readiness to do one's duty.

Das Grab geht auf, die Fahnen rauschen mächtig,
Und auf der Schwelle stehst du, stolz und prächtig.
Fridericus Rex, Nein, du verlässt uns nicht. . . .
Du kommst, das Reich in Hitler's Hand zu legen,
Dem tausendjährigen Frühlingstag entgegen.
Deutschland, üb immer Treu' und Redlichkeit.[3]

There could be no more striking proof of the merging of Prussian and Nazi ideas than these fantastic pictures of Frederick the Great rising up from the grave to place his beloved Prussia and the German Empire in Hitler's hands. And from a different standpoint these poems offer further confirmation of

[1] 'Thou art not dead, King Frederick. Thou art alive. And thy gaze has made us all aglow. Thou placest thy crooked stick in the hand of our Führer: "There, put things in order for me in Prussia. Thou art able to do it. Thou alone out of all the others. Thou shalt carry out my will." From afar the rolling drums resound in the clear winter-day. We shall rebuild thy Prussia! Frederick, my king, thou canst rely on us to do this.'

[2] 'Here, on the threshold of his grave, the conscience of the nation keeps alive for us.'

[3] 'The grave opens, the flags rustle powerfully, and on the threshold thou standest, proud and splendid. Oh King Frederick, thou wilt never desert us. Thou comest in order to put the Reich in Hitler's hands, who will create for it the millennium. Germany, always practise faithfulness and honesty.'

177

the theory which we have already put forward (see page 123 and footnote), namely, that the legend of Frederick Barbarossa has been largely superseded in recent years by the legend of Frederick the Great. Nowadays it is the Hohenzollern and not Barbarossa who lives on, and who in time of great need and danger will appear to protect and save the German people.

The volume includes several poems about East Prussia, the homeland of the poetess; one on 'The Battle of Tannenberg' begins with a glorification of the Teutonic Knights with their white cloaks and the black cross, and ends with the proud declaration that under the leadership of Hitler, and inspired by the black cross of a new order of knights (i.e. the swastika), East Prussians are ready to fight and win another Tannenberg for Germany.

We now turn to the dramatist Hans Rehberg, a writer whose literary achievement is of a much higher quality than that of Anne Marie Koeppen. Born in 1901, not much was heard of Rehberg until he began to produce his cycle of Prussian, or rather Hohenzollern, plays in 1934. The first of this cycle, *Der Grosse Kurfürst*, appeared in 1934; the second, *Friedrich I*, and the third, *Friedrich Wilhelm I*, in 1935; the fourth, *Kaiser und König*, in 1936; and the fifth, *Der Siebenjährige Krieg*, in 1937. The plays were later collected and published in one stout and very exhausting volume under the title *Die Preussen-Dramen*. For a time Rehberg was hailed as one of the great discoveries and hopes of the Nazi drama. His plays were quite often performed and were greeted with enthusiasm in the Goebbels press, although one could note at times a feeling of apprehension at the back of the Nazi theatre critic's mind lest the Hohenzollerns should step too much into the limelight.

One theme which runs right through the first three plays is that of the relationship between father and son [der Vater-Sohn-Konflikt or das Vater-Sohn-Problem], a theme which seems to have achieved far greater prominence in modern German than in modern English literature. (Perhaps German fathers and sons quarrel more than English fathers and sons, because in Germany the father is far more the head of the family, whereas in many English families something approaching matriarchy prevails?) The Great Elector quarrels with his

son Frederick because he is weak and vain; Frederick I despises
his son Frederick William because he is plain, rough, miserly;
Frederick William I struggles hard to win Fritz from his feminine and Frenchified and pleasure-loving mode of life. But in all
three cases the fathers act as they do because they are dominated
by the idea that the power and prestige of Prussia and the
Hohenzollern dynasty must be maintained and extended, and
each is afraid that his son will not understand and not be able to
cope with the great task before him. None of the four Hohenzollerns here portrayed is really happy. But happiness is of
secondary importance to them, so long as Brandenburg-Prussia
becomes great. Each is ready to strive and suffer to the utmost
for this end. In the play *Friedrich Wilhelm I*, Rochow, the officer
assigned to Fritz as a constant companion and tutor, says to
him: 'Your Highness, your family has renounced all ideas of
happiness. . . . Your Highness, the sufferings of the men and
women of your house have created the state. But you only wish
to enjoy life.'

The first play—like all the others—contains little or no plot,
but consists of a series of scenes loosely bound together by the
characters, and by such ideas as the father-son relationship and
the rise of Brandenburg-Prussia. The differences and rivalry
between Habsburg and Hohenzollern are greatly stressed, always to the advantage of the latter. Rehberg even goes so far as
to excuse the conduct of the Great Elector in allying with
Louis XIV against Habsburg and the Reich, and thus allowing
France to gain among other prizes Strassburg. The Great
Elector: 'I would not be lacking in loyalty, if only the accursed
Germany showed that it respected me. . . . I proved victorious
over the Swedes . . . and His Majesty the Emperor left me in the
lurch. . . . Am I not to learn (by experience)? . . . What concern
of mine is Germany?' It is true that after his great victory over
the Swedes at Fehrbellin in 1675 the Great Elector was able to
occupy the whole of Hither-Pomerania, and that at the Peace
of Saint-Germain in 1679 he was obliged to give back the greater
part to the Swedes, because his allies, the Emperor and Holland,
did not support him. But it is very unikely that he ever talked
about the 'accursed Germany' or declared 'Germany is no concern of mine'.

In another passage he says to his son: 'Discipline is making Brandenburg the nucleus of the Reich and the heir of Habsburg ... I can see that Habsburg is dying. I see in Habsburg my own enemy and the enemy of the Fatherland, and know that Hohenzollern must be strong in Germany, because otherwise the world will divide up Germany just as it pleases.' Again it is hard to believe that the Great Elector made up his mind to oppose Habsburg in order to save the 'Fatherland' and 'Germany', both of which terms appeared much later in German political history, and are anachronistic and vague when applied to the dynastic struggles of the seventeenth century. Rehberg makes the Great Elector declare: 'I have as my aim to create out of a land sadly lacking in power that which makes Germany eternal —and in order to achieve this aim I am ready to use force, treachery, and every possible means.' Once again it is highly improbable that the Great Elector said any such thing. It is simply the way Prussians and Nazis interpret history, and another instance of their habit of reading into history what is not there, so long as it suits their present and future ends. But such passages readily explain why the Nazis were quite eager to call Rehberg their own.

Apart from the general points discussed above the second play does not merit any special treatment here. The third play, however, is much more important, chiefly because of the idealized picture it gives of Frederick William I and of his efforts to make Prussia strong. The greater part of the play is taken up by the Katte episode, the treatment of which is reminiscent of Paul Ernst's drama, *Preussengeist*. Frederick William says rather unconvincingly to his son: 'Frederick, please, please, please—please, please—love your father; don't run away—even if I beat you.' And when Fritz and Katte finally make the attempt and are caught, it is Katte who is sacrificed. Katte's father and grandfather plead for him in vain. 'It is better that the whole world should perish rather than that justice should disappear. . . . Men like Katte do not die for my sake. I am not thinking of my own personal desires, nor the personal desires of others.' As in Paul Ernst's play the effect of Katte's death, which in accordance with the king's command Fritz witnesses from the window of his cell in Küstrin, is an immediate (and very unconvincing!)

reformation in his character. In the next scene the king is told that the 'sacrifice' of Katte has not been in vain; he is at once full of joy and addresses those around him thus: 'Comrades!' (surely a word which is much more suitable to the mouth of a Nazi Gauleiter than the Soldier-King!) 'My son has stood the test of the day of Küstrin! Comrades, my son is now a man!' The fiddles begin to play, and they all dance and sing. The king compels Katte's father to dance with him. 'Katte, the others will think you bear your king a grudge, if you won't dance. . . . Let's dance, Katte. Noble Katte. If you obey, then we (i.e. the Prussians) can never be overcome. If Europe knows that the sorrowing fathers dance with the king, then it (i.e. the 'sacrifice' of Katte) has not been in vain.' Here once again we encounter the essentially and typically Prussian idea, so heartily sponsored and so gladly propagated by the Nazis, that all personal desires, all humanitarian motives and feelings must be suppressed at the command of the head of the state, who is of course acting from the highest motives and must be obeyed. And it is in this way that the attitude and deeds of Hitler and the Nazi leaders were explained, excused, and justified by many otherwise normal human beings in Germany; they were still so dominated by the Prussian spirit that they could not do otherwise.

The last two plays represent above all an idealization and glorification of Frederick the Great. The tone is already set in the prologue to *Kaiser und König*, which contains lines like the following:

> *So gross ist Friedrich,*
> *Den ich nun beschreiben werde,*
> *Dass ich gestalten kaum,*
> *Zu schreiben wage.*
> *Mich drückt die Last.*[1]

The Austrian general Traun says to Maria Theresa: 'The King of Prussia is a god of war. . . . He loves war. More than that—he *is* war.' Frederick's own officers and servants address him in terms of highest praise, for example, a lieutenant-

---

[1] 'So great is Frederick, whom I shall now describe, that I hardly dare to write about him and to portray him. The heavy nature of the task weighs upon me.'

colonel, von Wedell, declares: 'Your Majesty, this war for Silesia and the greatness of our king will add admiration to love and eternal fame to admiration. That is the fundamental and irrevocable thought in the heart of every Prussian. Why should we therefore be unhappy? God is with us.' In the last play, Eichel, his secretary, in a moment of ecstatic veneration and prophecy tells his lord and master: 'Oh Frederick, even if this century curses you and does not understand your greatness, the time will come (after 1933?!) when Germans will proclaim your humanity (the German word is Menschlichkeit!) to the whole world. And this will continue for ever, to the day when the trumpets sound to summon the last of this divine race and people of the Germans.' It is doubtful whether Frederick the Great, in spite of all his vanity and ambition, would ever have listened to such fulsome flattery and compliments; and such speechifying is indeed much more like Hermann Göring back-slapping Hitler after a speech in the Reichstag. But it all goes to show how the Nazis 'cornered' and made great propaganda out of the best-known figure in Prussian history.

Finally, attention may be drawn to a passage in the last play which is a wonderful piece of Prussian and Nazi propaganda against England. The English envoy Mitchell announces that Lord Bute, who has just succeeded Pitt as Prime Minister, will no longer pay the subsidies to Prussia and intends to make peace with France.

Frederick: 'You have got firm hold of Canada?'

Mitchell: 'Yes.'

Frederick: 'You have definitely turned the French out of India?'

Mitchell: 'Yes, we now possess India.'

Frederick: 'Then the world is indeed divided up.'

Mitchell: 'Half of it is divided up.'

Frederick: 'I have had no other desire but this. Is England happy?'

Mitchell: 'I hope so, Your Majesty.'

Frederick: 'Then I am happy also. I am glad to have been England's friend, and to have helped her to conquer half the world.'

But at the end of the scene Frederick declares: 'The earth *will*

THE NAZI EXPLOITATION OF PRUSSIA

belong to us, or at any rate to those who come after us.' And this is a statement quite in keeping with the chorus of the popular Hitler Youth song: 'To-day Germany belongs to us, to-morrow the whole world' ['Heute gehört uns Deutschland, Morgen die ganze Welt']. One can imagine a Nazi audience being thrilled to the marrow on hearing that England obtained her 'colonies' chiefly through the help of the greatest of the Prussian kings. And what Frederick the Great did so generously, it was perhaps the destiny of his even greater successor Adolf Hitler to undo? Poor England!

Another writer worthy of special treatment because of his combination of Prussian and Nazi elements is Hans Schwarz. We have already encountered him as the editor of the works of Moeller van den Bruck and Director of the Moeller-van-den-Bruck-Archiv in Berlin; and this close association with one of the chief representatives of the Prussian spirit after 1918 would alone be sufficient indication of his Prussian attributes. Further proof may be sought in the fact that all Hans Schwarz's books were published by Korn of Breslau, with black and white bindings and dust covers, ornamented with the Prussian eagle. He achieved considerable fame in Nazi Germany as a lyric poet; for example, the collection of poems which he published in 1932 under the title *Götter und Deutsche* ['Gods and Germans'] was hailed by a critic of the *Altonaer N(ational)-S(ozialistisches) Tageblatt* with the following words: 'We have here a political poet of our own time, who gives expression to the incidents in Germany's awakening with the strength of Kleist (!) and the greatness of Hölderlin(!). His poems breathe the spirit and the fighting will of the new-born German people.' The first poem is called 'Der Held', and begins: 'Der Held ist tot? So steigen tausend neue!' ['The hero is dead? Then a thousand new heroes rise up!'] There are poems on Siegfried, Hagen, Parsifal, Hutten, Luther, the Battle of Leuthen, 'Das Brandenburger Tor', and several poems on war, one of which begins:

Am Himmel ritten
behelmte Jungfrauen
auf roten Rossen
im Licht des Abends

183

PRUSSIA AND THE THIRD EMPIRE

die Adler schrieen
und murmelnd sprachen
die Völker: Krieg.[1]

These lines are typical of the Germanic broodings, the romantic heroics, and the patriotic fulminations in which Schwarz excels. But we are concerned here not so much with his lyrics as with the best-known of his dramas, *Prinz von Preussen*, and the way in which Louis Ferdinand and the Prussia of 1806 were harnessed to the chariot of Adolf Hitler.

The play was published in 1934 by Wilhelm Gottlieb Korn. In the prologue symbolical figures declaim verses like the following in praise of Prussia:

> *In der Nacht*
> *Erstrahlt kein Stern so hell wie Preussens Ruhm.*
> *Sein Banner hält an Rhein und Weichsel Wacht.* . . . .
> *Unendlich deutsch und doch geheimnisvoll*
> *So wurde Preussen, was es werden soll,*
> *Von der Unsterblichkeit schon angerührt.*[2]

At the end of the prologue drums are heard, and gradually they merge into a Prussian military march.

The play is divided up into 'Pictures' ['Bilder'] the first of which reveals a room in the palace of Louis Ferdinand. His mistress, Pauline Wiesel, is giving vent to her jealousy of certain other of the prince's lady friends, and what threatens to become a really first-class lovers' quarrel is interrupted by a servant who announces the arrival in a steady procession of practically all the popular Prussian heroes of the uprising against Napoleon, including Stein, Blücher, Gneisenau, Scharnhorst, Friedrich Ludwig von der Marwitz. By a wonderful stroke of poetic licence they have all been invited to dinner. Of course they are all in uniform, which gives great scope to the producer for a really colourful historical pageant, so dear to Prussian and Nazi hearts. A long discussion takes place of which the following

---

[1] 'Helmeted virgins rode across the sky on red horses in the light of evening, the eagles shrieked, and the peoples murmured: War.'

[2] 'No star shines so bright in the night as Prussia's fame. Its banner keeps guard on the Rhine and on the Vistula. . . . Infinitely German and yet full of mystery, Prussia developed according to its destiny; already touched by immortality.'

wordy duel is typical. The die-hard Prussian nobleman, Marwitz, accuses Stein of being far too much concerned about his social reforms. 'You have too much humanism about you, Stein! You ought to be in Weimar, and not in Berlin!' As if already in 1805 the spirit of Weimar and the spirit of Berlin had recognized their hostility to each other! Other typical statements are—Marwitz: 'What would become of Germany, if Prussia renounced its role as leader?' Or Louis Ferdinand: 'Our encirclement is complete' (cf. Hitler). Finally Pauline reappears, greets the guests wittily and announces that dinner is served.

The second 'Picture' takes us to the Garrison Church in Potsdam. It is just the end of the service and the soldiers are filing out of the pews. Louis Ferdinand talks with a colonel, and asks him if he had not found the sermon revolting ['empörend']. 'Are we soldiers or old women?' The colonel agrees that the sermon was rather soft ['pflaumenweich']. Louis Ferdinand replies with the simple but drastic word 'Friedensschleim', which might perhaps be translated as 'pacifist slime or drivel', and he proceeds to give the pastor, who has approached in the meantime, a piece of his mind. 'What on earth do you think you are doing—misusing the Potsdam Garrison Church for such a pacifist demonstration?' Louis Ferdinand is obviously on much better terms with the verger: 'You served in the army of Frederick the Great?' 'Of course I did,' the verger proudly replies. 'And I was decorated' (he points to his medals). 'Ah,' says Louis Ferdinand with a sigh, 'at that time we were the centre of the world.' Queen Luise appears; they enter the crypt, and stand for a time in prayer before the coffin of Frederick the Great. Then they have a long discussion on current topics. Louis Ferdinand: 'It is a question of the rebirth of Prussia (cf. Germany in 1933?). The king is in the hands of evil counsellors—I demand your help.' The queen promises.

The third 'Picture' reveals the dwelling of the prince at Magdeburg, to which town he was in fact banished by Frederick William III for his rebellious and insolent conduct. Once again Schwarz allows his imagination to run riot, and describes how Louis Ferdinand is visited by all kinds of important people, including Heinrich von Kleist, whom he welcomes with enthusiasm as a fellow spirit, realizing apparently with a prophetic insight denied to practically all his contemporaries Kleist's greatness and immortality. Louis Ferdinand: 'I know that you are a patriot, Kleist.' They both agree that Prussia's position is very grave, but that a new age is dawning and that the German people is at last beginning to move. Kleist: 'Your Royal Highness—you are our hope—we depend on you alone to pursue a Prussian policy which will give back the German nation its honour.' Kleist describes the terrible things he has seen in France and the necessity of opposing the evil world of the French Revolution in the spirit of Arminius (cf. the *Hermannsschlacht*, which Kleist was *soon* to write!), the Great Elector (cf. Kleist's *Prinz von Homburg*), and Frederick the Great. 'In Hermann, in Frederick we did only one thing—we rescued freedom—our greatest, our everlasting task is again and again to rescue freedom (cf. Hitler) . . . Prince Louis Ferdinand, Prussia stands where Hermann stood! You are the uncrowned King of Prussia.'

The fifth 'Picture' is a stormy Royal Council in Berlin at which Louis Ferdinand demands war on Napoleon.

In the sixth 'Picture' Queen Luise stands at the open window of the palace in Potsdam, dressed in the uniform of her own regiment, and watches full of enthusiasm the march past of the soldiers who are on their way to fight against Napoleon, to the inspiring accompaniment of military bands. She says to her chief lady-in-waiting: 'Voss, wave to them. You are also a soldier's child. Let yourself go just for once. Whose heart does not melt at the sight of so many uniforms? My regiment, my wonderful regiment!' (She bursts into tears.)

The seventh and last 'Picture' finds Louis Ferdinand with his officers on the eve of the engagement at Saalfeld, at which he met his death. He proposes a toast—the health of the queen and of the king, and adds: 'Let us swear an oath, that we shall do our duty to-morrow! Prussia will stand the test. . . . Long live Prussia! Long live Germany.' The prince, left alone, plays the piano. Good night, and curtain.

Fourth and lastly, a brief account of one of the most successful short stories to appear in Nazi Germany: Werner Beumelburg's *Preussische Novelle*, of which many thousands of copies have been sold since it was first published in 1935. Beumelburg's life and literary achievement offer striking parallels with

Ernst Jünger. Born in 1899, he left school in the spring of 1916 when he was just seventeen and joined the army as an 'ensign' ['Fahnenjunker'] in a Rhineland regiment. By September 1917 he had won the Iron Cross, Second Class, and had been made lieutenant, and soon afterwards he won the Iron Cross, First Class. When the War ended in November 1918 he was only nineteen. Apart from some historical sketches centring round the River Rhine (published in 1925 under the title *Der Strom*), Beumelburg's first important literary work was to edit some of the official accounts, based on 'documents', of the battles of the Great War, for example, *Ypres 1914* (published 1925), *Flanders 1917* (published 1928). His *Sperrfeue rum Deutschland* ['The Barrage round Germany'] (1929) and *Gruppe Bosemüller* (1930), which told the story of a non-commissioned officer and his men in the prolonged fighting round Verdun, rivalled the success of Jünger's war stories, and Beumelburg quickly came to be regarded, like Jünger, as a mouthpiece of the war-generation and of ex-servicemen. With such credentials it was natural that the Nazis should welcome him with open arms, and in 1933 he was made General Secretary of the German Academy of Letters ['Deutsche Akademie der Dichtung'].[1]

Preussische Novelle, reduced to its essentials, is the story of a Prussian Junker who overcomes all love of self and every trace of self-will, and finally sacrifices his life for the 'idea of Prussianism' ['die Idee des Preussentums']. It is also a transposition and exposition of the problem of duty which found its classical treatment in Kleist's *Prinz von Homburg*.

The story opens with an idyllic description of the return home one afternoon in October 1760 of young Werner von Romin, ensign in the regiment of his father, Colonel Franz von Romin. He is bent on making the most of his leave: enjoys a long sleep and good food, puts on civilian clothes, talks with his mother,

---

[1] This was the name given to the reorganized and 'purified' German Writers' Academy—Deutsche Dichter-Akademie. It was the great fashion in 1933 to change names in this way, just to stress that the organization or institution or association had been 'vaccinated' or 'impregnated' with the new spirit. An 'English Club' which had functioned under this name in a large town since 1885 was renamed with much Nazi ceremony and many patriotic speeches 'Deutsche Gesellschaft für englische Sprachpflege'—'German Association for the Cultivation of the English Language'!

who obviously longs for peace, visits the pastor and his daughter, with whom he is in love. Suddenly a letter arrives from his father, ordering him to leave within six hours and rejoin the regiment. The scene changes to the eve of the battle of Torgau. Frederick has decided to attack an army much larger than his own. He summons his officers and tells them that the battle next day will be no ordinary battle. It was not only a matter of defeating the enemy; the outcome would decide the fate of the army, and the fate of Prussia. He must demand, therefore, from his officers and soldiers blind obedience, the greatest daring, and the most ruthless readiness for sacrifice. He realized that on the following night he would see round him only a small number of the men now listening to him, but he was confident that each of them would do his duty. Then, leaning on his stick, because his gout gave him great pain, he dictated in a quiet voice his orders for the attack. Once again it is the familiar picture of Old Fritz, the heroic king, who in spite of his sufferings is determined to fight on: the model for all good Prussians and Nazis in the new Germany of the Third Empire.

During the battle young Romin finds himself in command of a forward post, with orders to hold up the Austrians as long as possible. When he decides the position is no longer tenable and gives the order to retire, an old soldier reminds him that as long as possible means—in the Prussian interpretation of the phrase —to the very last man. Romin replies that it is his duty not to sacrifice lives unnecessarily, and that it is for him to command and for those under him to obey. He is wounded, and left lying on the battlefield. He dreams that he is far away on the sea, and that the captain of the ship talks with him about the necessity of obedience. 'It is not only one's father whom one is obeying, but a long line of ancestors. And it is even more than that. It is an idea, to which one is sacrificed.'

In the best Prussian tradition Colonel Romin reported to the king that his regiment had failed in its duty, that one of his officers had acted against orders and had given up a position, although he knew that it was his son who was responsible. Young Romin is found on the battlefield, put under arrest, brought before a court-martial, and condemned to death. The father—again in true Prussian fashion—signs the verdict him-

self, and refrains from making any request for pardon or leni-
ency. In a letter to his mother young Romin asks to be forgiven
for bringing such disgrace on his family and his name, and
declares he now wishes he could have shared the fate of his
brother Ferdinand, who had died fighting. In other words, he
had now found his true Prussian self, and had come to realize
the necessity of sacrificing everything to the glorious idea of
Prussianism. The king graciously pardons him, and a few
months later he is able to put his newly won principles and
faith into practice by dying at his post in the defence of Schweid-
nitz, long after the rest of the garrison had retired.

In all this Nazi exploitation of Prussia, the great name and
the great figure, the focal point and the presiding genius, was
Frederick the Great. It is impossible to attempt here anything
like a survey of the literature on Frederick the Great since 1933:
the task is too huge and too tiresome. We must content ourselves
with a typical quotation from the introduction to yet another
'selection' from the writings of Frederick the Great (*Friedrich der
Grosse. Aus seinen Schriften*. Ausgewählt von Franz Riedweg.
Nibelungen-Verlag, Berlin-Leipzig, 1940). 'For present-day
Germany, which by the National Socialist Revolution has inaugurated a new European epoch, the life and deeds of Frederick the Great are no longer of historical interest only—they
represent a testament and a legacy.'[1]

Many Germans attached special significance to the year 1940
because it marked the two-hundredth anniversary of Frederick
the Great's accession to the throne; and they were probably not
at all surprised that it proved to be a year of remarkable victories and conquests. The ghost of Old Fritz must have been well
pleased with the achievements of German arms in 1940, and
happier than at any time since 1871! For our part we may express the hope that 1940 witnessed the climax of the legend of
Frederick the Great, and that in the years to come its unhappy
influence on German political life will decline, and finally disappear. But it is to be feared that all such hopes are vain.

---

[1] 'Das Leben und die Taten Friedrichs des Grossen bedeuten dem heuti-
gen Deutschland, das mit der nationalsozialistischen Erhebung ein neues
Zeitalter Europas eingeleitet hat, nicht mehr nur Geschichte, sie sind
Vermächtnis.'

Chapter XII

The Prussian Spirit in Opposition

1. Spengler's 'Decisive Years'

Among the few Prussians who raised their voices in protest was Oswald Spengler, whose *Preussentum und Sozialismus* had done so much to prepare the way for Hitler and the Nazis. In the preface to his book *Jahre der Entscheidung*,[1] which he dated July 1933, he expressed his disapproval and his doubts and suspicions in words which were carefully chosen and restrained, but the meaning of which was perfectly clear. He began by saying: 'Nobody could have longed for the national uprising of this year more than I. I have hated the dirty revolution of 1918 from the very first day and have fought against it.' But a few lines lower down he was pointing out that the man of action often fails to see far enough ahead, that he is driven along without knowing what he is aiming at, and that if he is wise he will allow creative criticism and heed the warnings of philosophers and students of history. The man of action is obviously Hitler, who had already shown his obstinate narrow-mindedness and his refusal to listen to others. Spengler went on: 'I shall not scold or flatter. I abstain from any judgement about the things which have only just *begun* to take their rise. History itself will judge when all those taking part in present movements are dead.' How galling for the man who was soon to rave at Schuschnigg and tell him he was in the presence of the greatest German who

---

[1] An English translation was published by Allen & Unwin in 1934 under the title *The Hour of Decision*.

had ever lived, and for the puffed-up pride and insolent cock-sureness of the other Nazi creators of the empire of a thousand years: to be reminded that they were mere beginners, that they too would die, and that historians would weigh up their achievements! Spengler next informed those responsible for the revolution of 1933 that they must above all realize that 'it was no victory, for there were no opponents; it was a promise of *future* victories (again the italics are Spengler's) which could only be won by hard fighting, and for which the ground must first of all be prepared'. This was no time for, and there was no cause for, ecstasies and feelings of triumph. 'Woe to those who mistake mobilization for victory! The danger for enthusiasts is that they regard the situation as too simple. I note with misgiving that the assumption of power is daily celebrated with much noise. It would be better if they saved all that for the day of real successes, that is to say, successes in foreign politics, for there are no successes of any other kind. When these have been achieved, the man of the moment (i.e. Hitler), the man who took the first step, will perhaps have long been dead, perhaps forgotten and scorned.' And so on. When one remembers the precarious situation of Hitler in his relationships with other countries in the first few months of power, and how eagerly he grasped at a Concordat with the Papacy, and a non-aggression pact with Poland, the significance of Spengler's warning becomes doubly clear. It was all like a sensible uncle reminding the vain schoolboy who had carried off all the prizes that the battle of life had not yet begun.

But of even greater importance for my thesis is Spengler's insistence that the greatness of the Revolution of 1933 lay in the fact that it was 'Prussian' through and through; and he went on to declare that if a lasting foundation (N.B., only a foundation!) for a great future was to be laid here and now, then it was not possible without the continued working of old traditions. 'What I years ago described as "Prussianism" is all-important—it has just proved its worth—not *any* kind of "Socialism" (e.g. "National" Socialism?). We need to be educated to bear ourselves like the Prussians in 1870 and 1914.' He concluded: ' My fears for Germany have not become less (the colossal cheek of the man, when the Nazis had only just announced the advent of the golden age!). The victory of March 1933 was so easy that the eyes of the victors have not been opened to the dangers which still confront Germany.'

The book consists in the main of a comparative study of the position and prospects of the chief world powers, including Russia, Japan, the United States, France, and England; most of it, therefore, does not concern us here. But we may pause for a moment to consider some of Spengler's remarks on England, as a kind of postscript to the views already summarized in Chapter III. It is interesting to learn, for example, that the English nation is spiritually and racially no longer strong enough, young enough, or healthy enough to be confident about its ability to overcome the present crisis in world affairs. 'England has become tired.' In the nineteenth century she sacrificed too much valuable blood for her overseas possessions; and even more important is the lack of the racial and biological foundation which only a strong peasantry can provide. Furthermore, the social layer which has in the past provided leaders is now exhausted ['die Führerschicht ist verbraucht'], and the *rentier* spirit has triumphed over capitalistic imperialism. English people are now living on their capital, and the urge to win new wealth has disappeared. Industry and trade are declining, because of the old-fashioned methods still cherished, and the spirit of enterprise is dying out. The younger generation is showing unmistakable signs of spiritual and moral decline. The old cry of 'England expects every man to do his duty', which before the Great War every young Englishman of good family at Eton and Oxford felt was addressed personally to himself, falls to-day on deaf ears. The Oxford Union Society, the largest student club in the foremost English University, passed with an overwhelming majority the following motion: 'This house will under no circumstances fight for King and Country!' Young people dabble in Bolshevism, practise eroticism as a sport, and regard sport as a vocation and the main content of life. And members of the older generation ask in sorrow and despair: 'Who is to defend the ideal of Greater Britain after we are gone?' It is also interesting to note how quickly German commentators like Spengler seized upon and gloated over the Statute of Westminster of 1931 as a sure sign of weakness. England had placed the Dominions on complete equality and had renounced her position of leadership and dominance! Very soon Canada and Australia might turn to the United States! On the far side of Singapore England had already ceased to count, and if India were lost, then it would be futile for England to remain in Egypt and the Mediterranean. Spengler's malicious pleasure [Schadenfreude] in what he regarded as England's decline and fall culminated in the happy thought: 'It is not impossible that the Anglo-Saxon powers are on the point of passing away.'

After 1933 Spengler was snubbed and attacked by the Nazis for his 'Kulturpessimismus', his unwillingness to accept the new theories of race, and his critical and carping attitude in the early days of the revolution; but the Nazis continued to exploit many of his ideas when it suited them. At all events it is safe to say that such views on England as those we have just summarized played an increasing part in Nazi propaganda for home consumption and came more and more to be accepted as correct. The dignified, scholarly, and reasoned interpretation given by Professor Wilhelm Dibelius in his two-volume work on *England* (first published in 1925) receded further and further into the background after 1933, until it was almost forgotten.

2. *The Legend of Frederick William I*

We have seen how the legend of Frederick the Great was cherished and cultivated in the years of the Weimar Republic and how the Nazis gleefully seized upon it and exploited it after 1933. But at the same time the legend of Frederick William I, the less illustrious father of the greatest Prussian king, was slowly but surely taking shape, above all in the hearts and minds of those who most genuinely and worthily represented the Prussian spirit. Long before 1933, but increasingly afterwards, the following rather strange but very significant development could be observed: the more Frederick the Great was lauded and made the instrument of party-warfare and nationalist propaganda, the greater the revulsion of feeling against him among the real Prussians, and the more they turned to Frederick William I. The awakening of interest in Frederick William I probably goes back, like so many other features of Prussianism since 1918, to

Moeller van den Bruck, who it will be remembered described him in *Der preussische Stil* as 'the only real Prussian, the original and authentic model' ['der Nur-Preusse, der Ur-Preusse'], and altogether painted a novel and idealized portrait of him. Frederick William I had hitherto figured chiefly as the uncouth tyrant on the Prussian throne who prepared the way for his son's far more glorious reign. Here at any rate he stepped out of the background and more into that limelight his son had always enjoyed; he was given independent treatment and his own halo, and he was even placed above Frederick the Great as the chief creator of Prussianism and as the great model for Prussian character. After 1933 this change in the Prussian centre of gravity, as one might call it, continued at an even more rapid rate. For there was much in the life of Frederick the Great which made him a blood-brother of Hitler, and there was much in the life of Frederick William I which could not possibly be reconciled with Hitlerism, for example, his honesty and love of truth, and above all his religious beliefs and practices, his Prussian piety. It was these things which appealed to the Prussian opponents of Hitler after 1933; and the increased attention they paid to Frederick William I, to the partial neglect of Frederick the Great, was to a large extent an expression of their opposition to National Socialism. Admittedly, it was an opposition far more passive than active, an opposition veiled and implied rather than open and aggressive, but it was nevertheless there, and represented one of the few good omens for Germany's future.

The literary climax of this idealization of Frederick William I came with the publication in 1937 of a novel called *Der Vater*, with the sub-title, 'Der Roman des Soldatenkönigs' ['The Father—The Novel of the Soldier-King'], by Jochen Klepper, a young and almost unknown Silesian writer. Klepper began by writing short stories, and then in 1933, when he was thirty, he published his first novel *Der Kahn der fröhlichen Leute* ['The Boat of the Merry People']: a light and amusing story consisting of scenes from the lives of bargees on the river Oder. In 1937, after a silence of four years, he astonished the German reading public and even his friends, by publishing a historical novel of over a thousand pages on Frederick William I. By the summer of 1939 nearly a hundred thousand copies had been sold, a remarkable achievement for a serious work of literature in Nazi Germany.

It was at once clear to anyone reading the novel that the author had made a most thorough and scientific study of the sources, but further proof of this was forthcoming in two small volumes which appeared a year later (1938): *Der Soldatenkönig und die Stillen im Lande* ('the Quiet People in the Land', i.e. the Pietists), and *In Tormentis Pinxit*, in which Klepper edited in a most interesting way much of the material he had collected for his *magnum opus*. The first contains the accounts written down by August Hermann Francke (1663–1727), his son Gotthilf August Francke, and his son-in-law Freylinghausen, and Count Zinzendorf (1700–60), of their conversations with Frederick William I, and also some of the correspondence they had with him. All these men were leaders of the religious movement known as Pietism, and their relations with the Soldier-King had never before been thrown into such high relief. The second volume is at bottom a psychological study of Frederick William I on the basis of his weird and wonderful oil-paintings, many of which are reproduced: here again Klepper was giving prominence to a little-known aspect of the king's life, in order to use it skilfully and convincingly in his novel. The explanation of the title is that Frederick William did most of the paintings towards the end of his life, when his body was entirely broken by dropsy and gout, so that it was no exaggeration for him to sign them 'F.W.painted this in torment'.

These subsidiary publications provide a ready key to the interpretation of Frederick William I's character and significance which Klepper gives in his major work. The main point of this interpretation is that he can only be understood in his relationship to Pietism; and in order to make this clear it is necessary to consider briefly what Pietism involved. It was a religious movement which began in Germany in the seventeenth century, a reform movement inside Protestantism, started by a minority who were dissatisfied less with doctrine than with practice, and who desired greater stress on the personal and individual side of religion. The idea of a spiritual rebirth was prominent and also the idea of the chosen few, whose religious life was much deeper than that of the easy-going majority. The chief defects of Pietism—if defects is the right word—were similar to those of Puritanism: contempt for learning, the insistence on a set and uniform kind of conversion, an unnatural renunciation of all 'fleshly lusts', including worldly books, theatrical performances, and dancing. In South Germany, for example in Württemberg, Pietism was taken up chiefly by citizens and peasants, but in North Germany it spread above all among the nobility and landowners, and was thus one of the main sources of that piety which characterized great Prussians like Bismarck and Hindenburg, and a characteristic manifestation of the Prussian spirit.

The movement was at first opposed by Protestant orthodoxy, but the Pietists managed to establish themselves in the University of Halle, which had been founded in 1694; August Hermann Francke was appointed Professor of Theology at Halle in 1698. He founded a school for the poor, an orphanage, and later a Latin school and a boarding school; he also began the Lutheran mission in India and the publication of cheap Bibles. Francke's educational foundations at Halle (the so-called Franckeschen Stiftungen) soon obtained, and have succeeded in maintaining right up to the present day, a very good reputation. (It will be remembered that Spengler was a pupil there, and how he lauded Pietism to the great discredit of English Puritanism in his *Preussentum und Sozialismus*, see pages 65 f.) The church of the Moravian Brothers developed very largely under the influence of Pietism: they were originally Protestants expelled from Moravia and Bohemia, who after many wanderings settled in 1722 at Herrnhut in Saxony on the estate of Graf Zinzendorf, who became their leader.

A final point about Pietism before we return to Klepper: one of its most characteristic ideas is summed up in the German word 'Busse', of which the nearest English equivalent is 'penitence'. It signifies a change of heart, coming from an introspective humility, a ready and strict attention to the stirrings and qualms of conscience, a full and unquestioning recognition of individual responsibility, and an ever-present and overwhelming consciousness of guilt. These ideas spread in varying degrees to the whole of Prussian Protestantism and are still to be found everywhere in Prussia, so much so that the special day set aside in the church calendar for 'penitence and prayer' ['Buss- und Bettag'] is

196

recognized by the state as a public holiday. The day always falls in November, when the weather is usually in conformity with the religious mood. In the Protestant churches in Prussia it is one of the most important religious festivals and church holidays, standing second only to Good Friday.

Now according to Klepper penitence was the dominating factor in Frederick William's unhappy life, and the idea which was always uppermost in his mind. One of his favourite sayings was: 'Kings must be able to suffer more than other men' ['Könige müssen mehr leiden können als andere Menschen'], and this is the motto and ever-recurring refrain of the book. Klepper describes in great detail his difficulties with his wife, who was vain, pleasure-loving, ambitious; with his son Fritz, who refused to be trained as a Prussian soldier and official, as a landowner and a Christian; and with his subjects, who would not work and pray hard enough, cultivate the land properly, serve willingly in the army, and pay their taxes punctually. He knew they all hated him: his family, the court, soldiers, officials, peasants, merchants, craftsmen. Did he not in bursts of uncontrollable rage slap the Crown Prince in the face, and beat with his stick any subject who failed in his duty, or annoyed him? Everybody in Prussia toiled on and was silent—like the rowers in a galley. Prussia had become a land of hard and never-ceasing work, a joyless land of penitence.

Frederick William bore all these feelings of loneliness, opposition, and hatred with a calm fortitude; he never allowed them to interfere with what he considered to be his duty, and his decisions as to where his duty lay were always guided and shaped in the last resort by religious considerations. He believed that kings must be hard judges for the sake of law and order, but even more for the simple reason that they are kings, and therefore directly responsible to God, and to God alone. Kings must not only be able to suffer more intensely than other men; they must also realize that it is their bounden duty on occasions to sin more gravely than ordinary mortals. And for this reason they are more dependent than their subjects on God's grace, and in greater need of the forgiveness of God. This is how Klepper explains—and explains away—much of Frederick William's harshness and what a non-Prussian observer would at once condemn as tyranny and cruelty and inhumanity. The following is a typical example; an incident which Klepper, true to the Prussian spirit and tradition, relates without turning a hair, and without a trace of criticism or disgust. Once when reviewing his troops the king noticed that the eyes of one of the soldiers were fixed on him with a gaze full of hate. He stopped. The soldier stood motionless, and held his gun just like the others. But it was clear from the bluish-green marks on his hands that they had been beaten by the corporal's stick. 'What is your name?' asked the king. 'Bleuset.' 'Is there anything wrong?' 'I miss my freedom,' was the prompt and unheard-of reply. 'You have been told that bold answers from my soldiers do not annoy me.' 'No, Your Majesty, but I have been told Your Majesty likes to hear the truth.' The king began to move on, but as he did so he said: 'I too am not free.' 'But you are not ill-treated, Your Majesty.' To which the king replied: 'Oh yes, I am—in some ways.' Soon afterwards it was announced that a deserter had been captured. It was Bleuset. The punishment for the great crime of desertion had been fixed long ago, namely, running the gauntlet ['Spiessruten laufen']; so there was no need for consideration of the case or for a lengthy trial. Klepper describes the punishment scene in detail. Two hundred soldiers stood so as to form a narrow lane, each with a switch, and the sentence demanded that the culprit should be driven down this lane eight times. His shirt was soon torn to shreds and stripped off his bleeding back. But still the blows rained on him, until finally he fell down dead.

Klepper interprets—and excuses—the famous Katte episode, in a similar way. In his shame and chagrin and rage that Fritz should have shown so openly and unmistakably to all the world his hatred for his father by attempting to flee the country, Frederick William exaggerated his son's connexions with foreign powers and made out of Katte a rebel who had plotted to get rid of him and to put Fritz on the throne, in order to make it all appear more heinous and treasonable than it really was. From the very first he was convinced that a sacrifice was necessary for the sake of the outraged law and order: the point to be decided was whether both of the culprits should suffer, or only one, and how? Why is it that a king cannot forgive, just as other men forgive? This was the question which continually presented itself to his troubled mind. 'His crown had become a crown of thorns, and his sceptre a cross'—such is Klepper's heightened, and rather blasphemous, description. He listened anxiously for God's voice. Day after day and night after night he read in his Bible the story of Abraham and Isaac, David and Absalom. Finally the court-martial declared they had no right to sit in judgement upon the king's son and the future king, and supported by this decision, Frederick William also came to the conclusion that God did not wish him to take revenge for the crime on his first-born son and heir. But he was now even more certain that Katte must be sacrificed. The voting in the court-martial for and against Katte's death was equal: Frederick William decided he must die. Katte wrote a letter humbly suing for pardon, but received no answer. His father, a highly placed and trusted officer, pleaded in vain, and so did Katte's grandfather, the senior member of the family, the Marshal von Wartensleben. Frederick William explained in an audience which he graciously granted the Marshal why the law must be satisfied, and why the punishment, the atonement, the sacrifice must take place. 'It is better that one man should die than that justice should perish from the earth,' he declared. 'And once again he broke out into lamentations: why kings cannot forgive like other men, and why for them alone the Son of God did not speak the words of the prayer: And forgive us our trespasses, as we forgive them that trespass against us.' As the Marshal came out from the audience the tears were running down his withered cheeks. To the officers and others who were waiting anxiously outside, he said: 'What a wonderful king we have!' The comment of most foreign readers might well be: 'That may be typically Prussian! But Heaven preserve us from such a king or such a ruler!' At the same time, after encountering many such incidents and interpretations in German literature, one begins dimly to understand why some of Hitler's ghastly crimes on the personal side roused so little indignation and protest, and were indeed blandly and unquestioningly accepted by the great mass of the German people. For example, the famous blood bath or Nazi Saint Bartholomew's Eve, of the 30th June 1934, when Hitler, like the merest Chicago gangster-leader, caused to be 'bumped off' men who had for years been among his most intimate associates and helpmates in the struggle for power. The incident called forth a scathing leading article in *The Times*, with the apt heading 'Medieval Methods'; but in Germany— quite apart from the determined and efficient repression of opposition—the attitude of most people with whom one talked was strictly and correctly 'Prussian': a shrug of the shoulders, a grave 'Hitler-knows-best', and 'It-must-have-been-hard-for-him to-do-it, but-it-had-to-be-done'. It may also be noted that the case of one of those shot on the 30th June 1934 provides a close parallel with Klepper's account of how Katte's father pleaded in vain with Frederick William I for the life of his son. General Litzmann (1850–1936), who fought with distinction throughout the Great War, was the first general of the old army openly to espouse the Nazi cause after Ludendorff quarrelled with Hitler, and before the Nazis came to power in 1933. He was a very popular and highly ornamental figure, and his support proved a great asset to Hitler. His son was involved in the affair of the 30th June, and he begged Hitler to show mercy. Hitler refused to receive the father, and the son was shot.[1]

Klepper paints a sympathetic and moving picture of the sad end of Frederick William's tragic life. Stricken with disease, he knew he must soon die. But he bore his sufferings with patience and submissiveness, regarding them as a sign of God's grace: God wished to remind him of his weakness and mortality, and to give him time to prepare for the life after death. In the last few weeks before his death he wrote several letters to Zinzendorff and received letters in return. They had become really intimate, so that Zinzendorff could assume without hesitation the role of spiritual adviser and father-confessor. In a letter to Zinzendorff dated the 5th March 1740, Frederick William wrote: 'I repent my sins from the bottom of my heart and will strive with God's grace and as far as is humanly possible to give up sinning and will try to be thankful to God. I hope through the mercy of God and the mediation of Jesus Christ to attain eternal bliss.' In his letter of the 4th April 1740 Zinzendorff enclosed an exposition of

---

[1] General Litzmann won his most famous victory near Lodz in December 1914. Soon after the defeat of Poland in 1939, it was announced that Lodz had been renamed Litzmannstadt.

Psalm 116, the psalm which is so full of the expectation of death, alternating with confidence in deliverance. He explained that there comes a time when even a king is bent and bowed down with suffering, and with the consciousness of his heavy load of sin; the 116th Psalm describes this unhappy state, and how relief may be obtained. 'As soon as the poor sinner, whether he is a beggar or a prince (for that does not matter in the slightest), obtains and assimilates God's grace, then he is glad like a little child and is in Heaven and worships the Lamb of God, as if he were already in His presence.' Frederick William left instructions forbidding any word either of praise or blame to be said about him to the people after his death, except that he had died as a great and miserable sinner, who had sought the grace of God and of the Saviour. He also expressed the wish to be buried in his uniform, and without pomp and ceremony.

The novel contained no patriotic tub-thumping, no blood and soil ecstasies, no mock heroics about the glory of war and the life of the soldier: to mention but a few of the themes so favoured by the Nazi leaders, and so cunningly propagated by them among a long-suffering and credulous people. The whole atmosphere was grim, unhappy, tragic, full of doubts, heart-burnings, and searchings of conscience: the very antithesis of the specious confidence, the defiant and shrieking optimism of the Nazis. Klepper gave expression to the sad thoughts and feelings, the joyless mood, of many of his good Prussian contemporaries; a consciousness of suffering, a resigned preparedness for worse things to come, and a determination to keep firm hold on the consolations of a most strict religious belief and practice. It was a dignified retreat from the present into the distant Prussian past, and into the depths of the Prussian soul. There are undoubtedly some similarities between the hero of the novel and the dominating figure of the Germany in which it was written; but the differences and contrasts are very great. It is impossible to reconcile the Prussianism of Frederick William I with the views and practices of Adolf Hitler.

3. *Pastor Niemöller and Prussianism*

Many readers may be rather surprised, and not a few shocked, to find Pastor Niemöller described here as a Prussian. It does not fit in with the idea that everything Prussian is bad, and that anything good cannot possibly be Prussian. In the early days of the second Great War a dear old lady was perusing an illustrated weekly in the train, when suddenly she turned to a fellow passenger and said: 'I say, I *am* surprised to find that Göring is a Bavarian. I know such nice Bavarians. I was sure Göring was a Prussian.' In the conversation which followed she refused to believe that Niemöller was in any way Prussian, because she had never met and never heard of any 'nice' Prussians.

The best proofs of Niemöller's Prussianism are to be found in the autobiography he wrote in the summer of 1934, and which appeared in an English translation in November 1936, with the title: *From U-Boat to Pulpit*. The first part describes in simple but thrilling language his experiences during the Great War. He had been in the Navy since 1910 and when war broke out was an officer on a battleship. The inactivity of his ship soon filled him with boredom and made him volunteer for service in submarines. After a period of training and experience in various submarines he was made navigator of U39, and later he became commander of U151, which sank many Allied ships both in the Mediterranean and the North Sea. He was, indeed, one of the most successful of the German submarine commanders, and received high praise and many decorations. At the same time he seems to have been one of the most chivalrous.

Niemöller deplores what he calls 'the suicidal orgy of internal strife' which was the 'great crime' of 1918. 'It was clear to me from the first that I was, and would remain, as far apart as are the poles from the wire-pullers of this "Revolution".' When ordered to take his submarine to an English port he replied: 'I have sailed in submarines for three years, fighting against England, sir; I have neither sought nor concluded this armistice. As far as I am concerned, the people who promised our submarines to England can hand them over. I will not do it.' In words which express even more strongly this Prussian truculence and dogged refusal to accept Germany's defeat, Niemöller describes how it became increasingly clear to him that he could not continue to serve as an officer. He realized that with the abolition of conscription an officer's career had no further attractions for him, and that he could not reconcile himself to serving the new state. He thought for a time of emigrating to South America, and learnt Spanish for that purpose; eventually he decided to use the small capital he possessed to make a start in sheep-farming in his native Westphalia, and with typical thoroughness set about learning his new job by working as a farm labourer. For several months he was happier than he had ever been before, but suddenly he made up his mind to become a Protestant pastor, like his father and many of his ancestors. By a great effort of concentration he passed the matriculation examination, and was thus able to begin his theological studies at the University of Münster. His life as a student was far from uneventful. From the very first he worked hard with a few kindred spirits to form a group of 'nationally minded' students: 'I gave all my leisure hours to this movement.' He took part in the Kapp Putsch of March 1920; helped to organize the local branch of the 'National Union of German Officers'; and for a time worked as a platelayer on the railways in order to earn money for the maintenance of himself and his wife, and to pay his university fees. He succeeded in passing his examinations and was ordained. Almost immediately he was appointed to the staff of the Home Mission [Innere Mission], a very important organization within the German Protestant Church, revivalist in spirit and famous for its social work, a kind of orthodox Salvation Army. In 1931 he became pastor of the church at Dahlem, a large suburb of Berlin.

I now wish to quote a passage from *Pastor Niemöller and His Creed*, the brief biography which was written in German by his former curate at Dahlem for publication in Switzerland, and which appeared in an English translation in November 1939. 'The national ideal was always foremost in his upbringing, and by nature he had leanings to the Right. Love of his profession as an officer was a matter of course to him, and he was in his element in the War, which demanded the pledge of his life. At the end of 1918 he felt it was morally impossible for him to continue his service, for he belonged with his heart to the enemies of the

Weimar Republic, and to the ranks of those who were fighting for national resurrection. It was only by chance that he, unlike his brother, did not become a member of the National Socialist Party. Their programme for a national revival was fundamentally his own, with its vehement denial of all that was meant by individualism, parliamentarism, pacifism, Marxism, and Judaism. And so from 1924 onwards he voted for this party.' The author speaks of Niemöller's 'hereditary conservatism' and points out that it was characteristic of Niemöller to think and speak in military terms. There is surely no better way of summarizing all this than by saying that Niemöller, both in character and way of life, was essentially and typically Prussian. This view is at any rate accepted by the Dean of Chichester, and expressed in no uncertain language in the chapters he added to the English version of Niemöller's autobiography, and in which he tells Niemöller's 'further story' since 1934. 'In his political outlook he was a strong conservative. Earlier chapters have shown that, as a former Prussian officer, Niemöller believed in the old Prussian ideal of honour, industry, obedience, and simplicity, an ideal which, of course, also included the belief in might, in a state essentially military, a state founded on responsible rather than representative government, guided by one man, the ideal in short of Bismarck and Treitschke.'

We now turn to Niemöller's sermons, some of which have been translated and collected under the title *First Commandment*, first published in 1937.[1] As the Dean of Chichester points out, the sermons Niemöller preached in the spring and summer of 1933 are full of evidence of his sympathy with the eagerly awaited rejuvenation of Germany which the Nazis proclaimed had now been achieved. The following passage from his sermon on the Third Sunday after Easter is typical. The text was: 'Rejoice! Make a joyful noise, all ye lands!' 'Yes, that is what we feel like doing, for outside we see the spring with its verdure and its

---

[1] Early in 1941 the same publisher (William Hodge) brought out an English translation of the last twenty-eight sermons preached by Pastor Niemöller before his arrest, with the title *The Gestapo Defied*. They were taken down in shorthand, and smuggled out of Germany; copies were passed round in typescript among the members of the Confessional Church living in England and their friends. All these sermons are now easily accessible to English readers.

flowers, and around us, in our people and our country, we see the national awakening, and in spite of all its storms and stress, in spite of all its effervescence and fermentation, that awakening tells us that we are still a young nation which does not wish to be drawn into the collapse of Western civilization: we wish to live! May God speed us on our way!' Even here there is a slight note of doubt and opposition, and this note soon became predominant, and the initial enthusiasm was lost in bitter disillusionment and an unflinching determination to resist. When the Confessional Church came into being in April 1934 Niemöller at once became one of its leaders, and he stood his ground and carried on the fight until he was arrested on the 1st July 1937.

Niemöller, like many others, had hoped that the national rebirth would also be a rebirth of Christianity within the nation, and he was convinced that the national rebirth could not be real without a corresponding and indeed all-pervading religious revival. In a sermon preached on the 5th March 1933 he declared: 'When our German nation became a nation, God gave it as a soul the Christian faith; our national development has— whether we like the idea or not—been inwardly based upon Christianity, and from this Christianity of the German national soul have come all the forces which made our nation develop and grow. Our nation would not be our nation but for the Reformation, and for the positive Christianity of the Lutherans and the Calvinists and the Catholics. Therein lives the soul of our nation, and it would literally be of no avail to us if we were to gain the whole world and in so doing lose our soul. That is the real reason why there never has been and never will be for our German nation any national rebirth which is not inwardly based upon the revival of the Christian faith. This nation—our nation—will be either a Christian nation or it will cease to exist.'

Hitler's speech to the Reichstag on the 23rd March 1933 contained the following reassuring statement: 'The National Socialist Government sees in the two Christian confessions most vital factors. Their rights will not be touched. The government will accord and secure to the Christian confessions the influence that is due to them in schools and education. Its aim is the genuine inter-relation of Church and State.' But it became increasingly clear that these words were empty of meaning, and that the promises they expressed were worthless. The Nazis interfered more and more in Church affairs, commanding and intriguing and not hesitating to use force. The result was that men like Niemöller were reluctantly forced to recognize in National Socialism a denial of religion and a challenge to Christianity.

In a sermon preached early in 1935 (Fourth Sunday after Epiphany) Niemöller boldly declared: 'Many of our hopes have been shattered in these two years; we see more and more clearly how there is being propagated a new paganism which wishes to have nothing to do with the Saviour who was crucified for us, while the Church which acknowledges that Saviour as its only Lord is exposed to the reproach of being an enemy of the state, and has difficulty in obtaining a hearing for its most earnest assurances to the contrary.' On the 15th November 1936 Niemöller dared to take for his text: 'Render unto Cæsar the things that are Cæsar's and unto God the things that are God's'; and on another occasion he roundly asserted that in their religious adoration of the Führer many Germans were forgetting Jesus of Nazareth. He denounced the Nazi racial teaching and the doctrine of 'Blood and Soil' as un-Christian. He even defended the Old Testament: 'It is undoubtedly possible to produce a number of reasons for treating the Old Testament with reverence; it contains a great wealth of genuine piety, and not only did Jesus pray in the words of the Old Testament psalms, but even men like Luther and Paul Gerhardt used the words of these psalms in their hymns, which are still alive among us.'

In all this Niemöller was living up to the very best traditions of German, and more particularly of Prussian, Protestantism. Patriotism was a virtue and a necessity, but Christ must come first, and after Christ comes Luther. Niemöller's sermons, and indeed the whole of the Confessional Church movement represented a harking back to the Reformation and the Augsburg Confession (1530) as far as beliefs and doctrines are concerned, and to eighteenth-century Pietism for religious practice and mode of life. The link with 'Pietism' is revealed clearly in Niemöller's frequent stress on penitence. On the Day of Penitence ['Buss- und Bettag'] in November 1934, he declared: 'The word "penitence" has, I admit, depreciated greatly in value nowadays; indeed, it seems as though it has been outlived and proscribed in our Protestant Church. And the terrible thing about what has happened in the Church at this time is that there has been no visible sign of what God's word calls "penitence" and "conversion". There is no faith without penitence, and there is no church without penitence.'

Niemöller never allowed Nazi threats to prevent him from reading from his pulpit the names of those pastors and lay-members of the Confessional Church who were suffering persecution, and to ask his congregation to join with him in praying for them. He knew that his own turn to be arrested would soon come. Probably it would have come earlier than it did if he had not had such a large and influential following at Dahlem and elsewhere, and if the Nazis had not hesitated to lay hands on a man whose past life was so well-known and had been so patriotic. Niemöller had made himself indeed one of the chief centres and pillars of the Prussian opposition. But by the 1st July 1937 Hitler's patience with this fearless and mighty opponent was 'exhausted', and the Gestapo was allowed to do its work. In typical Nazi fashion the trial was delayed for several months, and when finally it did take place and the court declared its verdict on the 7th February 1938 many Germans uttered a sigh of relief. Niemöller was sentenced to seven months' imprisonment and a fine of a thousand marks for transgression of the so-called 'Pulpit Decrees'. Nothing was said about treason, and as Niemöller had already been confined for over seven months it was clear that the court intended he should at once be set free. But immediately after the trial, and just when he was preparing to go away with his family for a holiday, he was again arrested and taken to the concentration camp at Sachsenhausen, near Berlin. No doubt he would soon have been released if he had promised to give up his preaching. But all reliable reports go to show that Niemöller has persistently refused to give in and that his spirit has remained unbroken. He is too great a man, and too great a Prussian, to waver in his faith and his duty.

4. Ernst Wiechert on the Simple Life

Another genuine Prussian who at first welcomed and supported Hitler, and later, after his disillusionment, had the courage to protest openly, was Ernst Wiechert. Born in East Prussia in 1887, his ancestors had been mainly foresters and minor civil servants. He went to a classical high school [Gymnasium] at Königsberg, and then to the university there. For a time he taught in a 'Middle School', and just before the Great War he gave up teaching in order to devote himself entirely to writing. He fought throughout the War on the various eastern fronts, and when peace came he returned to his writing, a greatly changed and much more mature personality. Several of his novels and short stories achieved a limited success, for example, *Die Majorin* (1934) and *Hirtennovelle* (1935). Wiechert was probably too specifically East Prussian to have a universal appeal in Germany: too serious, too melancholy, too much given to monkish brooding; too much of what in German is called 'grey-in-grey' ['Grau in Grau'].

Wiechert seems to have fallen foul of the Nazis and to have merited the attentions of the Gestapo several times after 1934, but the climax came early in 1938, when it became known that he had lodged a protest with the Nazi Winter Relief Organization. He wrote them a letter in which he called to mind Hitler's proud boast, often repeated by other Nazi leaders and their underlings, that 'No German was to be allowed to suffer from hunger or from cold' ['Kein Deutscher darf hungern oder frieren']. It had come to his notice, however, that the wife of Pastor Niemöller was almost destitute and suffering from both calamities. He proposed, therefore, to withdraw his regular monthly contribution to the Winter Relief Fund, and send it direct to Frau Niemöller. Wiechert was this time arrested and sent to the concentration camp at Sachsenhausen, where he was kept for about five months.

His novel, *Das einfache Leben*, appeared in 1939. It was at once a tremendous success. The director of a special library for students [Studentenbücherei] at a German university declared in the summer of 1939 that the students were simply tearing the book out of each other's hands in their eagerness to read it, and that several extra copies had been provided. It is undoubtedly Wiechert's greatest novel so far, and will probably come to be recognized as one of the greatest novels in twentieth-century German literature, worthy to be set alongside Thomas Mann's

Buddenbrooks (1902) and Gerhart Hauptmann's *Der Narr in Christo Emanuel Quint* (1911). Wiechert's period in the concentration camp, and the spiritual and mental stress this involved, seemed to bring out his finest qualities as a man and a writer; and his opposition to Hitlerism threw him back upon his Prussian origins, and made him even more than before the conscious and defiant representative of the finest Prussian spirit, the highest Prussian values, and the noblest Prussian tradition. The novel is an epitome of Prussianism in the best sense of the word. Further, there would seem to be very good grounds for regarding it as a monument to Niemöller. There can therefore be no doubt about its claims to be considered in some detail here.

The hero of the novel is Thomas von Orla, a retired naval captain in his forties when the story begins. The Great War robbed him of all his self-confidence, took the ground from under his feet, left him with nothing to hold on to; with no ambition, little hope, and not much faith. He finds new strength and happiness in a simple, strenuous life in a land of lakes and woods in the north-east corner of Germany, far away from Berlin. (Wiechert is obviously referring to his own native land, East Prussia, and probably to the lakes of Masuren.) Hard manual work, patience, and a joyful heart are the main factors in his new beginning, his fresh lease on life; above all a joyful heart. 'To be able to lie down at night with a joyful heart, that was perhaps the whole secret.'

The story opens in Berlin just after the War. Orla feels miserably alone; nobody understands him; his wife, a weak character badly shaken by the War, has given herself up to a life of pleasure, goes out a great deal, invites many guests, uses powder and paint (both decidedly non-Prussian habits!), and even takes drugs. His son Joachim is too young to understand him. (Joachim, by the way, is a very Prussian name, common above all in East Germany.) Suddenly, the impulse to begin life anew is given him by the verse of the psalm: 'We bring our years to an end, as it were a tale that is told.' It is part of the ninth verse of Psalm 90, which begins: 'Lord, thou hast been our refuge: from one generation to another.' Verse 9 reads: 'For when thou art angry all our days are gone: we bring our years to an end, as it were a tale that is told.' (The German version is: 'Wir bringen unsere Jahre zu wie ein Geschwätz', and in this case the English is superior to the German.) In the evening of the day on which he encountered this verse Orla went off on his own to avoid the guests his wife had invited, and wandered for several hours through the streets of Berlin. All around him he saw misery and depression, the aftermath of war. It made him feel more than ever that he was lonely and hopeless among accursed and forlorn people. He was forced to admit that he had not stood the test of war, and that life had lost its meaning. Somehow at the back of his mind he knew that he was engaged expectantly in a search for a vision, for some revelation, for peace. On reaching home he saw lights in the windows and knew that the guests were still there, so he turned away again, and suddenly made up his mind to call on a pastor who lived near by. Wiechert's monument to Niemöller is firstly Orla, who—to mention only two of the striking parallels and similarities—was like Niemöller a naval captain in the war and struggled hard to find his true self in the years that followed. It is secondly the pastor, who received Orla kindly, filled him with hope and resolve, and set him irrevocably on his new path. The following description might be applied almost equally well to Niemöller. 'He looked as if his ancestors had been peasant farmers. His forehead and mouth were wrinkled and tormented with care, but one almost expected to see above his smooth grey hair a halo like that over the crucifix on the wall. The expression of his face was one of reserve, but the eyes were friendly, eyes that had seen much and knew much, so that Orla felt young and foolish under their gaze.' He began with an apology: 'I am not a church-goer.' But the pastor interrupted him: 'Let's talk about the important things.' Then Orla told him how he had begun once again to read his Bible, and how he had been struck by the words: 'We bring our years to an end, as it were a tale that is told.' What would the pastor advise him to do? Should he try to become pious, to believe? Pastor: 'Become pious? Believe?' He bent forward and looked at Orla in astonishment. 'How did you get that idea? Work is what you want, work! Do you understand? Nothing but work!' 'What kind of work?' asked Orla, and the pastor went on: 'In this parish live both Cabinet Ministers and road-sweepers. Neither come to church, but both work, and I regard the work they do of equal value. I believe, too, that the road-sweeper is happier in his work than the Cabinet Minister.'

Orla decided to leave Berlin without further delay, as if it were a city of the plague, although it meant giving up home, wife, and greatest loss of all, his son. He set off to the north-east, allowing instinct and fate to guide him, until he eventually came to a lonely lake surrounded by woods, where he was told that the post of fisherman and huntsman on the estate of General von Platen was vacant. Orla went to see the General at the castle. The door was opened by a giant in an old-fashioned uniform, who looked as if he had stepped straight out of the period of Frederick the Great. In the huge entrance-hall Orla noticed antlers, portraits of the General's ancestors, old cannons, eagle banners, swords and other weapons from the battles of Frederick the Great. The General is a wonderful Prussian type in every way, and not least in his short, sharp, military way of talking, with all unnecessary words and often the verbs left out. 'He spoke in a hoarse voice, which ejected the words as if out of the barrel of a gun.' 'Name Orla?' 'Yes, sir' ['Jawohl']. 'Been in the army?' 'Yes, sir.' 'Decorated?' 'Yes, sir.' They then talked about the duties and privileges of the job. 'Maintain discipline and order! Still a soldier, though dressed as a fisherman, is that clear?' 'Yes, sir.' 'By no means a bad motto: I serve' ['Ich dien'].

Orla soon made himself at home in the tiny cottage, little more than a hut, on an island in the lake, and settled down to his new life. There were no exciting events, no heroic roles to play, no laurel wreath round his head. He had work to do which he loved, and his hands became hard from rowing. His daily round was fixed by the chiming of the clock in the castle tower, and was made up of such actions as putting out the nets and pulling them in again, keeping the house and island clean, reading a few pages from a favourite book when work was done, and sitting in the late evening on the bench outside the cottage or on a tree-stump at the water's edge, watching the sun go down. It was in such moments as this that Orla was really happy. 'Only as a child had he felt in this way how beautiful the world is, so beautiful that his heart ached. The last red glow on the lake, the sleeping forest, the young leaves of the birch-trees against the white sky, and their scent which is not to be compared with anything else. And now the owls begin to hoot, the mist rises, the stars begin to appear, the peace of night spreads out like the ripples of a stone in a pond, growing wider and wider, and in the middle he himself is sitting motionless and he can feel his blood surging and murmuring like a fountain in a dream.'[1] It was indeed a simple life, demanding nothing but hard work and willing obedience: no wasting of one's energies, no tumult, no idle talk, but goodness and wisdom and the absence of all desires.

One day the General came to the island to call on Orla. 'Thought I would come and see how you are getting on,' said the General, looking round him with piercing, threatening eyes. 'You look well. It all looks well. All correct' ['Alles in Ordnung']. He stepped up to the posts on which the nets were hung up to dry, and standing in front of the first post he looked carefully along the line to see if it was straight. It was as straight as an arrow. 'Knew it would be,' said the General, and leaning on his stick he surveyed the island as if he were looking at a parade-ground. 'Knew it would be. Old soldier. Reliable.' The two men became great friends, Orla of course always maintaining an attitude of deference. And the General told Orla one day that he could live on the island as long as he liked. Obviously he had found in Orla a man after his own heart, and he once described him as 'an officer and a nobleman who would have given much pleasure to the great king' (i.e. Frederick the Great). This was no doubt the highest tribute of which the General's Prussian mind and limited vocabulary were capable.

In one of their many talks the General said quietly: 'Lost much, Orla; Emperor and Reich, wife and two sons. But so

---

[1] 'Nur als Kind hat er so gewusst, wie schön die Welt ist, so schön, dass es in der Brust schmerzt. Das letzte rote Licht auf dem See, der schlafende Wald, das junge Birkenlaub vor dem weissen Himmel und sein Duft, der keinem andern zu vergleichen ist. Und nun beginnen die Eulen zu rufen, der Nebel steigt, Sterne zünden sich an. Die Ruhe der Nacht breitet sich aus wie Wellenkreise von einem Stein, weiter und weiter, und in der Mitte sitzt er selbst, regungslos, und sein Blut rauscht und singt wie ein Brunnen im Traum.' There are many such passages of natural description, written in language of great simplicity but wonderful poetic beauty. This particular passage is like a prose version of the poem by Matthias Claudius, 'Der Mond ist aufgegangen'.

much at any rate still remains—sunset and one's own land. No use complaining. Begin again at the beginning.' He suddenly asked Orla: 'Why did you come here?' And then Orla told him how the verse of the psalm had struck him with hammer blows, and that he had gone to a pastor whose advice was work, work, work, nothing but work. With this gospel Orla had gone out into the world, determined to live a simple life, and to win if possible a contented heart. 'Good plan,' was the General's comment. 'Be satisfied with what one has. The beginning of wisdom. Men strive and fight for glory, but best of all is the sweat of one's brow.' Orla tells him that some English friends had written to him about a man who conquered the whole of Arabia and Palestine, and who after the War gave up his titles and even his name in order to work as a simple soldier in an aeroplane factory [*sic!*]. 'It seems to me that this man is one of the few wise men left over to us from the War.' In this way Lawrence of Arabia is also given his monument in Wiechert's novel, and held up as a protagonist and model of the 'simple life'. They often talk about religion. Orla's mind is full of doubts and difficulties. The General tells him: 'Too much thinking makes life difficult, dear Orla. Things were much more simple in the old days. "With God for King and Fatherland!" ["Mit Gott für König und Vaterland!"]. Even the simplest man understood.' The General's relationship to God is like that of a child to a father; and here, too, as in so many other ways, he is representative of a fine Prussian type, and one is often reminded of that other great East Prussian landowner, nobleman, and soldier—Hindenburg.

There are many other genuinely Prussian characters and ideas and incidents in the book, but space only allows the brief mention of one of them here. The military authorities wrote to ask a relative of the General, who had already lost five sons in the War, if she would like them to send her only remaining son home. The proud Prussian mother replied that she would be grateful if they would refrain from making such suggestions in future. She had brought her sons into the world not for the 'house' and the family, but for the Fatherland and the Reich.

One final quotation, wonderfully expressive of Prussianism in the very best sense of the word and particularly of that new and noble Prussianism which opposition to Hitlerism has called forth at any rate among a minority of Germans, and which the experiences of the second Great War may very well strengthen. Towards the end of the book Orla is asked why he does not go to live in a house he has inherited. He replies: 'We don't need any possessions; we need work, poverty, and a little time.' ['Wir brauchen keinen Besitz. Wir brauchen Arbeit, Armut und ein bisschen Zeit.']

Chapter XIII

Retrospect and Prospect

---

1. Misconceptions

Some of the most frequent misconceptions about the problem of Germany have already been specifically dealt with; it is hoped that others will have been dispelled indirectly and by inference. A brief list and summary may be attempted here.

That most useful reference book, the *Oxford Companion to English Literature* (2nd edition, 1938), defines 'Prussianism' as 'the national spirit or political system of Prussia, with reference to the arrogant and overbearing character attributed to the former, and to the militarism of the latter'. This definition is a work of art: so terse and compact, so much of importance in such a small nutshell, and superficially so accurate and comprehensive. At the same time such a definition is unfortunate and misleading, because it takes the line of least resistance and the accepted view, and makes Prussia and Prussianism appear to be an easy and straightforward matter, whereas it is in reality most difficult and complicated.

All such 'easy' definitions and solutions are, therefore, to be regarded with suspicion, and most of them deserve to be treated as misconceptions. For example, that the Prussians can simply be condemned and dismissed as Slavs. Or that Prussians and Nazis can be clearly distinguished from the rest of the Germans and from the 'real' Germans, as the theory of the 'Two Germanys' would have it. It is significant that Emil Ludwig and Oswald Spengler, two writers whose characters and views are so fundamentally different and so antagonistic, should agree that

Prussianism is not a question of locality and birth, or even of race, but an attitude of mind and spirit, a type of character and a mode of life, which is to be found among Germans everywhere. From this it follows that any suggestions for separating the 'Two Germanys' or for 'exorcizing' Prussianism are futile, no matter how attractive they may appear at first sight.

Another unsatisfactory way of approach to the problem of Germany may be nailed down by brief reference to Professor F. J. C. Hearnshaw's recent book, *Germany the Aggressor Throughout the Ages*. When reviewing it for the *Sunday Times* (21st April 1940) Sir John Marriott spoke of the 'one criticism' he had to make of Professor Hearnshaw's 'admirable and apposite book'. 'He relies on his erudition, which is indisputable, to prove that from the days of Julius Cæsar down to Hitler's the Germans have been a "savage and aggressive people". Though aggressiveness may be ingrained in the German nature, Professor Hearnshaw's case would, I think, have been strengthened had he concentrated rather on Prussia than on a Germany, which, as a National State with a national consciousness, hardly existed before 1871. Modern Germany is the creation of Prussia.' (Incidentally this review greatly encouraged the present writer to continue his researches into the Prussian spirit from 1914 to 1940.)

Similarly, all plans for splitting up Germany into a number of small states at the conclusion of the second Great War may be treated as proof of wishful thinking, an over-developed anti-German bias, and an inadequate knowledge of the facts of the German and of the European situation on the part of those who put them forward. Such a case was reported in the weekly paper published by the students of a certain university, under the date 15th June 1940, just two days before Marshal Pétain announced the surrender of France. A distinguished visitor, well known as a 'Conservative' historian, prominent in the work of the British Council, and indeed Director of the British Institute in a great European capital, had addressed the students a few days before on 'France and the War'. The following extracts have been culled from the account given of his speech. 'The Speaker thought that the annexation of the Rhineland by France was the first step in the safeguarding of her integrity.' 'The Speaker then discussed the question of what was to become of Germany after the War. . . . The Speaker thought that the only remedy to protect France from further invasions was to destroy Germany as a single state, and set up small principalities such as existed before the rule of Bismarck.' 'By these methods the Speaker was absolutely confident that the Allies would be victorious and lasting peace would be secured for future generations.' I do not wish to comment on these 'realistic' and 'constructive' proposals, except to point out that if there is one thing which justifies Bismarck and even more Adolf Hitler in the minds of almost *all* Germans, and not only Prussians, it is their work for German unity. This does not of course justify Bismarck and Hitler to the outside world, and most certainly not the annexation of Austria, Czechoslovakia, Poland, and Heaven only knows how many other lands under Hitler's fantastic concept of 'Great Germany' ['Grossdeutschland']. But it is just as well to see clearly and admit that this is all very attractive to Germans, and that although it may and indeed must be possible to make the monster of Hitler-Germany disgorge its ill-gotten gains, any attempt at splitting up Germany and destroying the unity so long and so fervently desired is bound to lead to more Hitlers and further wars. German unity would not have been achieved without the centralizing effects of the first Great War, and the second Great War and future wars can only serve to strengthen it still further. This may be tiresome and unfortunate, but it is true.

A final misconception may be dealt with here, namely, that 'no good ever came out of Prussia'. This idea, which is of course entirely contrary to Burke's famous observation that 'you cannot indict a whole nation', is often unthinkingly rather than deliberately expressed, as the following typical instance goes to show. Soon after the naval action off the Norwegian coast in February 1940 which resulted in the release of three hundred British sailors from the German prison-ship *Altmark*, a pamphlet appeared with the title, *I Was an Altmark Prisoner*, written by Thomas Foley, able seaman of the *Doric Star*, one of the British ships sunk by the *Graf Spee*. After describing the appearance, character, and conduct of Captain Dau of the *Altmark*, who must have been the very worst type of German one can imagine, Mr. Foley gave by way of contrast a brief portrait of Captain

Langsdorff of the *Graf Spee*. 'A man of medium height, clean-shaven, smart-looking, with a sort of sad look in his eyes. You could see at a glance that he was an officer and a gentleman, and we all agreed that he could not possibly be a Prussian. He was wearing an Iron Cross on his tunic. As Mr. Underwood, the *Doric Star*'s cook, once remarked: "The fellow looks so decent he might almost be British."' Mr. Foley was using the word Prussian in its customary and accepted sense as a term of abuse, although it is probable that Captain Langsdorff was a Prussian officer of the very finest type, and was regarded by many Germans as such. Mr. Underwood, on the other hand, was paying him that well-meant, but naïve and back-handed, kind of compliment which English people often pay to foreigners, and which usually succeeds in annoying them.

Once again it must be denied that this book is an attempt to 'whitewash' the Prussians, and to prove that they are angels or model beings, because most of them are not. But at the same time it is only fair and scientifically accurate to point out that there are many notable exceptions, and that it is hopeless to try to solve the problem of Germany with the aid of sweeping statements, and convenient condemnations of the whole people, or one entire section of it.

2. *Prussianism as a Political Religion*

In one of the essays already quoted (see pages 19 f.) G. K. Chesterton wrote: 'We have used fire and sword, death and destruction, slander and surrender, diplomacy and flattery, suspicion and oblivion, to solve the supposed problem of Germany; and we find that we still have not solved the problem of Prussia. The reason is that the thing involved belongs to the history of thought. The thing is not a nation; it is rather a religion, or perhaps an irreligion.'

There is a great and fundamental truth expressed in the words: 'The thing is a religion'; although the idea is difficult to grasp and to explain. But it can be illustrated by reference to Walter von Molo's novel *Luise* (1919). This is the second novel in the trilogy 'Ein Volk wacht auf', of which the first—*Fridericus* —has already been discussed in the chapter on 'The Legend of

Frederick the Great' (see pages 118 ff). About the contents of this novel we have nothing to say except that the main theme is Luise's development from a gay, superficial, and coquettish girl into a serious, mature, and responsible queen. It is only the conclusion which claims our attention. Walter von Molo discovers Luise one night when she is on her flight to East Prussia, crouching before the flickering fire in her lowly quarters, dressed in her night attire and a fur coat. She prays. 'Our Father, which art in Heaven . . . Art Thou really in Heaven? Yes, He is! . . . Give us this day our daily bread. But how are the Prussians to get their daily bread now that we are slaves? . . . We have been defeated and destroyed, we have become cowardly and small. . . . Punish us, oh God, so that we become better, so that we become Germans. . . .' She kneels down, and puts her face in her hands, and sobs, and her loose hair tumbles down over her shoulders like a reddish-gold cry of distress ['wie ein rotgoldener Notschrei'] gleaming in the light of the fire. She continues her Prussian commentary to the Lord's Prayer. 'Deliver us from evil, deliver us from evil, deliver us . . .' At this point she raised her despairing figure and knelt upright. Her gleaming hair streamed like a halo round her head, and she pressed her fingers on her breast as if that gave her strength. 'For Thine is the kingdom, the power and the glory, for ever and ever, Amen. For Thine is the —kingdom?' Luise's eyes lit up, they smiled—'Thine is—the kingdom of the Germans!' ['Dein ist das *Deutsche Reich?*' N.B. In 1806 there was no Reich at all.] She raised her arms triumphantly and stretched forth her hands to the starry heavens (apparently there was a hole in the roof of the lowly cottage). 'Oh, God! create this Germany!' This is just as if an English novelist had made Queen Victoria pray during the Crimean War: 'For Thine is the United Kingdom, the power and the glory of the British Empire (including India), for ever and ever, Amen!'

Another example of this strange mingling of religious and political motifs is provided by Luther's well-known hymn, 'A safe stronghold our God is still' ['Ein' feste Burg ist unser Gott']. In Carlyle's translation (1831) the last line reads: 'The city of God remaineth', which is really very close to the German original: 'Das Reich muss uns doch bleiben'; for Luther is of course referring to the Kingdom of God. It may seem a bold statement to make, but I am convinced that many Germans have been singing this last line with special enthusiasm during the last two decades because they were thinking far less of religion than of politics, and far less of the Heavenly Kingdom than of the German Reich, and since 1933 of the Third Reich of Adolf Hitler.

It may or may not be true that an Englishman takes his pleasures sadly: it is most certainly true that a Prussian and a Nazi takes his politics sadly, and the reason is doubtless very largely that he always tends to turn them into a religion. Bismarck and Hindenburg are always portrayed as the sternest and gravest of men, and Hitler's wooden visage is seldom lit up by a normal, human smile, although sometimes in a speech he barks out a short, derisive laugh. A Prussian or a Nazi becomes fervent and ecstatic when he ought to be cold and calculating; a kind of political mysticism usurps the place of common sense; a blind faith overcomes healthy scepticism. He practises ancestor-worship, and hears (or pretends he hears) the voice of his German and Aryan blood. He renders unto Cæsar the things that are God's; he makes a demigod out of a nervous, abnormal creature like Hitler, and attributes to him an infallibility far surpassing that claimed by even the most staunch Roman Catholics for the Pope. We are here concerned with a German idiosyncrasy which amounts to a curse and disease. Religious fanatics have always been hard to get on with; it is almost impossible to treat with, or live with, the fanatical devotees of a political religion.

3. Prussianism and Romantic Imperialism

It will be remembered how Moeller van den Bruck declared in *Der preussische Stil* (see page 46 above) that the spirit of Germany as a whole was essentially 'romantic' and that Prussianism was a necessary counterbalance and antidote. He spoke with contempt of the Romanticism which 'for a thousand years and longer' accompanied German history in the old Empire, and which eventually robbed German political life of all sense of reality and reduced it to a mere sham ['Scheinleben']. Prussia, however, had made a new beginning, and represented from the start realistic political principles and methods. Later (see page

51) he described how after 1871 German 'Romanticism' spread to Prussia, and destroyed the Prussian style and Prussian character. In a word Prussia was 'Teutonized'. But as a matter of fact, by creating the Prussian myth, and even more by reviving the idea of the 'Third Empire', Moeller van den Bruck showed that he was himself a first-class Romanticist, and provided some of the most remarkable examples of Romanticism in the whole history of German political thought. This would be amusing, if it were not so typically German, and so tragic in its consequences. For it was just this combination of Prussianism with Romanticism in Germany since 1871, and increasingly since 1919, which has proved so dangerous, not only to Germany itself, but to the rest of Europe and the world.

Romantic Imperialism, the century-old idea, or rather ideal, of the 'Reich', was far from vicious in itself and left to itself. Up to 1860 there was seldom any special stress on the 'German' nature of the Reich; as in the Middle Ages the 'Reich' remained in many ways the secular counterpart of the Papal and religious rule over Christendom; it lacked almost entirely political and military activism, unless it was a question of throwing back the infidel Turks from the gates of Vienna; and it rarely caused unneighbourliness, wars of aggression, or the suppression of peoples. It was only when the ideal of the Reich became linked up with Prussian nationalism, partly as a result of the struggle against French nationalism embodied in the person and warlike genius of Napoleon, that it became a curse; but a curse it has remained ever since. As the nineteenth century proceeded this intermingling and union of Prussian nationalism and Romantic imperialism became ever more evident and somehow ever more inevitable. In the years just previous to the first Great War this amalgamation of forces so strangely different produced militant Pan-Germanism; under Hitler it has adopted a strong racial bias and has also taken on a marked economic tinge. We know the results only too well: the essentially romantic but at the same time dangerously aggressive ideas of 'Great Germany' ['Grossdeutschland'] and of the German 'living-space' ['der deutsche Lebensraum'], two closely related conceptions and programmes which were among the main causes of the second Great War. Stern-Rubarth described Hitler in his book *Exit*

221

Prussia as the Arch-Prussian; it would be almost equally true to describe him as the Arch-Romanticist in the troubled course of German politics. Hitler has been from the start the discontented visionary, as well as the ambitious and ruthless egoist; and it was because he embodied and expressed the longings of Germans for unity and political power and a glorious empire that so many Germans felt bound to support him.

It is worthy of note that ·Prussian nationalism and modern German Romanticism both had their origins in the east of Germany, and primarily in East Prussia. At the same time as Frederick the Great was enlarging and consolidating the Prussian State as the dominating factor, along with Austria, in German political life, writers like Hamann (1730–88), for many years Professor of Philosophy at the University of Königsberg, and Herder (1744–1803), who migrated from East Prussia to Weimar, were laying the foundations of Romanticism. The Romantic period in German literature is usually relegated for convenience to the first three decades of the nineteenth century; but Romanticism began earlier than this, and it is a broad stream which has never ceased to flow in German life and literature ever since. It was the Romanticists who discovered the glories of the German past, and above all, of the Middle Ages; stressed the specific and unique nature of the German 'Volk' and nation, and its outstanding cultural achievements; and dreamt· of the final achievement of unity and of an even more glorious imperial future.

A good illustration from recent German literature of the combination of Prussianism and Romantic Imperialism is to be found in Professor Julius Petersen's essay on 'Die Sehnsucht nach dem Dritten Reich in deutscher Sage und Dichtung', which appeared first of all in the periodical *Dichtung und Volkstum*,[1] and was then extended and published in book form in 1934. Professor Petersen, for many years Professor of German Literature at the University of Berlin, had built up for himself a great reputation as a scholar and a literary historian; and it

[1] 'The Longing for the Third Empire in German Legend and Literature.' *Dichtung und Volkstum* was the new name given in 1933 to the old-established and highly reputable literary, philosophical, and cultural periodical *Euphorion*: just to show that it had been 'gleichgeschaltet', i.e. reorientated, or brought into line with the Nazis.

came as a shock to many of his friends and admirers to find him 'sailing with the Nazi wind', and indulging in patriotic effusions which might perhaps have done credit to a Hitler Youth Leader. But the fact of the matter was that he belonged to the 'Prussian' tradition, and was at heart an opponent of the Weimar Republic; so that when Hitler seized power he cast aside his doubts, and rushed like so many other good Prussians to welcome him.

Significantly enough, he began his essay with Moeller van den Bruck's revival of the idea of the Third Empire; and in the second paragraph he gave expression to his great joy at the National Socialist Revolution. 'And now to-morrow has become to-day; the Doomsday mood has changed into an eager desire to start life anew; the final goal can be discerned by the eyes of the present . . . and the dream-pictures, with which the past lulled itself to sleep, are again brought by revolutionary conservatism to the light of day.'[1] This use of the term 'revolutionary conservatism' also showed that Professor Petersen owed much to Moeller van den Bruck.

In the six chapters which followed, Professor Petersen dealt in turn with the six main conceptions of earthly bliss: (1) the Golden Age (or mythical conception); (2) the Kingdom of God (theocracy); (3) World Monarchy (the imperialistic conception); (4) the Kingdom of the Spirit (the humanistic conception); (5) a League of Nations (the federative conception); (6) the Anarchist or Communist idea of a future state based on common ownership, etc. And all this was simply meant to lead up to the final and more glorious National Socialist conception of the *Volksreich*, or the Empire of the (German) People. The conclusion of this learned jumble of romanticism and special pleading contained a graceful reference to Hitler. 'The new Empire has been set up. The leader, whose coming has been prophesied and longed for, has appeared.' ['Das neue Reich ist gepflanzt. Der ersehnte und geweissagte Führer ist erschienen.'] It seems hardly necessary to point out that if the professors and

---

[1] 'Nun ist das Morgen zum Heute geworden; Weltuntergangsstimmung hat sich in Aufbruch gewandelt; das Endziel tritt ins Blickfeld der Gegenwart, . . . und die Traumbilder, in denen die Vergangenheit sich wiegte, werden durch den revolutionären Konservatismus neu an den Tag gezogen.'

the flower of German learning and culture allowed themselves to be carried away on such waves of Romanticism in 1933, then it is not to be wondered at if the rank and file, the 'men and women in the street', and the gullible, unthinking German masses were overwhelmed by them.

In all probability the sufferings of the second Great War, and the consequences—spiritual, psychological, and economic—of a defeat far greater than in 1918, will destroy at any rate for a time such romantic elements in German political life. And it is possible that many Germans will turn more and more to the solid and ascetic side of Prussianism: like Orla in Ernst Wiechert's novel they will perhaps seek after the simple life, and ask for nothing more than 'work, poverty, and a little time'. Such at any rate was the hope and faith of some of the best of the Prussians as they braced themselves in the summer of 1939 to meet the relentless and inevitable avalanche!

4. Prussia and the Heart-Land

Early in 1919 a book appeared by H. J. Mackinder, M.P. (later Sir Halford John Mackinder), with the rather misleading title *Democratic Ideals and Reality, A Study in the Politics of Reconstruction*. It was not, as one might imagine, an abstract and theoretical essay on democracy, but a matter-of-fact, realistic inquiry into the world situation after the first Great War, as moulded by the interplay of geographical and historical factors. It soon came to be regarded as one of the primary works in the new and developing science of 'Geopolitics', a word which signifies that foreign policy should be based on geography.

Mackinder wrote: 'The joint continent of Europe, Asia, and Africa, is now effectively, and not merely theoretically, an island. . . . Let us call it the World-Island.' Within this World-Island lies the Heart-Land, a vast region extending for more than four thousand miles from the mouth of the Elbe on the North Sea to the mouth of the Amur on the Pacific Ocean, and from the icy wastes in the north to the torrid mountain ranges of Persia, India, and China in the south. Control of the Heart-Land under a single political system would be a tremendous step towards dominion over the World-Island, but such control is dependent on the position in East Europe. Mackinder laid down the following geopolitical axioms:

(1) Who rules East Europe commands the Heart-Land.

(2) Who rules the Heart-Land commands the World-Island.

(3) Who rules the World-Island commands the world.

As he proceeded to explain, the main point behind these rather Delphic words was that a union of German genius for organization and exploitation with Russian sources of man-power and raw materials must at all costs be prevented. Such a combination of two hundred and fifty millions would eventually be capable of outbuilding and outmanning the aggregate sea-power of Great Britain and the United States. With control of the Baltic and the Black Sea, the huge area would be inaccessible to direct attack from the sea, and would possess internal resources with which to defy blockade. It would be in a position to outflank and attack from the rear British possessions overseas. Mackinder therefore concluded: 'It is essential that we should focus our thought on the stable resettlement of the affairs of East Europe, and the Heart-Land.'

The validity of Mackinder's main point, namely, that a political, economic, and offensive union between Germany and Russia must be prevented at all costs, can hardly be called in question. Nor is it possible to deny the rightness of concentrating on the stable resettlement of the affairs of East Europe in any attempts to visualize and promote peace in Europe. Germany's western frontier has remained fairly stable since very early times: in spite of the struggle between France and Germany since the days of Richelieu for the Rhine frontier the demarcation-line between the two countries has not materially changed since 880, when Ludwig III, King of the East Franks, concluded a treaty at Ribemont with Ludwig and Karlmann, Kings of the West Franks, whereby Lorraine fell to the territory of the former. But Germany's eastern frontier has always been in a state of flux, due to the steady advance eastwards. Perhaps this can best be realized by bearing in mind that Berlin lies within territory which was Slav in the earlier Middle Ages, and by tracing on a map the three main lines of German advance, namely, north-eastwards along the Baltic coast, and south-eastwards along the Oder and the Danube. German political history has been dominated for over eleven hundred years by the 'Drang nach dem Osten', and this tremendous 'urge towards the east' is likely to continue.

Mackinder's chief suggestion for the 'stable resettlement of the affairs of East Europe' in 1919 was simple and drastic. The German population of East Prussia and Danzig was to be exchanged in a body for the Polish population of West Prussia! In this way Poland would be strengthened, and more important, the bridge between Russia and Germany afforded by East Prussia would be destroyed. 'By some means the new Poland must be given access to the Baltic Sea, not only because it is essential to her economic independence, but also because it is desirable to have Polish ships on the Baltic, which strategically is a closed sea of the Heart-Land, and further, there must be a complete buffer between Germany and Russia.' Of course this was not done, and the ill-fated 'Polish Corridor' was created instead.

Now one can readily agree with the necessity for a strong Poland and for a buffer between Germany and Russia, but it is quite a different matter to suggest that Poland should include East Prussia. Similar suggestions will no doubt be made at the end of the second Great War. If so, it is earnestly to be hoped that they will not be carried out! To forecast peace terms at such an early stage in this desperate struggle is difficult and rather futile; but the opinion may be ventured that to wrest East Prussia from Germany would have just as disastrous consequences as an attempt to split up Germany into small states, and would very rapidly breed more Hitlers and even worse kinds of Prussianism and Hitlerism. The romanticism of the Marienburg and Königsberg to which Wilhelm Stapel refers (see page 74), backed by the powerful and unalterable conception of East Prussia as the birthplace and pillar of German political might, would unite the Germans as never before and make them even worse to deal with than in the past. Put limits once and for all to the policies of 'Great Germany' and the 'German living space'. Restore Czechoslovakia and transfer to the Reich the Germans on the Bohemian fringe (Hitler has himself created sufficient precedents for such wholesale transfers of population!). Restore Poland, and turn out the Germans in Posen and Upper Silesia, including the newly arrived settlers from the Baltic States; give Poland absolute control of the Vistula, even to the extent of compelling the Germans to evacuate Danzig. Restore the independence of Austria; or better still, make Austria part of a 'Danubian Federation'. But do not attempt to split up Germany, or to take away East Prussia.

Mackinder was looking at Prussia from the standpoint of geopolitics. We have looked at Prussia from the standpoint of literature, art, mythology, history, and 'political' religion. Regarded in this way it becomes abundantly clear that Prussianism is a matter of the spirit, of character, temperament, tradition, and mode of life, and that it cannot be checked, purified, or destroyed simply by the drawing of frontier lines and the amputation of provinces. It is because of my different approach that I find it difficult to agree with the 'solution' offered by Mackinder, just as I found it difficult in an earlier section (see pages 21 ff.) to accept the proposals of Stern-Rubarth and Emil Ludwig.

5. *Propaganda to Prussians*

This book has been written in the belief that the Prussian spirit and Prussianism represent a crucial and in many ways fundamental aspect of the problem of Germany, and that it is an aspect which deserves to be placed in the forefront of informed discussion and enlightened policy. It should be the task of our propaganda, therefore, to link up the first Great War against Prussianism with the second Great War against Hitlerism. And this should be done, firstly, with reference to the home and allied fronts, and secondly, as part of our propaganda to Germany. It can certainly do no harm, and it might conceivably do a great deal of good, if English people at home, and our allies and well-wishers in the British Commonwealth of Nations and in the United States, are made to realize the Prussian nature of our present opponents. They should be constantly reminded of the Prussian vices—and the virtues—which made Germany such a mighty opponent in the last war, and which in an even more developed and perverse form make her such a mighty opponent to-day. They should be frankly told that we are faced with the same kind of efficient and often brilliant German General Staff, with the same well-organized and highly trained military machine, with the same policies of ruthlessness and brutality, the same obedience to authority and sense of duty on the German home front, as in 1914–18. This would do much to destroy the feelings of complacency, the tendency to under-estimate the power of the enemy and to overestimate our own power, which have done so much to delay and hamper the war-effort here—and the war-effort in America. It would also dis-pose of the naïve and wishful thinking which above all in the early stages of the war and periodically since then has pro-phesied revolution in Germany; for it would make clear that the Prussians will not countenance or participate in a revolution until they have suffered a resounding military defeat. At the same time, whilst strengthening the will to win, this propaganda would strengthen confidence in ultimate victory, by stressing the simple parallel that just as Prussian-Germany was defeated in 1918, so Nazi-Germany can and will be defeated in the present struggle.

Secondly, in our propaganda to Germany, an attempt should of course be made, as in the last war, to influence the non-Prussian and anti-Prussian elements, for example, the Austrians, the Roman Catholics of the Rhineland and Bavaria, the Socialist workers, the trade unionists, and the Communists. But at the same time, with quite different methods and with ever-increasing pressure, an attempt should be made to influence the Prussians; that is to say, our propaganda to Germany should aim at the Right, as well as at the Left and the Centre.[1] Propa-ganda to the Left and the Centre was no doubt an intelligible and justifiable policy for the start of the propaganda war, because it represented the line of least resistance. But an assault must also be made on the main stronghold, in full realization of the fact that it is on the Prussian elements that the Nazi war-

[1] In an article on 'The Propaganda Problem' (*Horizon*, January 1941) Peter Cromwell wrote: 'The first stage in the construction of a propaganda campaign is, in the words of Doctor Goebbels: "to diagnose with an almost scientific precision the people's soul, to be informed of all psychology in citizenry". When we have this, it is possible to decide on our propaganda objectives.' This is the kind of diagnosis I have attempted—on the basis of recent German literature. Hence my views on 'our propaganda objectives'.

effort primarily depends. Propaganda to non-Prussians is comparatively easy and far more certain of success; when the time and the opportunity come they will readily become our allies. Propaganda to Prussians, on the other hand, must be steady, patient, and 'long-term' in character; based on the assumption that it will probably achieve only minor successes until the tide of military events has turned in our favour. At the outset it should be directed chiefly at those Prussians who have lost their initial enthusiasm for Hitler, and who now realize—even if they are loath to admit it—that they have been betrayed and exploited, and whose state of mind is such that they are ready to see the comparison between the course of the last great struggle and the course of the present. In other words our propaganda must make the most use of what might be called the 'Prussian dilemma': the struggle between their spirit of sacrifice, their sense of duty, their traditions of obedience to the state and authority, and the ever-present and gnawing thought that the Nazi leaders and the whole Nazi régime and philosophy are unworthy of their support, because they are destructive of order, efficiency, real community life, culture and religion, and ultimately of Germany itself. At the same time it should be made clear to the Prussians—and indeed to all Germans—that Germany will not be split up after the war, nor will East Prussia be wrested from her. The Prussians let Hitler and the Nazis in; but in a spirit of restrained optimism and hope one may surely look forward to the time when they will help to throw them out.

It is impossible at this stage to visualize with any certainty or in any detail the political situation in Germany after the end of the second Great War. The most pressing demand may well be for a way out of terrible chaos, and for a temporary solution until the evil effects of Prussianism and Hitlerism can be modified, if not eradicated. Perhaps the most probable and most suitable form of government for Germany in the months immediately after the War will be a military dictatorship.[1] Such a

[1] Such a government, working in close co-operation with our own military commission, would ensure the rapid and thorough disarming of Germany, and would prevent the army leaders and the big industrialists from evading responsibility and making a hasty but cunning retreat behind the forces of 'democracy', as they did in the early years of the Weimar Republic.

government might well represent and encourage the best rather than the worst kind of Prussianism, get rid of the Nazis, and at the same time hold in check the Communists. For it is certain that the Prussians, because of their tradition, their character, and their spirit, will never accept Communism for long, even if there is a successful Communist revolution in Germany at the end of the war; and it is on them that we may have to rely in order to avert the prospect of a solid German-Russian block stretching from the Rhine to Vladivostok, a prospect which has now become much more fraught with dangers than when Mackinder wrote his book in 1919.

It must be recognized, however, that a military dictatorship or any kind of dictatorship in post-war Germany will only represent a temporary and unsatisfactory solution. The Prussians will continue in Germany, and will probably continue to dominate it politically, long after Hitler and his henchmen have disappeared; and in view of this, English policy for a considerable period after the end of the second Great War should be to regard and treat Germany and the Germans in all matters of politics as if one were dealing with Prussians. This may seem rather hard on the non-Prussians and the representatives of the spirit of Weimar, but it is simply the unhappy recognition of the fact that during the last eighty years—partly through lack of political interest and political ability, partly through bad luck and force of circumstances—they have not been able to assert themselves sufficiently to control the government and policy. As soon as the initial period has come to an end, therefore, and the difficult task of saving Germany for democracy has begun, it will be necessary to give as much help as possible—and far more help than was granted to the Weimar Republic—to those Germans who are eager to create and work successfully a democratic system in Germany; but it will be equally necessary for our propaganda to try to convert the Prussians. It must be made clear to all Germans, and particularly to the Prussians, that Prussian aggressiveness ('the pike in the pond', in Lord Rosebery's phrase), excessive and uncontrolled militarism, an overweening confidence in the rights of Germans to 'lord it' over their neighbours (the conception of the Herrenvolk), will not be tolerated for a moment, and that as soon as they show themselves they will be attacked. In a word, there will be no more policies of 'appeasement'. At the same time it must be made equally clear by word and deed that we do not contemplate the thankless and impossible task of keeping down the Germans permanently by force, and that we are ready and eager to co-operate with a Germany which is trying to work out its own salvation and the salvation of others in a democratic way. We must freely admit that we are not satisfied with our own democracy, in so far as it permits of stock-exchange gambling, class privilege, gross inequality of wealth, and insecurity of work and income for millions of our people. But we must try to convert the Prussians and the Nazis to the view which we ourselves—and many Germans—have for several decades held, namely, that democracy is the only 'humane' system of government and society, the only system which is in line with the dignity and well-being of the individual, with the achievement of international concord, and with the continuation of human progress. In a sense an attempt must be made to sublimate Prussianism and Hitlerism; to harness such Prussian qualities as hard work, discipline, efficiency, obedience, self-sacrifice, in the service of a great and worthy world-idea; to put the Prussian virtues to creative and constructive use instead of allowing them to be wasted in the destructive pursuit of outmoded and narrow nationalist aims.

Finally, it must be fully realized and never lost sight of that in political affairs Germany has been for several decades past, and is likely to remain for several decades to come, the 'Sick Man of Europe'. From 1871 to 1933 the disease was Prussianism; after 1933 it took on a more serious form, and developed into Hitlerism. The result has been that what is potentially one of the finest nations in the world has become one of the most tormented, one of the most tragic, and with good reasons one of the best hated. '*Corruptio optimi pessima*' ['There is nothing so bad as the best gone wrong']. Unless and until the German nation can cure itself of its 'disease' and develop a sane, healthy, and decent political outlook and practice, this unhappy state of affairs is likely to continue, to the serious detriment of Germany itself, and indeed of Europe and the whole world. And the sad verdict of history may then well be: that the great German contributions to civilization and culture in the fields of religion, philosophy, music, literature, and science were overwhelmed and nullified in a welter of political crimes, fruitless revolutions, and internecine wars, and that Luther, Kant, Beethoven, Goethe, and Robert Koch were relentlessly persecuted and even finally murdered by Hitler, Bismarck, and Frederick the Great.

Index

INDEX

Niemöller, M., 55, 82, 202 ff., 208, 209, 210

Petersen, J., 168, 222 f.
Pietism, 65, 66, 195 f., 206
Potsdam, 20, 37, 38, 39, 41, 51, 99, 101, 113, 131, 136, 148, 152, 177, 185, 186
Puritanism, 65, 66, 196

Ranke, 129, 130
Rauch, 45
Rehberg, H., 178 ff.
Robertson, 165
Rococo, 48 f., 51 f., 75
Rome, 47, 49, 53, 70, 75, 95, 127, 166
Rosebery, Lord, 18, 230
Rosenberg, A., 41, 136, 138, 139 ff.

Schinkel, F., 147, 156 ff., 160, 173
Schinkel, K. F., 46, 53, 54
Schlüter, 49, 54
Schwarz, H., 45, 46, 183 ff.
Slav, 24, 27 ff., 47, 63, 215, 225
Socialism, Prussian, 60 ff., 156 ff., 173
Sparta, 52, 53, 73, 75, 95
Spengler, O., 41, 55, 60 ff., 74, 95, 112, 139, 154, 155, 156, 158, 159, 160, 173, 190 ff., 193, 196, 215
Stapel, W., 41, 72 ff., 226

Stern-Rubarth, E., 21 f., 25, 28, 221, 227

Tannenberg, 32, 113, 150, 153, 178
Teutonic Knights, 16, 27, 30 ff., 47, 63, 66, 67, 77, 178
Thoma, L., 97 f., 112 f.
Treitschke, 130, 204

Unruh, F. von, 41, 78, 82 ff.

Versailles, 19, 20, 37, 40, 45, 56, 57, 61, 149, 150, 176
Vikings, 63 f., 66 ff., 139

Weimar, 10, 17, 27, 37 ff., 61, 72, 73, 90, 98, 105, 112, 113, 117, 124, 125, 135, 136, 138, 150 f., 156 ff., 170, 185, 193, 204, 223, 230
Wiechert, E., 82, 207 ff., 224
Wieland, 117
William I, 65, 149
William II, 18, 23, 98, 113, 127, 157
Winckelmann, 117, 132
Winckler, J., 120 ff.
Winnig, A., 147, 160 ff.
Wolters, F., 52

Zimmern, A., 16
Zinzendorff, 195 f., 200
Zopf, 49, 51, 53
Zuckmayer, C., 41, 55, 98 ff.